About the Author

Brené Brown, PhD, LMSW, is a research professor at the University of Houston Graduate College of Social Work. She is the author of the Number 1 *New York Times* bestseller *Daring Greatly* (2012), the Number 1 *New York Times* bestseller *The Gifts of Imperfection* (2010), and *I Thought It Was Just Me (but it isn't)* (2007). She is the founder and CEO of The Daring Way™, an organization that brings her work on vulnerability, courage, shame, and worthiness to organizations, schools, communities, and families. She lives in Houston with her husband, Steve, and their two children, Ellen and Charlie.

brenebrown.com

Facebook.com/BreneBrown

@BreneBrown

BY BRENÉ BROWN

Rising Strong

Daring Greatly

The Gifts of Imperfection

I Thought It Was Just Me

RISING STRONG

RISING STRONG

BRENÉ BROWN

Vermilion
LONDON

16

Vermilion, an imprint of Ebury Publishing,
20 Vauxhall Bridge Road,
London SW1V 2SA

Vermilion is part of the Penguin Random House
group of companies whose addresses can be found
at global.penguinrandomhouse.com

Copyright © Brené Brown 2015
Illustrations copyright © Simon Walker 2015

First published in the United Kingdom by Vermilion in 2015
First published in the United States in 2015 by Spiegel & Grau, an imprint
of Random House, a division of Penguin Random House LLC, New York

www.eburypublishing.co.uk

A CIP catalogue record for this book is available from the British Library

ISBN 9780091955038

Printed and bound in Great Britain by Clays Ltd, Elcograf S.p.A.

Penguin Random House is committed to a sustainable future
for our business, our readers and our planet. This book is made
from Forest Stewardship Council® certified paper.

To the brave and brokenhearted who have taught us
how to rise after a fall.
Your courage is contagious.

Contents

SIX

SEVEN

EIGHT

NINE

TEN

ELEVEN

A Note on Research
AND STORYTELLING AS METHODOLOGY

In the 1990s, when I began studying social work, the profession was in the midst of a polarizing debate about the nature of knowledge and truth. *Is wisdom derived from experience more or less valuable than data produced by controlled research? What research should we allow into our professional journals and what should we reject?* It was a heated debate that often created considerable friction between professors.

As doctoral students, we were often forced to take sides. Our research professors trained us to choose evidence over experience, reason over faith, science over art, and data over story. Ironically, at the exact same time, our non-research professors were teaching us that social work scholars should be wary of false dichotomies—those "either you're this or you're that" formulations. In fact, we learned that when faced with either-or dilemmas, the first question we should ask is, *Who benefits by forcing people to choose?*

If you applied the *Who benefits?* question to the debate in social work, the answer was clear: Traditional quantitative researchers benefited if the profession decided their work was the only path to truth. And tradition had the upper hand at my college, with little to no training in qualitative methods available and the only dissertation option quantitative. A single textbook covered qualitative research, and the book jacket was light pink—it was often referred to as "the girls'" research book.

This debate became personal to me when I fell in love with qualitative research—grounded theory research, to be specific. I responded by pursuing it anyway, finding a few faculty allies inside and outside my college. I chose as my methodologist Barney Glaser, from the University of California San Francisco Medical School, who, along with Anselm Strauss, is the founder of grounded theory.

I am still deeply affected by an editorial I read in the 1990s titled "Many Ways of Knowing." It was written by Ann Hartman, the influential editor of one of our most prestigious journals at the time. In the editorial, Hartman wrote:

> This editor takes the position that there are many truths and there are many ways of knowing. Each discovery contributes to our knowledge, and each way of knowing deepens our understanding and adds another dimension to our view of the world. . . . For example, large-scale studies of trends in marriage today furnish helpful information about a rapidly changing social institution. But getting inside one marriage, as in *Who's Afraid of Virginia Woolf?*, richly displays the complexities of one marriage, leading us to new insights about the pain, the joys, the expectations, the disappointments, the intimacy, and the ultimate aloneness in re-

lationships. Both the scientific and the artistic methods provide us with ways of knowing. And, in fact, as Clifford Geertz . . . has pointed out, innovative thinkers in many fields are blurring the genres, finding art in science and science in art and social theory in all human creation and activity.

I succumbed to fear and scarcity (the sense that my chosen research method wasn't enough) for the first couple of years of my career as a tenure-track professor and researcher. I felt like an outsider as a qualitative researcher, so for safety I stood as close as I could to the "if you can't measure it, it doesn't exist" crowd. That served both my political needs *and* my profound dislike of uncertainty. But I never got that editorial out of my head or my heart. And today I proudly call myself a researcher-storyteller because I believe the most useful knowledge about human behavior is based on people's lived experiences. I am incredibly grateful to Ann Hartman for having the guts to take this position, to Paul Raffoul, the professor who handed me a copy of that article, and to Susan Robbins, who bravely led my dissertation committee.

As you read through this book, you will see that I don't believe faith and reason are natural enemies. I believe our human desire for certainty and our often-desperate need to "be right" have led to this false dichotomy. I don't trust a theologian who dismisses the beauty of science or a scientist who doesn't believe in the power of mystery.

Because of this belief, I now find knowledge and truth in a full range of sources. In this book, you'll come across quotes from scholars and singer-songwriters. I'll quote research and movies. I'll share a letter from a mentor that helped me get a handle on what it means to get your heart broken and an editorial on nostalgia by a sociologist. I won't set up Crosby, Stills & Nash as academics, but I also won't diminish the ability of artists to capture what is true about the human spirit.

I'm also not going to pretend that I am an expert on every topic that emerged as important in this book's research. Instead, I will share the work of other researchers and experts whose work accurately captures what emerged in my data. I can't wait to introduce you to some of these thinkers and artists who have dedicated their careers to exploring the inner workings of emotion, thought, and behavior.

In early 2013, I received an angry email from a man upset about my quoting a lyric from a Rush song in *Daring Greatly*. He wrote, "I don't want complex research summarized with rock lyrics." I thought about responding with an elaborate explanation about the nature of conceptualizing in grounded theory research, but then I decided there was a simpler, more truthful answer: "You can't always get what you want, but if you try sometimes, you just might find, you get what you need" (Professors Jagger and Richards, 1969).

For more information on my methodology and current research, visit my website, brenebrown.com.

Thank you for joining me on this adventure.

Brené

The truth is that

FALLING HURTS.

THE DARE IS TO

keep being

BRAVE

and FEEL YOUR WAY

BACK UP.

Truth and Dare

AN INTRODUCTION

During an interview in 2013, a reporter told me that after reading *The Gifts of Imperfection* and *Daring Greatly,* he wanted to start working on his own issues related to vulnerability, courage, and authenticity. He laughed and said, "It sounds like it could be a long road. Can you give me the upside of doing this work?" I told him that with every ounce of my professional and personal being, I believe that vulnerability—the willingness to show up and be seen with no guarantee of outcome—is the only path to more love, belonging, and joy. He quickly followed up with, "And the downside?" This time I was the one laughing. "You're going to stumble, fall, and get your ass kicked."

There was a long pause before he said, "Is this where you tell me that you think daring is still worth it?" I responded with a passionate *yes,* followed by a confession: "Today it's a solid *yes* because I'm not lying facedown after a hard fall. But even in the midst of struggle, I would still say that doing this work is not only worth it, it is *the work* of living a wholehearted life. But I promise that if you asked me about this in the midst of a fall, I'd be far less enthusiastic and way more pissed off. I'm not great at falling and feeling my way back."

It's been two years since that interview—two years of practicing being brave and putting myself out there—and vulnerability is still uncomfortable and falling still hurts. It always will. But I'm learning that the process of struggling and navigating hurt has as much to offer us as the process of being brave and showing up.

Over the past couple of years, I've had the privilege of spending time with some amazing people. They range from top entrepreneurs and leaders in Fortune 500 companies to couples who have maintained loving relationships for more than thirty years and parents working to change the education system. As they've shared their experiences and stories of being brave, falling, and getting back up, I kept asking myself: *What do these people with strong relationships, parents with deep connections to their children, teachers nurturing creativity and learning, clergy walking with people through faith, and trusted leaders have in common?* The answer was clear: They recognize the power of emotion and they're not afraid to lean in to discomfort.

While vulnerability is the birthplace of many of the fulfilling experiences we long for—love, belonging, joy, creativity, and trust, to name a few—the process of regaining our emotional footing in the midst of struggle is where our courage is tested and our values are forged. Rising strong after a fall is how we cultivate wholeheartedness in our lives; it's the process that teaches us the most about who we are.

In the past two years, my team and I have also received emails every week from people who write, "I dared greatly. I was brave. I got my butt kicked and now I'm down for the count. How do I get back up?" I knew when I was writing *The Gifts* and *Daring Greatly* that I would ultimately write a book about falling down. I've collected that data all along, and what I've learned about surviving hurt has saved me again and again. *It saved me and, in the process, it changed me.*

Here's how I see the progression of my work:

The Gifts of Imperfection—Be you.

Daring Greatly—Be all in.

Rising Strong—Fall. Get up. Try again.

The thread that runs through all three of these books is our yearning to live a wholehearted life. I define *wholehearted living* as engaging in our lives from a place of worthiness. It means cultivating the courage, compassion, and connection to wake up in the morning and think, *No matter what gets done and how much is left undone, I am enough.* It's going to bed at night thinking, *Yes, I am imperfect and vulnerable and sometimes afraid, but that doesn't change the truth that I am brave and worthy of love and belonging.*

Both *The Gifts* and *Daring Greatly* are "call to arms" books. They are about having the courage to show up and be seen even if it means risking failure, hurt, shame, and possibly even heartbreak. Why? Because hiding out, pretending, and armoring up against vulnerability are killing us: killing our spirits, our hopes, our potential, our creativity, our ability to lead, our love, our faith, and our joy. I think these books have resonated so strongly with people for two simple reasons: We're sick of being afraid and we're tired of hustling for our self-worth.

We want to be brave, and deep inside we know that being brave requires us to be vulnerable. The great news is that I think we're making serious headway. Everywhere I go, I meet people who tell me how they're leaning in to vulnerability and uncertainty—how it's changing their relationships and their professional lives.

We get thousands of emails from people who talk about their experiences of practicing the Ten Guideposts from *The Gifts*—even the hard ones like cultivating creativity, play, and self-compassion. I've worked alongside CEOs, teachers, and parents who are mounting major efforts to bring about cultural change based on the idea of showing up and daring greatly. The experience has been more than I ever imagined sixteen years ago when my husband, Steve, asked me, "What's the vision for your career?" and I answered, "I want to start a global conversation about vulnerability and shame."

If we're going to put ourselves out there and love with our whole hearts, we're going to experience heartbreak. If we're going to try new, innovative things, we're going to fail. If we're going to risk caring and engaging, we're going to experience disappointment. It doesn't matter if our hurt is caused by a painful breakup or we're struggling with something smaller, like an offhand comment by a colleague or an argument with an in-law. If we can learn how to feel our way through these experiences and own our stories of struggle, we can write our own brave endings. When we own our stories, we avoid being trapped as characters in stories someone else is telling.

The epigraph for *Daring Greatly* is Theodore Roosevelt's powerful quote from his 1910 "Man in the Arena" speech:

> It is not the critic who counts; not the man who points out how the strong man stumbles, or where the doer of deeds could have done them better. The credit belongs

to the man who is actually in the arena, whose face is marred by dust and sweat and blood; who strives valiantly; . . . who at the best knows in the end the triumph of high achievement, and who at the worst, if he fails, at least fails while *daring greatly.*

It's an inspiring quote that has truly become a touchstone for me. However, as someone who spends a lot of time in the arena, I'd like to focus on one particular piece of Roosevelt's speech: "The credit belongs to the man who is actually in the arena, whose face is marred by dust and sweat and blood"— STOP. (Imagine the sound of a needle scratching across a record.) Stop here. Before I hear anything else about triumph or achievement, this is where I want to slow down time so I can figure out exactly what happens next.

We're facedown in the arena. Maybe the crowd has gone silent, the way it does at football games or my daughter's field hockey matches when the players on the field take a knee because someone is hurt. Or maybe people have started booing and jeering. Or maybe you have tunnel vision and all you can hear is your parent screaming, "Get up! Shake it off!"

Our "facedown" moments can be big ones like getting fired or finding out about an affair, or they can be small ones like learning a child has lied about her report card or experiencing a disappointment at work. Arenas always conjure up grandeur, but an arena is any moment when or place where we have risked showing up and being seen. Risking being awkward and goofy at a new exercise class is an arena. Leading a team at work is an arena. A tough parenting moment puts us in the arena. Being in love is definitely an arena.

When I started thinking about this research, I went to the data and asked myself, *What happens when we're facedown? What's going on in this moment? What do the women and men who have successfully staggered to their feet and found the courage to try again have in common? What is the process of rising strong?*

I wasn't positive that slowing down time to capture the process was possible, but I was inspired by Sherlock Holmes to give it a shot. In early 2014, I was drowning in data and my confidence was waning. I was also coming off a tough holiday, when I had spent most of my scheduled vacation time fighting off a respiratory virus that hit Houston like a hurricane. One night in February, I snuggled up on the couch with my daughter, Ellen, to watch the newest season of Masterpiece's *Sherlock* with Benedict Cumberbatch and Martin Freeman. (I'm a huge fan.)

In Season 3, there's an episode where Sherlock is shot. *Don't worry, I won't say by whom or why, but, wow, I did not see it coming.* The moment he's shot, time stops. Rather than immediately falling, Sherlock goes into his "mind palace"—that crazy cognitive space where he retrieves memories from cerebral filing cabinets, plots car routes, and makes impossible connections between random facts. Over the next ten minutes or so, many of the cast of recurring characters appear in his mind, each one working in his or her area of expertise and talking him through the best way to stay alive.

First, the London coroner who has a terrific crush on Sherlock shows up. She shakes her head at Sherlock, who seems completely taken aback by his inability to make sense of what's happening, and comments, "It's not like it is in the movies, is it, Sherlock?" Aided by a member of the forensics team at New

Scotland Yard and Sherlock's menacing brother, she explains the physics of how he should fall, how shock works, and what he can do to keep himself conscious. The three warn him when pain is coming and what he can expect. What probably takes three seconds in real time plays out for more than ten minutes on the screen. I thought the writing was genius, and it re-energized my efforts to keep at my own slow-motion project.

My goal for this book is to slow down the falling and rising processes: to bring into our awareness all the choices that unfurl in front of us during those moments of discomfort and hurt, and to explore the consequences of those choices. Much as in my other books, I'm using research and storytelling to unpack what I've learned. The only difference here is that I'm sharing many more of my personal stories. These narratives grant me not only a front-row seat to watch what's playing out onstage, but also a backstage pass to access the thoughts, feelings, and behaviors that are taking place behind the scenes. In my stories, I have the details. It's like watching the director's cut of a movie or choosing the bonus feature on a DVD that allows you to listen to the director talk through decisions and thought processes. This is not to say that I can't capture details from other people's experiences—I do it all the time. I just can't weave together history, context, emotion, behavior, and thinking with the same density.

During the final stages of developing the rising strong theory, I met with small groups of people familiar with my work to share my findings and gather feedback from their perspectives on the fit and relevance of the theory. Was I on the right track? Later, two of the participants in those meetings reached out to share their experiences of applying the rising strong process in their lives. I was moved by what they shared and asked if I could include it in this book. They both agreed, and I'm grateful. Their stories are powerful examples of rising.

On a cultural level, I think the absence of honest conversation about the hard work that takes us from lying facedown in the arena to rising strong has led to two dangerous outcomes: the propensity to gold-plate grit and a badassery deficit.

GOLD-PLATING GRIT

We've all fallen, and we have the skinned knees and bruised hearts to prove it. But scars are easier to talk about than they are to show, with all the remembered feelings laid bare. And rarely do we see wounds that are in the process of healing. I'm not sure if it's because we feel too much shame to let anyone see a process as intimate as overcoming hurt, or if it's because even when we muster the courage to share our still-incomplete healing, people reflexively look away.

We much prefer stories about falling and rising to be inspirational and sanitized. Our culture is rife with these tales. In a thirty-minute speech, there's normally thirty seconds dedicated to "And I fought my way back," or "And then I met someone new," or, as in the case of my TEDx talk, simply "It was a street fight."

We like recovery stories to move quickly through the dark so we can get to the sweeping redemptive ending. I worry that this lack of honest accounts of overcoming adversity has created a Gilded Age of Failure. The past couple of years have given rise to failure conferences, failure festivals, and even failure awards. Don't get me wrong. I love and continue to champion the idea of understanding and accepting failure as part of any worthwhile endeavor. But embracing failure without acknowledging the real hurt and fear that it can cause, or the complex journey that underlies rising strong, is gold-plating grit. To strip failure of its real emotional consequences is to scrub the concepts of grit and resilience of the very qualities that make them both so important—toughness, doggedness, and perseverance.

Yes, there can be no innovation, learning, or creativity without failure. *But failing is painful. It fuels the "shouldas and couldas," which means judgment and shame are often lying in wait.*

Yes, I agree with Tennyson, who wrote, "'Tis better to have loved and lost than never to have loved at all." *But heartbreak knocks the wind out of you, and the feelings of loss and longing can make getting out of bed a monumental task. Learning to trust and lean in to love again can feel impossible.*

Yes, if we care enough and dare enough, we will experience disappointment. *But in those moments when disappointment is washing over us and we're desperately trying to get our heads and hearts around what is or is not going to be, the death of our expectations can be painful beyond measure.*

The work being done by Ashley Good is a great example of how we must embrace the difficult emotion of falling. Good is the founder and CEO of Fail Forward—a social enterprise with the mission to help organizations develop cultures that encourage the risk taking, creativity, and continuous adaptation required for innovation. She got started as a development worker in Ghana with Engineers Without Borders Canada (EWB) and was integral to the development of EWB's failure reports and AdmittingFailure.com, a kind of online failure report where anyone can submit stories of failure and learning.

These first reports were bold attempts to break the silence that surrounds failure in the nonprofit sector—a sector dependent on external funding. Frustrated by the learning opportunities missed because of that silence, EWB collected its failures and published them in a glossy annual report. The organization's commitment to solving some of the world's most difficult problems, like poverty, requires innovation and learning, so it put achieving its mission before looking good, and sparked a revolution.

In her keynote address at FailCon Oslo—an annual failure conference in Norway—Good asked the audience for words they associated with the term *failure*. The audience members shouted out the following: *sadness, fear, making a fool of myself, desperation, panic, shame,* and *heartbreak.* Then she held up EWB's failure report and explained that the thirty glossy pages included fourteen stories of failure, proving that EWB had failed at least fourteen times in the last year. She then asked the same audience what words they would use to describe the report and the people who submitted their stories. This time the words shouted out included: *helping, generous, open, knowledgeable, brave,* and *courageous.*

Good made the powerful point that there's a vast difference between how we think about the term *failure* and how we think about the people and organizations brave enough to share their failures for the purpose of learning and growing. To pretend that we can get to *helping, generous,* and *brave* without navigating through tough emotions like *desperation, shame,* and *panic* is a profoundly dangerous and misguided assumption. Rather than gold-plating grit and trying to make failure look fashionable, we'd be better off learning how to recognize the beauty in truth and tenacity.

THE BADASSERY DEFICIT

I know, *badassery* is a strange term, but I couldn't come up with another one that captures what I mean. When I see people stand fully in their truth, or when I see someone fall down, get back up, and say, "Damn. That really hurt, but this is important to me and I'm going in again"—my gut reaction is, "What a badass."

There are too many people today who instead of *feeling hurt* are *acting out their hurt;* instead of *acknowledging pain,* they're *inflicting pain* on others. Rather than risking *feeling disappointed,* they're choosing to *live disappointed.* Emotional stoicism is not badassery. Blustery posturing is not badassery. Swagger is not badassery. Perfection is about the furthest thing in the world from badassery.

To me the real badass is the person who says, "Our family is really hurting. We could use your support." And the man who tells his son, "It's okay to be sad. We all get sad. We just need to talk about it." And the woman who says, "Our team dropped the ball. We need to stop blaming each other and have some tough conversations about what happened so we can fix it and move forward." People who wade into discomfort and vulnerability and tell the truth about their stories are the real badasses.

Daring is essential to solve the problems in the world that feel intractable: poverty, violence, inequality, trampled civil rights, and a struggling environment, to name a few. But in addition to having people who are willing to show up and be seen, we also need a critical mass of badasses who are willing to dare, fall, feel their way through tough emotion, and rise again. And we need these folks leading, modeling, and shaping culture in every capacity, including as parents, teachers, administrators, leaders, politicians, clergy, creatives, and community organizers.

So much of what we hear today about courage is inflated and empty rhetoric that camouflages personal fears about one's likability, ratings, and ability to maintain a level of comfort and status. We need more people who are willing to demonstrate what it looks like to risk and endure failure, disappointment, and regret—people willing to feel their own hurt instead of working it out on other people, people willing to own their stories, live their values, and keep showing up. I feel so lucky to have spent the past couple of years working with some true badasses, from teachers and parents to CEOs, filmmakers, veterans, human-resource professionals, school counselors, and therapists. We'll explore what they have in common as we move through the book, but here's a teaser: They're curious about the emotional world and they face discomfort straight-on.

My hope is that the process outlined in this book gives us language and a rough map that will guide us in getting back on our feet. I'm sharing everything I know, feel, believe, and have experienced about rising strong. I'll tell you once more that what I learned from the research participants continues to save me, and I'm deeply grateful for that. The truth is that falling hurts. The dare is to keep being brave and feel your way back up.

RISING
STRONG

WE ARE
BORN MAKERS.
We move
WHAT WE'RE LEARNING
from our
HEADS
to our
HEARTS
through our
HANDS.

One

THE PHYSICS
OF VULNERABILITY

When it comes to human behavior, emotions, and thinking, the adage "The more I learn, the less I know" is right on. I've learned to give up my pursuit of netting certainty and pinning it to the wall. Some days I miss pretending that certitude is within reach. My husband, Steve, always knows I'm mourning the loss of my young-researcher quest when I am holed up in my study listening to David Gray's song "My Oh My" on repeat. My favorite lyrics are

What on earth is going on in my head?
You know I used to be so sure.
You know I used to be so definite.

And it's not just the lyrics; it's the way that he sings the word *def.in.ite*. Sometimes, it sounds to me as if he's mocking the arrogance of believing that we can ever know everything, and other times it sounds like he's pissed off that we can't. Either way, singing along makes me feel better. Music always makes me feel less alone in the mess.

While there are really no hard-and-fast absolutes in my field, there are truths about shared experiences that deeply resonate with what we believe and know. For example, the Roosevelt quote that anchors my research on vulnerability and daring gave birth to three truths for me:

I want to be in the arena. I want to be brave with my life. And when we make the choice to dare greatly, we sign up to get our asses kicked. We can choose courage or we can choose comfort, but we can't have both. Not at the same time.

Vulnerability is not winning or losing; it's having the courage to show up and be seen when we have no control over the outcome. Vulnerability is not weakness; it's our greatest measure of courage.

A lot of cheap seats in the arena are filled with people who never venture onto the floor. They just hurl mean-spirited criticisms and put-downs from a safe distance. The problem is, when we stop caring what people think and stop feeling hurt by cruelty, we lose our ability to connect. But when we're defined by what people think, we lose the courage to be vulnerable. Therefore, we need to be selective about the feedback we let into our lives. For me, if you're not in the arena getting your ass kicked, I'm not interested in your feedback.

I don't think of these as "rules," but they have certainly become guiding principles for me. I believe there are also some basic tenets about being brave, risking vulnerability, and overcoming adversity that are useful to understand before we get started. I think of these as the basic laws of emotional physics: simple but powerful truths that help us understand why courage is both transformational and rare. These are the rules of engagement for rising strong.

1. **If we are brave enough often enough, we will fall; this is the physics of vulnerability.** When we commit to showing up and *risking* falling, we are actually committing to falling. Daring is not saying, "I'm willing to risk failure." Daring is saying, "I know I will eventually fail and I'm still all in." Fortune may favor the bold, but so does failure.

2. **Once we fall in the service of being brave, we can never go back.** We can rise up from our failures, screwups, and falls, but we can never go back to where we stood before we were brave or before we fell. Courage transforms the emotional structure of our being. This change often brings a deep sense of loss. During the process of rising, we sometimes find ourselves homesick for a place that no longer exists. We want to go back to that moment before we walked into the arena, but there's nowhere to go back to. What makes this more difficult is that now we have a new level of awareness about what it means to be brave. We can't fake it anymore. We now know when we're showing up and when we're hiding out, when we are living our values and when we are not. Our new awareness can also be invigorating—it can reignite our sense of purpose and remind us of our commitment to wholeheartedness. Straddling the tension that lies between wanting to go back to the moment before we risked and fell and being pulled forward to even greater courage is an inescapable part of rising strong.

3. This journey belongs to no one but you; however, no one successfully goes it alone. Since the beginning of time, people have found a way to rise after falling, yet there is no well-worn path leading the way. All of us must make our own way, exploring some of the most universally shared experiences while also navigating a solitude that makes us feel as if we are the first to set foot in uncharted regions. And to add to the complexity, in lieu of the sense of safety to be found in a well-traveled path or a constant companion, we must learn to depend for brief moments on fellow travelers for sanctuary, support, and an occasional willingness to walk side by side. For those of us who fear being alone, coping with the solitude inherent in this process is a daunting challenge. For those of us who prefer to cordon ourselves off from the world and heal alone, the requirement for connection—of asking for and receiving help—becomes the challenge.

4. We're wired for story. In a culture of scarcity and perfectionism, there's a surprisingly simple reason we want to own, integrate, and share our stories of struggle. We do this because we feel the most alive when we're connecting with others and being brave with our stories—it's in our biology. The idea of storytelling has become ubiquitous. It's a platform for everything from creative movements to marketing strategies. But the idea that we're "wired for story" is more than a catchy phrase. Neuroeconomist Paul Zak has found that hearing a story—a narrative with a beginning, middle, and end—causes our brains to release cortisol and oxytocin. These chemicals trigger the uniquely human abilities to connect, empathize, and make meaning. Story is literally in our DNA.

5. Creativity embeds knowledge so that it can become practice. We move what we're learning from our heads to our hearts through our hands. We are born makers, and creativity is the ultimate act of integration—it is how we fold our experiences into our being. Over the course of my career, the question I've been asked more than any other is, "How do I take what I'm learning about myself and actually change how I'm living?" After teaching graduate social work students for eighteen years; developing, implementing, and evaluating two curricula over the past eight years; leading more than seventy thousand students through online learning courses; and interviewing hundreds of creatives, I've come to believe that creativity is the mechanism that allows learning to seep into our being and become practice. The Asaro tribe of Indonesia and Papua New Guinea has a beautiful saying: "Knowledge is only a rumor until it lives in the muscle." What we understand and learn about rising strong is only rumor until we live it and integrate it through some form of creativity so that it becomes part of us.

6. Rising strong is the same process whether you're navigating personal or professional struggles. I've spent equal time researching our personal and our professional lives, and while most of us would like to believe that we can have home and work versions of rising strong, we can't. Whether you're a young man dealing with heartbreak, a retired couple struggling with disappointment, or a manager trying to recover after a failed project, the practice is the same. We have no sterile business remedy for having fallen. We still need to dig into the grit of issues like resentment, grief, and forgiveness. As neuroscientist Antonio Damasio reminds us, humans are not either thinking machines or feeling machines, but rather feeling machines that think. Just because you're standing in your office or your classroom or your studio doesn't mean that you can take the emotion out of this process. You cannot. Remember those badasses I referenced in the introduction? One more thing they have in common is that they don't try to avoid emotions—they are feeling machines who think and engage with their own emotions and the emotions of the people they love, parent, and lead. The most transformative and resilient leaders that I've worked with over the course of my career have three things in common: First, they recognize the central role that relationships and story play in culture and strategy, and they stay curious about their own emotions, thoughts, and behaviors. Second, they understand and stay curious about how emotions, thoughts, and behaviors are connected in the people they lead, and how those factors affect relationships and perception. And, third, they have the ability and willingness to lean in to discomfort and vulnerability.

7. Comparative suffering is a function of fear and scarcity. Falling down, screwing up, and facing hurt often lead to bouts of second-guessing our judgment, our self-trust, and even our worthiness. *I am enough* can slowly turn into *Am I really enough?* If there's one thing I've learned over the past decade, it's that fear and scarcity immediately trigger comparison, and even pain and hurt are not immune to being assessed and ranked. *My husband died and that grief is worse than your grief over an empty nest. I'm not allowed to feel disappointed about being passed over for promotion when my friend just found out that his wife has cancer. You're feeling shame for forgetting your son's school play? Please—that's a first-world problem; there are people dying of* *starvation every minute.* The opposite of scarcity is not abundance; the opposite of scarcity is simply enough. Empathy is not finite, and compassion is not a pizza with eight slices. When you practice empathy and compassion with someone, there is not less of these qualities to go around. There's more. Love is the last thing we need to ration in this world. The refugee in Syria doesn't benefit more if you conserve your kindness only for her and withhold it from your neighbor who's going through a divorce. Yes, perspective is critical. But I'm a firm believer that complaining is okay as long as we piss and moan with a little perspective. Hurt is hurt, and every time we honor our own struggle and the struggles of others by responding with empathy and compassion, the healing that results affects all of us.

8. You can't engineer an emotional, vulnerable, and courageous process into an easy, one-size-fits-all formula. In fact, I think attempting to sell people an easy fix for pain is the worst kind of snake oil. *Rising Strong* doesn't offer a solution or a recipe or step-by-step guidance. It presents a theory—grounded in data—that explains the basic social process men and women experience as they are working to rise after falling. It is a map meant to orient you to the most significant patterns and themes that emerged from the research. In my interviews with others and my own experiences, I've seen the process take twenty minutes, and I've seen it take twenty years. I've seen people get stuck, set up camp, and stay in one place for a decade. While the process does seem to follow a few patterns, it presents no formula or strictly linear approach. It's a back-and-forth action—an iterative and intuitive process that takes different shapes for different people. There is not always a relationship between effort and outcome in this process. You can't game it or perfect it so it's fast and easy. You have to feel your way through most of it. The contribution I hope to make is to put language around the process, to bring into our awareness some of the issues that we may need to grapple with if we want to rise strong, and to simply let people know that they're not alone.

9. Courage is contagious. Rising strong changes not just you, but also the people around you. To bear witness to the human potential for transformation through vulnerability, courage, and tenacity can be either a clarion call for more daring or a painful mirror for those of us stuck in the aftermath of the fall, unwilling or unable to own our stories. Your experience can profoundly affect the people around you whether you're aware of it or not. Franciscan friar Richard Rohr writes, "You know after any truly initiating experience that you are part of a much bigger whole. Life is not about you henceforward, but you are about life."

10. Rising strong is a spiritual practice. Getting back on our feet does not require religion, theology, or doctrine. However, without exception, the concept of spirituality emerged from the data as a critical component of resilience and overcoming struggle. I crafted this definition of spirituality based on the data I've collected over the past decade: *Spirituality is recognizing and celebrating that we are all inextricably connected to one another by a power greater than all of us, and that our connection to that power and to one another is grounded in love and belonging. Practicing spirituality brings a sense of perspective, meaning, and purpose to our lives.* Some of us call that power greater than ourselves God. Some do not. Some people celebrate their spirituality in churches, synagogues, mosques, or other houses of worship, while others find divinity in solitude, through meditation, or in nature. For example, I come from a long line of folks who believe that fishing is church, and one of my closest friends believes that scuba diving is the holiest of experiences. As it turns out, our expressions of spirituality are as diverse as we are. When our intentions and actions are guided by spirituality—our belief in our interconnectedness and love—our everyday experiences can be spiritual practices. We can transform teaching, leading, and parenting into spiritual practices. Asking for and receiving help can also be spiritual practices. Storytelling and creating can be spiritual practices, because they cultivate awareness. While these activities *can be* spiritual practices, it appears that rising strong after falling *must be* a spiritual practice. Rising demands the foundational beliefs of connection and requires wrestling with perspective, meaning, and purpose. I recently came across this quote on Liz Gilbert's Instagram feed—and I think it sums this up perfectly: "Grace will take you places hustling can't."

THE MIDDLE

is

MESSY,

BUT IT'S ALSO

WHERE THE

magic

HAPPENS.

Two
CIVILIZATION STOPS AT THE WATERLINE

I once made a map of my heart, and smack-dab in the center of that map I drew Lake Travis. Nestled in the gorgeous Texas Hill Country, right on the western edge of Austin, the lake is a sixty-five-mile-long reservoir of the Colorado River. It is a place of rocky banks, breathtaking cliffs, and mesquite trees, all surrounding cold turquoise water.

I spent every summer of my childhood at Lake Travis. It's where I learned how to fish for perch and largemouth bass, run a catfish trotline, whittle, build tree houses, and set a proper table. My great-aunt Lorenia and her husband, Uncle Joe, had a house in Volente. Back then the area around the lake was rural, home to country folk with trucks and fishing poles who didn't consider themselves residents of Austin—they just lived "at the lake." Today the same area is considered a suburb of Austin and studded with mansions and gated neighborhoods.

Aunt Bea lived next door to Aunt Lorenia, and Ma and Pa

Baldwin lived in the next house down with their daughter and son-in-law, Edna Earl and Walter. Edna Earl and Aunt Lorenia were best friends until they died. I spent hours running barefoot from house to house, screen doors slamming behind me. I'd play cards with Aunt Bea, then run back to Aunt Lorenia's to bake a pie. I would collect rocks and catch fireflies with Ma and Pa. Edna Earl loved to listen to my knock-knock jokes.

Aunt Lorenia was the local Avon lady. Helping her pack up the goods and "work her route" was the highlight of my summers. From the time I was in fourth grade, we'd jump in the pickup, her on the driver's side and me in the passenger seat with my Red Ryder BB gun, the bags of cosmetics, perfumes, and creams piled between us. I was in charge of the lipstick samples—a shiny vinyl box filled with what seemed like hundreds of tiny white tubes of lipstick in every imaginable color and formulation.

We'd travel down long gravel roads, then park at a customer's metal gate. Aunt Lorenia would get out first to open the gate and check for wild animals and rattlesnakes. Once she'd made her assessment, she'd yell back, "Bring the lipstick. Leave the gun." Or "Bring the lipstick. Grab the gun." I'd slide down out of the truck, lipstick and sometimes Red Ryder in hand, and we'd walk up to the house.

After long mornings of delivering Avon, we'd make sandwiches, pack them up, and grab a handful of worms from the worm farm Uncle Joe had made in a converted 1930s Westinghouse Coca-Cola ice chest in their backyard. With our lunch and bait, we'd head down to the dock to fish and float in inner tubes on the lake. I was never happier anywhere in my life than I was floating around on Lake Travis. I can still close my eyes and remember what it felt like to drift along in my tube, feeling the warm sun on my skin as I watched dragonflies skip along the water and kicked away perch nibbling at my toes.

THE BIG DOOR PRIZE

Lake Travis was magic for me—the kind of magic you want to share with your own kids. So, when Steve and I were planning our 2012 summer vacation, we decided to rent a house about half an hour from Aunt Lorenia and Uncle Joe's. We were excited because it was the first time we had blocked out such a long stretch for a vacation—we'd be gone for two whole weeks. Lawless one-week vacations are fine, but our family functions better with a few limits in place. So we decided for this vacation that we'd monitor technology with the kids, keep reasonable bedtimes, cook and eat relatively healthy meals, and work out as often as possible. Our siblings and parents were coming to spend time with us over the course of the vacation, so we put everyone on notice about the "healthy vacation" plans. Flurries of emails detailing meal planning and grocery lists ensued.

The rental house was tucked away along a deepwater cove on the lake and had a long stretch of stairs leading down to an old dock with a corrugated tin roof. Steve and I committed to swimming across the cove every day of our vacation. It was about five hundred yards each way. The day before we left, I went out and bought a new Speedo and replaced my goggles. It had been a long time since Steve and I had swum together. Twenty-five years, to be exact. We met when we both were lifeguarding and coaching swimming. While I still swim every week, it's more of a "toning" endeavor for me. Steve, on the other hand, was a competitive swimmer in high school, played club water polo in college, and is still a serious swimmer. I gauge the differences in our current abilities this way: He still does flip turns. I touch and go these days.

Early one morning, before any of our tribe was up, Steve and I headed down to the dock. My sisters and their families were visiting, so we felt comfortable leaving the kids up at the house. We dove in and started our trek across the cove. About halfway across, we both stopped to perform the basic open-water swimming check for boats. As we treaded water and looked for lake traffic, our eyes met. I was overwhelmed by gratitude for the surrounding beauty and the gift of finding myself swimming in my magic lake with the guy I met in the water some twenty-five years ago. Feeling the intense vulnerability that always accompanies deep joy for me, I let my sentiments roam free, tenderly telling Steve, "I'm so glad we decided to do this together. It's beautiful out here." Steve is so much better at putting himself out there that I prepared myself for an equally gushing response. Instead he flashed a noncommittal half smile and replied, "Yeah. Water's good." Then he started swimming again.

We were only about fifteen feet apart. *Didn't he hear me?* I thought. *Maybe he just heard something other than what I said. Maybe my unexpected touchy-feely-ness took him off guard, and he was so overwhelmed with love that he was rendered speechless?* Whatever the case, it was weird and I didn't like it. My emotional reaction was embarrassment, with shame rising.

I reached the rocky shore on the other side a few minutes

after Steve, who'd paused to catch his breath but was already preparing to swim back. We were only a few feet from each other. I took a deep breath and weighed the option of going in *again*. One poetic bid for connection was already outside of my comfort zone—but reaching out again felt really scary and possibly stupid. But I knew Steve would do it. He'd try twenty times, but then he's braver than I am. In his song "Hallelujah," Leonard Cohen writes:

> *Maybe there's a God above*
> *But all I've ever learned from love*
> *Was how to shoot at someone who outdrew you.*

That's how I was raised: Hurt them before they hurt you or, at the very least, as soon as they do. If you go in once and you get hurt, consider yourself schooled. If you go in twice and get hurt, consider yourself a sucker. Love is by far my scariest arena.

I couldn't reconcile the fear I felt, standing there in the lake muck, with the fact that I had just written a book about vulnerability and daring. So I told myself, *Put your heart where your mouth is.* I flashed a smile in hopes of softening him up and doubled down on my bid for connection: "This is so great. I love that we're doing this. I feel so close to you."

He seemed to be looking through me rather than at me when he replied, "Yep. Good swim." Then he took off again. *This is total horseshit,* I thought. *What's going on? I don't know if I'm supposed to feel humiliated or hostile.* I wanted to cry and I wanted to scream. Instead, fueled by anxiety, I took a deep breath and started swimming back across the cove.

I beat Steve back to the dock by a few strokes. I was physically and emotionally exhausted. I was even a little light-headed. Once Steve reached the dock, he went straight to the rickety metal ladder and started pulling himself out of the water.

"Can you get back in the water?" I said to him. It's all I could manage. He stopped climbing and turned his head toward me with both hands still on the ladder. "Get back in the water, please." He lowered himself into the lake.

"What's up?" he asked as we faced each other and treaded water next to the dock.

What's up? I thought. *He wants to know* what's up*? I have no idea what's up.* All I knew was that I had already scripted the rest of the morning on the swim back, and without an intervention we were headed toward a terrible day. We'd done this fight a thousand times.

We'd climb up onto the dock, dry off, and head to the house. We'd throw our towels over the porch rail, walk into the kitchen, and Steve would say, "What's for breakfast, babe?"

I'd look at him and fire off a sarcastic, "I don't know, *baaabe.* Let me ask the breakfast fairy." Then I'd raise my eyes to the ceiling and put my hands on my hips. "Oh, breakfast fairy! What's for breakfast?" And after a sufficiently long dramatic pause, I'd launch into this oldie but goodie: "Gee, Steve. I forgot how vacation works. I forgot that I'm in charge of breakfast. And lunch. And dinner. And laundry. And packing. And goggles. And sunscreen. And bug spray. And groceries. And . . ." Somewhere in the litany, Steve would scrunch up his face and insert a genuinely confused, "Did something happen? Did I miss something?" Then, somewhere between four and twenty-four hours of cold-war maneuvering would unfold.

We could do this argument with our eyes closed. But this was Lake Travis and this was our special vacation. I wanted something different. I looked at him and, rather than launching into blaming, I tried a new approach. "I've been trying to connect with you and you keep blowing me off. I don't get it."

He just stared at me. The water was about thirty feet deep at the dock, and we were treading water the entire time.

So I had to think quick. This was all new to me. In the course of what felt like an hour but was probably thirty seconds, I went back and forth in my head. *Be kind.* No, get him! *Be kind.* No, self-protect; take him down.

Opting for kind and trusting, I relied completely on a technique I had learned from my research, a phrase that emerged in numerous variations over and over again. I said, "I feel like you're blowing me off, and *the story that I'm making up* is either that you looked over at me while I was swimming and thought, *Man, she's getting old. She can't even swim freestyle anymore.* Or you saw me and thought, *She sure as hell doesn't rock a Speedo like she did twenty-five years ago.*"

Steve seemed agitated. He doesn't lash out when he's frustrated, he takes deep breaths, purses his lips, and nods his head. This probably serves him well in his job as a pediatrician, but I know his tells—he was agitated. He turned his back to me, then turned back around before saying, "Shit. You're being vulnerable, right?"

This answer took no time. "Yes. I am. But I'm right on the edge of rage. So what you say matters. A lot." The phrase "the story that I'm making up" may have emerged from the research as an important tool, but this was my first time using it and I felt literally and emotionally out of my depth.

Steve turned away again and back again. And after what seemed like another eternity, he finally said, "I don't want to do this with you. I really don't."

My immediate reaction was panic. *What's going on? What does that mean*—I don't want to do this with you? *Holy crap. Does that mean he doesn't want to swim with me? Or talk to me?* Then it flashed into my head that maybe the *this* he meant was being married. Time slowed down, and I went into slow-motion, frame-by-frame panic, only to be ripped back to reality when he said, "No. I really don't want to have this conversation with you right now."

I was out of tools and patience. "Too bad. We're having this conversation. Right now. See? I'm talking. Then you're talking. We're having this conversation."

After a few seconds of weird silence and turning away from me in the water, Steve finally faced me and said, "Look, I don't mind hanging out with the kids. I really don't."

What? I was so confused. "What do you mean? What are you talking about?"

Steve explained that he didn't mind taking the kids across the cove on the blow-up rafts. He actually enjoyed pulling them across so they could find "secret treasure," and he loved giving me time to hang out with my sisters.

Completely freaked out at this point, I raised my voice and said, "What are you talking about? What are you saying?"

Steve took a deep breath and, in a voice that was equal parts agitation and resignation, said, "I don't know what you were saying to me today. I have no idea. I was fighting off a total panic attack during that entire swim. I was just trying to stay focused by counting my strokes."

There was silence.

He continued, "Last night I had a dream that I had all five of the kids on the raft, and we were halfway across the cove when a speedboat came hauling toward us. I waved my hands in the air, and they didn't even slow down. I finally grabbed all five of the kids and went as deep as I could go. But, hell, Brené. Ellen and Lorna can swim, but Gabi, Amaya, and Charlie are little, and it's sixty feet deep. I grabbed them off the raft and pulled them as deep as I could go. I held them down there and waited for the boat to pass over us. I knew if we surfaced, we'd be killed. So I waited. But at one point I looked over at Charlie and I could tell he was out of breath. I knew he would drown if we stayed down one more minute. I don't know what you were saying. I was just counting my strokes and trying to get back to the dock."

My heart hurt and my eyes filled with tears. It made sense. We'd arrived at the house on a weekday, when the lake is pretty quiet. Today was Friday, traffic on the lake would double during the weekend, and drunk boaters would be a given. When you grow up around "water people," you hear a lot of stories about boating and skiing accidents caused by drinking, and, tragically, you often know people deeply affected by these events.

"I'm so glad you told me, Steve."

He rolled his eyes. "Bullshit."

Oh my God. Make this conversation stop. Now what? I couldn't believe it. "What are you saying? Of course I'm glad you told me."

Steve shook his head and said, "Look. Don't quote your research to me. Please. Don't tell me what you think you're supposed to say. I know what you want. You want the tough guy. You want the guy who can rescue the kids in the path of a speeding boat by throwing them to the shore and swimming so fast that he's there to catch them before they land. The guy who then looks over at you across the cove and shouts, 'Don't worry, babe! I got this!'"

He was hurting. I was hurting. We were both tired and at the absolute edge of our vulnerability. We owed each other the truth. I wouldn't quote my research at him, but I've been doing that research long enough to know that as much as we'd love to blame distant or cruel fathers, bullying buddies, and over-bearing coaches for the lion's share of shame that men feel, women can be the most fearful about letting men off the white horse and the most likely to be critical of their vulnerability.

I often say, "Show me a woman who can hold space for a man in real fear and vulnerability, and I'll show you a woman who's learned to embrace her own vulnerability and who doesn't derive her power or status from that man. Show me a man who can sit with a woman in real fear and vulnerability and just hear her struggle without trying to fix it or give advice, and I'll show you a man who's comfortable with his own vulnerability and doesn't derive his power from being Oz, the all-knowing and all-powerful."

I reached out and grabbed Steve's hand. "You know what? Ten years ago this story would have scared me. I'm not sure I could have handled it. I might have said the right thing, but a couple of days later, if something triggered it, I might have brought it up in a crappy way, like, 'Are you sure you're feeling up to taking the kids tubing?' I would have screwed up. I would have hurt you and betrayed your trust. I'm sure I have in the past, and I'm truly sorry. Five years ago I would have been better. I would have understood and been respectful, but probably still fearful. Today? Today I'm so grateful for you and our relationship, I don't want anything or anyone but you. I'm learning how to be afraid. You're the best man I know. Plus, we're all we have. We're the big door prize."

Steve smiled. I was speaking in code, but he knew what I meant. "The big door prize" is a line from one of our favorite songs—"In Spite of Ourselves" by John Prine and Iris DeMent. It's one of our favorite date songs, and the chorus always reminds me of Steve:

In spite of ourselves
We'll end up a-sittin' on a rainbow.
Against all odds,
Honey, we're the big door prize.
We're gonna spite our noses
Right off of our faces.
There won't be nothin' but big old hearts
Dancin' in our eyes.

We climbed up on the dock, dried off, and started up the stairs. Steve snapped me on the butt with his wet towel and smiled. "Just so you know: You still rock a Speedo."

That morning was a turning point in our relationship. There we were, both of us completely engulfed in our shame stories. I was stuck in appearance and body-image fear—the most common shame trigger for women. He was afraid I would think he was weak—the most common shame trigger for men. Both of us were scared to embrace our own vulnerabilities, even knowing full well that vulnerability is the only path out of the shame storm and back to each other. Somehow we managed to find the courage to trust ourselves and each other, avoiding both the hot sting of words we would never be able to take back and the withheld affection of a cold war. That morning revolutionized how we thought about our marriage. It wasn't a subtle evolution: It forever shifted our relationship. And that was a good thing.

For me, this became a story of great possibility, of what *could be* if our best selves showed up when we were angry or frustrated or hurt. Our fights didn't normally go so well—this was transformative. In fact, it was such a powerful story that I asked Steve what he thought about my using it as an example of the power of vulnerability when I speak in public. He said, "Of course. It really is a pretty amazing story."

We were able to resurrect some of these skills we learned at the lake in later arguments, but for some reason unknown to me at the time, those subsequent showdowns were never as good or as productive as the one that day. I was convinced that it was the magic of Lake Travis or the majesty of nature itself that made us more gentle and loving with each other. I would eventually learn that there was much more to the story.

YOU CAN'T SKIP DAY TWO

Fast-forward two years, and I find myself on a stage sharing the Lake Travis story with a standing-room-only crowd at Pixar Animation Studios.

First, like so many things in my life, synchronicity figured in to how I ended up at Pixar. I was in some U.S. airport waiting on a delayed plane when I went to the airport store to find something to read. I was surprised to see Eric Clapton on the cover of *Fast Company*—one of my favorite magazines—so I bought it and stuck it in my bag.

When we finally took off, I pulled out my magazine and upon closer examination realized it wasn't Eric Clapton. It was a rock 'n' roll photo of Ed Catmull, and the article was about his new book. Ed is the president of Pixar Animation and Walt Disney Animation Studios, and it's fair to say that his leadership book *Creativity, Inc.* would go on to influence me as much as anything I've ever read. His lessons, on how strong leaders must identify the things that kill trust and creativity in order to nurture cultures and conditions that allow good people to do what they do best, changed how I think about my role in my organization and even in my family. After I gave copies to everyone on my team, his ideas and concepts quickly became part of our vernacular at work.

I was so impressed by Ed's work that I reached out to my editor at Random House (also Ed's publisher) to ask for an introduction. I was hoping to interview him for this book. As it turned out, Ed and a core group of folks at Pixar had seen my TED talks. They promptly asked if I'd like to come out and spend the day with them. My first thought was, *Will it be too much if I show up dressed as Jessie from* Toy Story*?* Hell, yes, I'm coming for a visit.

Okay, many people would file our mutual interest in connecting under random coincidence. I file it under "God thing." Or, as novelist Paulo Coelho talks about in his book *The Alche-*

mist, when you're on your path, the universe will conspire to help you.

After giving my talk, I had lunch with Ed and some of the leaders at Pixar—mostly producers, directors, animators, and writers. The conversation focused on the unavoidable uncertainty, vulnerability, and discomfort of the creative process. As they were explaining how frustrating it is that absolutely no amount of experience or success gives you a free pass from the daunting level of doubt that is an unyielding part of the process, I thought about my own experiences with The Daring Way.

The Daring Way is a certification program for professionals in helping fields who want to facilitate my work. In our national training seminars, we use a three-day intensive model as our primary teaching tool. Our faculty members go through the curriculum with small groups of ten to twelve people, allowing new candidates both to experience the work as participants and to learn the research behind the curriculum. No matter how many times we've done it and how many people we've certified, day two of this three-day model still sucks. In fact, certified facilitators who go on to use the three-day model with their clients always tell us, "I thought I could do it better and make day two easier, but I can't. It's still so hard."

All of a sudden, when I was at Pixar, clarity struck. I looked at Ed and said, "Oh my God. I totally get this. You can't skip day two." Ed immediately knew I got it. He smiled in a way that conveyed, "Right. No skipping the middle."

Day two, or whatever that middle space is for your own process, is when you're "in the dark"—the door has closed behind you. You're too far in to turn around and not close enough to the end to see the light. In my work with veterans and active members of the military, we've talked about this dark middle. They all know it as "the point of no return"—an aviation term coined by pilots for the point in a flight when they have too little fuel left to return to the originating airfield. It's strangely universal, going all the way back to Julius Caesar's famous *"Iacta alea est"*—"The die is cast"—spoken in 49 BC as he and his troops made the river crossing that started a war. Whether it's ancient battle strategy or the creative process, at some point you're in, it's dark, and there's no turning back.

With the Daring Way groups, day two means we are moving into the shame and worthiness part of the curriculum, and people are feeling raw. The shine of a new undertaking and the sparkle of possibility have dulled, leaving behind a dense fog of uncertainty. People are tired. With our groups, and groups in general, you're also hitting the rocky part of what Bruce Tuckman, a group dynamics researcher, describes as the "form-storm-norm-perform" cycle. When a group or team first comes together (*form*), it's often rocky for a time while members figure out the dynamics (*storm*). At some point, the group finds its groove (*norm*) and starts to make headway (*perform*). *Storm* occupies the middle space. It's not only a dark and vulnerable time, but also one that's often turbulent. People find all kinds of creative ways to resist the dark, including taking issue with each other.

What I think sucks the most about day two is exactly what Ed and the Pixar team pointed out—it's a nonnegotiable part of the process. Experience and success don't give you easy passage through the middle space of struggle. They only grant you a little grace, a grace that whispers, "This is part of the process.

Stay the course." Experience doesn't create even a single spark of light in the darkness of the middle space. It only instills in you a little bit of faith in your ability to navigate the dark. The middle is messy, but it's also where the magic happens.

As we wrapped up our lunch conversation at Pixar, one of the writers in the room shared a keen observation about our discussion. "Day two is like the second act in our stories. It's always the toughest for our teams. It's always where we struggle with our characters and our narrative arc." Everyone in the room responded with an emphatic nod or a passionate "Yes!"

After I got back to Houston, Ed sent me an email saying that our conversation about day two had sent a jolt through the room. I had no idea at the time how the jolt and my entire Pixar visit would eventually affect me personally and professionally.

Hanging on the wall of Pixar's Story Corner display were these three sentences:

Story is the big picture.
Story is process.
Story is research.

An image of a crown was at the top of the wall, symbolizing the axiom that "story is king." When I got home, I used Post-it notes to re-create that wall in my study just to remind myself of the importance of story in our lives. It also turned out to foreshadow something important for me. I knew the trip to Pixar meant more than a great day with gifted people—there was something else to it. I just didn't know then how strong the reverberating power of that jolt would be.

Before my Pixar visit, I'd never thought much about the science of storytelling. I'd certainly never used any conscious storytelling calculus in designing my talks. In fact, when I read the occasional analysis of my TED talks, I'm shocked to see how people take the smallest gestures, from glances to pauses, and use them to apply labels and formulas to my work. *At minute four, Brené shifts her body to the left and gives a slight half grin. This is known as the Soft Smile Pivot and should be used with extreme care.* I'm exaggerating a bit, but not much. It's so weird.

I appreciate good storytelling and I know it's not easy. I assume that I learned storytelling from the long line of raconteurs from whence I came. I think my upbringing, combined with years of studying the science and art of teaching, led me to become an accidental storyteller. And while I might be able to make my way through a story, I knew I needed to learn more about the craft for one reason: Storytelling was emerging as a key variable in my most recent study. So I did what I do best—research.

I emailed Darla Anderson, a producer I had met at Pixar who was behind some of my favorite films, including *Toy Story 3, Monsters, Inc., A Bug's Life,* and *Cars.* I asked her if she could help me understand how people at Pixar think about the traditional three-act structure of storytelling. Even though I was amassing a growing number of books and articles on everything from the neuroscience of storytelling to screenwriting, I wanted to hear the process explained by someone who lives the work—someone who has it in her bones. That's where my richest data comes from: a person's lived experiences.

Darla was great. She had already emailed me about how her

team was still talking about vulnerability and how "Rock the Speedo" had become a touchstone among the Pixar crew. In a couple of emails, Darla helped me get my head around the three acts:

Act 1: The protagonist is called to adventure and accepts the adventure. The rules of the world are established, and the end of Act 1 is the "inciting incident."

Act 2: The protagonist looks for every comfortable way to solve the problem. By the climax, he learns what it's really going to take to solve the problem. This act includes the "lowest of the low."

Act 3: The protagonist needs to prove she's learned the lesson, usually showing a willingness to prove this at all costs. This is all about redemption—an enlightened character knowing what to do to resolve a conflict.

My first thought was, *Holy crap, this is Joseph Campbell's hero's journey.* Joseph Campbell was an American scholar, professor, and writer best known for his work on comparative mythology and religion. Campbell found that countless myths from different times and cultures share fundamental structures and stages, which he called the hero's journey, or the monomyth. He introduced this idea in his book *The Hero with a Thousand Faces,* which I read in my twenties and again in my midthirties. When I was growing up, my mom's bookshelves were stacked high with books by Joseph Campbell and Carl Jung. This new insight made me realize that in addition to my dad's campfire storytelling, I had been exposed to more about the art of story than I realized.

I shot an email to Darla, asking her if my Campbell comparison was on target, and she replied, "Yep! We reference Joseph Campbell and the hero's journey at the beginning of every film!" It started to make sense, and before I knew it, I had the opportunity to apply what I was learning to my own story.

One afternoon, after a really hard conversation with Steve about our seemingly different approaches to homework checking—an argument that did *not* end with a towel slap on the butt and a compliment but rather with my recommendation that we "stop arguing before we say something we'll regret"— I sat alone in my study, staring at my version of Pixar's Story Wall. *Maybe we should only fight when we're in the lake? Maybe I'm holding on to the Lake Travis story because it's an anomaly?* None of the arguments we'd had since then had ended that well. I started to play the story over in my head and glanced up at my story wall, where I had stuck a giant Post-it note outlining the three acts.

Increasingly frustrated about Steve's and my inability to show up and work things out the way we did in Austin, I decided to map our lake story into the three acts. Maybe I would learn something new. I came up with

Act 1: The call to the adventure of swimming across the lake. Inciting incident—Steve blows me off when I'm being vulnerable and trying to connect.

Act 2: Nothing, really. Just a crappy, anxiety-fueled swim back.

Act 3: We lean in to the discomfort and the vulnerability and we work it out.

Then the jolt coursed through my body, literally from the
top of my head to the bottoms of my feet. *You can't skip day
two. You can't skip day two. You can't skip day two. Where is the
messy middle? Where is Act 2?*

I had told this story fifty times, but I had never fleshed out
the second act, much less told it. *What about the crappy swim
back to the dock? What if the key to the lake story happened under
the water, not on it?* It popped into my head that both Carl Jung
and Joseph Campbell wrote about water as the symbol of the
unconscious. Symbolism and metaphor are embedded in our
storytelling genes, but I don't normally use terms like *con-
sciousness* and *the unconscious.* I believe in the concepts, but
those words don't feel very accessible or practical—they just
don't resonate with or speak to me. I prefer *awake* or *aware.*
Still, it was clear that something had been happening beyond
my awareness, and what better symbol exists for "beyond our
awareness" than deep water?

The anxiety that Steve and I both experienced while swimming that day is not uncommon for swimmers and divers. You
give up a lot when you venture into an environment that you
can't control and where your senses don't serve you in depend-
able ways. Hunter S. Thompson wrote, "Civilization ends at
the waterline. Beyond that, we all enter the food chain, and
not always right at the top." Was I just unaware of what really
transpired that day? Had I been telling the civilized version of
the story? Was something important happening beyond my
understanding until now?

I got out my research journal and started writing down everything I could remember from my swim back to the dock.

First, the swim back was terrible—it felt as if I were swimming through quicksand. Goggles kept the water out of my eyes, but you can't see two feet in front of you in Lake Travis. Even as a child, I wondered how the blue-green water could be so thick.

I remembered at one point, about halfway back to the dock, getting really anxious. I started thinking, *What's below me? Are there bodies under there? Are there snakes?* In a devastating turn, Pa, Aunt Lorenia's neighbor that I mentioned earlier, drowned in the lake when I was eight years old. He was fishing off the dock by himself, fell in the water, hit his head on the way down, and died. As I swam on, my imagination went wild, and I started freaking myself out (which, to be honest, doesn't take much for me in lakes or oceans). Just when I would feel the urge to flip onto my back and start floating until someone could rescue me from my own dammed-up reservoir of anxiety, I'd pull myself together.

In addition to battling the deepwater crazies, I was running through a series of random questions about Steve and the situation at hand. I was playing out scenarios and reality-checking myself as I made my way through the opaque water. I couldn't see anything, but I felt everything. It was as if the very emotion that my brain was generating had added fifty-pound weights around my ankles. I could barely get my legs to keep kicking. Normally I love the weightlessness of the water. On this swim I just felt like sinking.

The more I wrote in my journal, the more surprised I was by the vividness of the memories from that day. I switched to capturing the moments in a numbered list.

1. Early in the swim, I started off by telling myself a version of the story that allowed me to be the victim (and the hero) and that ended with Steve getting paid back when he least expected it.

2. I kept thinking to myself with each stroke, *I'm so pissed, I'm so pissed.* But after a few minutes, I fessed up. I had learned several years before that when I'm planning payback or rehearsing a conversation where I'm being super mean or trying to make someone feel bad, I'm normally not mad, I'm hurt, feeling uncomfortably vulnerable, or feeling shame. I was all three during that swim back. I was hurt that he had pushed me away and feeling shame over why.

3. I then started wrestling with the payback story. I hate that ending of Steve getting his, but it's the one I do best when I'm hurt. The only way I could possibly change the ending was to tell a different story, one where Steve's intentions were not bad. I bombarded myself with questions while I was swimming: *Could I be that generous? Do I have a part in this? Can I trust him? Do I trust myself? What's the most generous assumption that I can make about his response while still acknowledging my own feelings and needs?*

4. The question that was the hardest to answer that day involves the most vulnerable decision I have to make when I'm afraid or angry: What are the consequences of putting down the weapons and taking off the armor? *What if he was hurting me on purpose? What if he's really an insensitive person? If I give him the benefit of the doubt and I'm wrong, I'll be doubly shamed for being rejected* and *naïve.* Of course, this was the point in the swim when I started worrying about bodies in the water and krakens—the giant squids feared by generations of sailors. I actually remember thinking that morning about that scene in the second *Pirates of the Caribbean* film when Davy Jones yells, "Release the kraken!" It's no wonder I was light-headed by the time I got back.

5. I remember wishing I could talk to my sisters about this before I screwed it up.

Before I could write and punctuate number six in the growing list in my journal, a second big jolt hit me. Oh my God! Those weren't random questions that I had been trying to answer that morning. These questions were concepts emerging from my ongoing research on overcoming adversity. For a year, I had been telling this story as an example of vulnerability and shame resilience; little did I know that what lay beneath the story—in that murky water—was also the story of rising strong.

When I was writing *Daring Greatly,* I decided not to include what I was learning about overcoming adversity. Not only was it too much to include in a book that was already introducing huge concepts like vulnerability and scarcity, I also didn't fully understand it yet. I knew the elements of shame resilience and the role that vulnerability plays in being brave, but as far as the actual process of rising strong went, I was only clear on the basics. I had yet to sort out the process and label the pieces.

Looking back on how my research played out under the water that summer, I was caught off guard by the applicability of what I was learning about rising strong to smaller everyday situations—like the incident at the lake. I thought I was working on a process for addressing life's major struggles. Like everyone, I know failure and I know heartbreak—I've survived the kind of professional failures and personal heartbreaks that rearrange

your life. While a hallmark of grounded theory research is that it
generates basic social processes that have extremely broad application, I had worried about whether rising strong could address a wide range of issues, or if I even wanted it to. Would its
power be somehow diminished if we applied it to smaller events,
like the fight at the lake? The answer is no. Comparative suffering has taught me not to discount the importance of having a
process to navigate everyday hurts and disappointments. They
can shape who we are and how we feel just as much as those
things that we consider the big events do.

I still think Lake Travis is a magical place, but not because it
washed away Steve's and my conflict. It was a revolutionary
moment in our relationship that could happen only because
we had each owned our stories. We didn't just figure it out and
lean in to vulnerability. Like Darla had spelled out in her email,
our Act 2 was trying every comfortable way to solve the problem before we finally gave in to our truths. Having spent the
past two years drilling down into the smaller pieces of the rising strong process to understand how each part of it works and
how the pieces fit together, I can look back now and see exactly
why things happened that summer morning. I was working
through the process.

The Rising Strong Process

The goal of the process is to rise from our falls, overcome our mistakes, and face hurt in a way that brings more wisdom and wholeheartedness into our lives.

THE RECKONING: WALKING INTO OUR STORY

Recognize emotion, and get curious about our feelings and how they connect with the way we think and behave.

THE RUMBLE: OWNING OUR STORY

Get honest about the stories we're making up about our struggle, then challenge these confabulations and assumptions to determine what's truth, what's self-protection, and what needs to change if we want to lead more wholehearted lives.

THE REVOLUTION

Write a new ending to our story based on the key learnings from our rumble and use this new, braver story to change how we engage with the world and to ultimately transform the way we live, love, parent, and lead.

THE IRONY IS THAT WE *attempt to* DISOWN *our* DIFFICULT STORIES *to appear more whole or more* ACCEPTABLE, BUT OUR WHOLENESS – *even our wholeheartedness* – ACTUALLY DEPENDS ON THE INTEGRATION OF ALL OF OUR EXPERIENCES, *including the falls.*

Three
OWNING OUR STORIES

A map does not just chart, it unlocks and formulates meaning; it forms bridges between here and there, between disparate ideas that we did not know were previously connected.

—Reif Larsen

I love maps not because they dictate the route or tell me when or how to travel, but simply because they mark the waypoints I will eventually visit. Knowing that these places exist and that they are well traveled, even if they are unexplored by me, is powerful.

I have charted the map of the rising strong process from the stories and experiences of men and women who have found wholehearted ways to navigate struggle. This process teaches us how to own our stories of falling down, screwing up, and facing hurt so we can integrate those stories into our lives and write daring new endings.

"Owning our story and loving ourselves through that process is the bravest thing we'll ever do." I still believe in this quote from two of my previous books—maybe now more than ever. But I know that it takes more than courage to own your story. We own our stories so we don't spend our lives being defined by them or denying them. And while the journey is long and difficult at times, it is the path to living a more wholehearted life.

THE RISING STRONG PROCESS

The goal of this process is to rise from our falls, overcome our mistakes, and face hurt in a way that brings more wisdom and wholeheartedness.

The Reckoning—Men and women who rise strong are willing and able to reckon with their emotions. First, they recognize that they're feeling something—a button has been pushed, they're hooked, something is triggered, their emotions are off-kilter. Second, they get curious about what's happening and how what they're feeling is connected to their thoughts and behaviors. Engaging in this process is how we walk into our story.

The Rumble—Men and women who rise strong are willing and able to rumble with their stories. By *rumble,* I mean they get honest about the stories they've made up about their struggles and they are willing to revisit, challenge, and reality-check these narratives as they dig into topics such as boundaries, shame, blame, resentment, heartbreak, generosity, and forgiveness.

Rumbling with these topics and moving from our first responses to a deeper understanding of our thoughts, feelings, and behaviors gives birth to key learnings about who we are and how we engage with others. The rumble is where wholeheartedness is cultivated and change begins.

The Revolution—Unlike evolutionary change, which is incremental, revolutionary change fundamentally transforms our thoughts and beliefs. Rumbling with our story and owning our truth in order to write a new, more courageous ending transforms who we are and how we engage with the world. Men and women who rise strong integrate the key learnings that emerge from the rising strong process into how they live, love, lead, parent, and participate as citizens. This has tremendous ramifications not only for their own lives, but also for their families, organizations, and communities.

INTEGRATING

The Latin root of the word *integrate* is *integrare,* which means "to make whole." Integrating is the engine that moves us through the reckoning, the rumble, and the revolution, and the goal of each of these processes is to make ourselves whole. Participants spoke about the importance of feeling genuine, authentic, and whole rather than always compartmentalizing their lives or hiding parts of themselves or editing their stories. The tools they used to integrate their stories of falling are readily available to all of us because they are deeply human and part of our wholeness: storytelling and creativity (primarily writing about or taking notes on their experiences).

Integration Through Creativity

Steve Jobs believed that "creativity is just connecting things." He believed that creating was connecting the dots between the experiences we've had, to synthesize new things. He argued that this is only possible if we have more experiences or devote more time to thinking about our experiences. I agree—this is exactly why creativity is such a powerful integration tool. Creating is the act of paying attention to our experiences and connecting the dots so we can learn more about ourselves and the world around us. In addition to teaching creativity-based courses and learning from that process, I was able to interview more than one hundred creatives in this research. No group taught me more about the inherently tough middle space of processes and the power of integration.

For our purposes we need to do just a little writing—nothing formal, just jotting down some notes on our experiences. Of course, you're welcome to do something more elaborate, but it's not necessary. It's devoting time and attention to our experiences that really matters.

Among the professional storytellers I interviewed for this book was Shonda Rhimes, the creator and show runner of *Grey's Anatomy* and *Scandal,* and one of my favorite story writers. When I asked her about the role of struggle in storytelling, she said, "I don't even know who a character is until I've seen how they handle adversity. Onscreen and offscreen, that's how you know who someone is."

If *integrate* means "to make whole," then its opposite is to fracture, disown, disjoin, detach, unravel, or separate. I think many of us move through the world feeling this way. The irony is that we attempt to disown our difficult stories to appear more whole or more acceptable, but our wholeness—even our wholeheartedness—actually depends on the integration of all of our experiences, including the falls.

CURIOSITY
is a
SHIT-STARTER.
BUT THAT'S OKAY.
Sometimes we have to
RUMBLE
WITH A STORY
to find the truth.

Four

THE RECKONING

The big question is whether you are going to be able
to say a hearty yes to your adventure.

—Joseph Campbell

You may not have signed up for a hero's journey, but the second you fell down, got your butt kicked, suffered a disappointment, screwed up, or felt your heart break, it started. It doesn't matter whether we are ready for an emotional adventure—hurt happens. And it happens to every single one of us. Without exception. The only decision we get to make is what role we'll play in our own lives: Do we want to write the story or do we want to hand that power over to someone else? Choosing to write our own story means getting uncomfortable; it's choosing courage over comfort.

One of the truisms of wholehearted living is *You either walk into your story and own your truth, or you live outside of your story, hustling for your worthiness.* Walking into a story about falling down can feel like being swallowed whole by emotion. Our bodies often respond before our conscious minds, and they are hardwired to protect—to run or fight. Even with small, every-day conflicts and disappointments, physical and emotional intolerance for discomfort is the primary reason we linger on the outskirts of our stories, never truly facing them or integrating them into our lives. We disengage to self-protect.

In navigation, the term *reckoning,* as in *dead reckoning,* is the process of calculating where you are. To do that, you have to know where you've been and what factors influenced how you got to where you now are (speed, course, wind, etc.). Without reckoning, you can't chart a future course. In the rising strong process, we can't chart a brave new course until we recognize exactly where we are, get curious about how we got there, and decide where we want to go. Ours is an emotional reckoning.

There is a clear pattern among the women and men who demonstrate the ability to rise strong from hurt or adversity—they reckon with emotion. The word *reckon* comes from the Middle English *rekenen,* meaning to narrate or make an account. The rising strong reckoning has two deceptively simple parts: (1) engaging with our feelings, and (2) getting curious about the story behind the feelings—what emotions we're experiencing and how they are connected to our thoughts and behaviors.

First, rising strong requires us to recognize that we're experiencing a "facedown in the arena" moment—an emotional reaction. Remember, these moments can be small and we're susceptible to them anytime we're trying to show up and be seen. A button is pushed, a sense of disappointment or anger washes over us, our hearts race—something tells us that all is not well. We're hooked. The good news is that in our reckoning we don't have to pinpoint the emotion accurately—we just need to recognize that we're feeling something. There will be time to sort out exactly what we're feeling later.

> I don't know what's happening, but I just want to hide.
>
> I just know I want to punch a wall.
>
> I want Oreos. Lots of them.
>
> I feel _____ (disappointed, regretful, pissed, hurt, angry, heartbroken, confused, scared, worried, etc.).
>
> I am _____ (in a lot of pain, feeling really vulnerable, in a shame storm, embarrassed, overwhelmed, in a world of hurt).
>
> Steve ignored my bid for connection and now I'm feeling something between anger and fear.
>
> My stomach is in knots.

This sounds pretty easy, but you'd be surprised how many of us never recognize our emotions or feelings—we off-load instead. Rather than saying *I failed and it feels so crappy,* we move to *I am a failure.* We act out and shut down rather than reaching out.

The goal here is simply to recognize that emotions and feelings are in play. Some of us might be alerted to emotion by our bodies' responses. Others know that something emotional is happening because our thoughts start racing or we have the event on slow-motion replay. And others may recognize emotion is at hand only once their behavior sends up a flare, like yelling at their kids or firing off a shitty email to a colleague. For me, it all depends on the emotion. When I feel shame, sometimes my body's response is the first clue that I'm being hijacked by emotion. I can get tunnel vision and my heart races. My less-than-awesome blaming behavior is normally a sign that I'm resentful, and when I start rehearsing mean-spirited "gotcha" conversations, I'm normally feeling vulnerable or afraid.

Recognizing emotion means developing awareness about how our thinking, feeling (including our physiology), and behavior are connected. While some researchers and clinicians argue that you can change your life by just changing your thoughts, actions, or feelings, I have seen no evidence in my research that real transformation happens until we address all three as equally important parts of a whole, parts that are inextricably connected to one another, like a three-legged stool.

Second, rising strong requires getting curious about our experience. This means having the willingness to open a line of inquiry into what's going on and why. Again, the good news is that you don't need to answer those questions right off the bat. You just need to want to learn more:

Why am I being so hard on everyone around me
    today?
What's setting me off?
How did I get to the point that I want to punch this
    wall?
I want to dig in to why I'm so overwhelmed.
I can't stop thinking about that conversation at work.
    Why not?

I'm having such a strong emotional reaction—what's
   going on?
I know Oreos aren't going to work. What's really happening?
What's going on with my stomach?

For example, your face turns red and heat radiates across
your chest when you learn that your boss gave the lead for a
new project to your colleague. Rising strong requires you to
recognize that you're experiencing emotion and to get curious
about why: *I'm so pissed about her giving the lead to Todd. I need
to figure this out before I lose it with everyone on our team.* Or
maybe your father is once again critical of your parenting during a holiday get-together. You basically check out. You're
quiet and almost hiding the rest of the night. When you get
home you realize that you're full of emotion. You turn to your
partner and say, *"I'm so tired of feeling like crap around my father.
I expect it to get better, but he never lets up. Why do I keep walking
into this?"*

The reckoning sounds pretty straightforward, but like I said
earlier, that's deceptive and, frankly, it's not the default for
most of us. Don't forget that our bodies respond to emotion
first, and they often direct us to shut down or disengage. In
that first scenario, it's so much easier to steamroll right over
emotion: *My boss is an asshole. Todd's such a brownnoser. Who
cares? This job sucks and this company is a joke.* There's been no
recognition of emotion. No curiosity.

In the second scenario, there are a number of options that
are easier than engaging. We could buy into our father's criticism and stay completely withdrawn, we might start planning

how we're going to impress him the next time, we could discharge our emotion by yelling at our partner for no reason, we could drink another beer or three—whatever it takes to drown the criticism, we could easily rage and blame the kids for making us look bad, we could spend the entire ride home vowing to never see our dad again—the list goes on.

The opposite of recognizing that we're feeling something is denying our emotions. The opposite of being curious is disengaging. When we deny our stories and disengage from tough emotions, they don't go away; instead, they own us, they define us. Our job is not to deny the story, but to defy the ending—to rise strong, recognize our story, and rumble with the truth until we get to a place where we think, Yes. This is what happened. This is my truth. And I will choose how this story ends.

In the following sections I want to explore the two parts of the reckoning: recognizing emotion and getting curious. Specifically, I want to look at what gets in the way of both of these efforts and how we can develop new practices that give us both the tools and the courage to engage.

RECKONING WITH EMOTION

What gets in the way of reckoning with emotion is exactly what gets in the way of engaging in other courageous behaviors: fear. We don't like how difficult emotions feel and we're worried about what people might think. We don't know what to do with the discomfort and vulnerability. Emotion can feel terrible, even physically overwhelming. We can feel exposed, at risk, and uncertain in the midst of emotion. Our instinct is to run from pain. In fact, most of us were never taught how to hold discomfort, sit with it, or communicate it, only how to discharge or dump it, or to pretend that it's not happening. If you combine that with the instinctual avoidance of pain, it's easy to understand why off-loading becomes a habit. Both nature and nurture lead us to off-load emotion and discomfort, often onto other people. The irony is that at the exact same time that we are creating distance between ourselves and the people around us by off-loading onto others, we are craving deeper emotional connection and richer emotional lives.

Miriam Greenspan, a psychotherapist and the author of *Healing Through the Dark Emotions,* was interviewed by Jungian therapist Barbara Platek in *The Sun Magazine.* The article has been required reading in my classes since it first appeared in 2008. Greenspan explains why she believes our culture is "emotion phobic" and that we fear and devalue emotion. She cautions:

> But despite our fear, there is something in us that wants to feel all these emotional energies, because they are the juice of life. When we suppress and diminish our emotions, we feel deprived. So we watch horror movies or so-called reality shows like *Fear Factor.* We seek out emotional intensity vicariously, because when we are emotionally numb, we need a great deal of stimulation to feel something, anything. So emotional pornography provides the stimulation, but it's only ersatz emotion—it doesn't teach us anything about ourselves or the world.

I don't think we can learn much about ourselves, our relationships, or the world without recognizing and getting curious about emotion. Fortunately, unlike navigating using dead reckoning, we don't need to immediately be precise in order to find our way. We just need to bring our feelings to light. We just need to be honest and curious. *I'm having an emotional reaction to what's happened and I want to understand* is enough for the reckoning. But it's still difficult in our culture. Let's take a closer look at curiosity.

GETTING CURIOUS

Choosing to be curious is choosing to be vulnerable because it requires us to surrender to uncertainty. It wasn't always a choice; we were born curious. But over time, we learn that curiosity, like vulnerability, can lead to hurt. As a result, we turn to self-protecting—choosing certainty over curiosity, armor over vulnerability, and knowing over learning. But shutting down comes with a price—a price we rarely consider when we're focused on finding our way out of pain.

Einstein said, "The important thing is not to stop questioning. Curiosity has its own reason for existence." Curiosity's reason for existing is not simply to be a tool used in acquiring knowledge; it reminds us that we're alive. Researchers are finding evidence that curiosity is correlated with creativity, intelligence, improved learning and memory, and problem solving.

There is a profound relationship—a love affair, really—between curiosity and wholeheartedness. How do we come to those *aha* moments if we're not willing to explore and ask questions? New information won't transform our thinking, much less our lives, if it simply lands at our feet. For experiences and information to be integrated into our lives as true awareness, they have to be received with open hands, inquisitive minds, and wondering hearts.

A critical piece of my wholehearted journey has been moving from judgment to curiosity about my own path. Poet and writer William Plomer wrote, "Creativity is the power to connect the seemingly unconnected." Connecting the dots of our lives, especially the ones we'd rather erase or skip over, requires equal parts self-love and curiosity: *How do all of these experiences come together to make up who I am?*

Curiosity led me to adopt and live by the belief that "nothing is wasted"—a belief that shapes how I see the world and my life. I can now look back at my often rough-and-tumble past and understand how dropping out of school, hitchhiking across Europe, bartending and waiting tables, working as a union steward, and taking customer service calls in Spanish on the night shift at AT&T taught me as much about empathy as my career as a social worker, teacher, and researcher. I used to look back at those far-flung dots as mistakes and wasted time, but allowing myself to be curious about who I am and how everything fits together changed that. As difficult and dark as some of those times were, they all connect to form the real me, the integrated and whole me.

Curiosity is an act of vulnerability and courage. In this stage of the rising strong process—the reckoning—we need to get curious. We need to be brave enough to *want to know more.*

I say *brave* because getting curious about emotion is not always an easy choice. I have to take a deep breath and think through questions like, *What's at stake if I open myself up to investigate these feelings and realize I'm more hurt than I thought? Or, What if she's really not to blame and I was wrong? It's going to suck if it turns out that I'm the one who needs to make amends.*

But again, the upside of curiosity outweighs discomfort. A study published in the October 22, 2014, issue of the journal *Neuron* suggests that the brain's chemistry changes when we become curious, helping us better learn and retain information. But curiosity is uncomfortable because it involves uncertainty and vulnerability.

Curiosity is a shit-starter. But that's okay. Sometimes we have to rumble with a story to find the truth.

In his book *Curious: The Desire to Know and Why Your Future Depends on It,* Ian Leslie writes, "Curiosity is unruly. It doesn't like rules, or, at least, it assumes that all rules are provisional, subject to the laceration of a smart question nobody has yet thought to ask. It disdains the approved pathways, preferring diversions, unplanned excursions, impulsive left turns. In short, curiosity is deviant."

This is exactly why curiosity is so vital to this process: The diverse and sometimes erratic course of rising strong is also unruly. Embracing the vulnerability it takes to rise up from a fall and grow stronger makes us a little dangerous. People who don't stay down after they fall or are tripped are often troublemakers. Hard to control. Which is the best kind of dangerous possible. They are the artists, innovators, and change-makers.

The most common barrier to getting curious about emotion is having a **dry well.** In his groundbreaking 1994 article "The Psychology of Curiosity," George Loewenstein introduced his **information gap** perspective on curiosity. Loewenstein, a professor of economics and psychology at Carnegie Mellon University, proposed that curiosity is the feeling of deprivation we experience when we identify and focus on a gap in our knowledge.

What's important about this perspective is that it means **we have to have some level of knowledge or awareness before we can get curious.** We aren't curious about something we are unaware of or know nothing about. Loewenstein explains that simply encouraging people to ask questions doesn't go very far toward stimulating curiosity. He writes, "To induce curiosity about a particular topic, it may be necessary to 'prime the pump'"—to use intriguing information to get folks interested so they become more curious.

The good news is that a growing number of researchers believe that curiosity and knowledge-building grow together—the more we know, the more we want to know. The bad news is that many of us are raised believing that emotions aren't worthy of our attention. In other words, we don't know enough and/or we aren't sufficiently aware of the power of our emotions and how they're connected to our thoughts and behaviors, so we fail to get curious.

There are still no definitive research answers about how we develop curiosity, but what I can tell you for certain is this: The participants in my study who taught me the most about getting curious learned to investigate their emotions in one of three ways:

1. Their parents or another important adult in their lives (often a teacher, coach, or counselor) explicitly taught them about emotion and the importance of exploring feelings.

2. Their parents or another important adult in their lives (often a teacher, coach, or counselor) modeled curiosity about emotion.

3. They worked with a helping professional who taught them about the power of inquiry.

In other words, their pumps were primed with enough knowledge about emotion to serve as a foundation for getting curious.

There are numerous, complex reasons why the well is dry—why there's so little open discussion and engagement around emotion. The research made it clear that a lot of how much or little we value emotion comes from what we were taught or saw as we were growing up. That value usually results from a combination of several of the seven ideas listed below.

1. Being emotional is a sign of vulnerability, and vulnerability is weakness.

2. Don't ask. Don't tell. You can feel emotion all you want, but there's nothing to be gained by sharing it with others.

3. We don't have access to emotional language or a full emotional vocabulary, so we stay quiet about or make fun of it.

4. Discussing emotion is frivolous, self-indulgent, and a waste of time. It's not for people like us.

5. We're so numb to feeling that there's nothing to discuss.

6. Uncertainty is too uncomfortable.

7. Engaging and asking questions invites trouble. I'll learn something I don't want to or shouldn't know.

When I was a child, the smallest glimpse into a new world could unleash a torrent of curiosity within me. If I came across a word I didn't know in a book, I'd look it up. If a television show referenced an island in the Pacific, I'd run for our *Encyclopedia Britannica,* praying the entire way that there would be color photos. I wanted to know more about everything. Except emotion.

I grew up with a dry emotional well. I didn't want to know more because I didn't know there was more to learn—we didn't discuss feelings. We didn't do vulnerability. If we happened to get so overwhelmed by emotion that tears or a look of fear physically breached our tough veneer, we were promptly and not-too-subtly reminded that emotions don't fix problems—they make them worse. Doing, not feeling, fixes problems.

My emotional education started in my late teens, when I watched my mother break every taboo in our family and go to therapy. Our family was like many others I knew—quietly imploding. It was the early 1980s and we lived in a suburb of Houston. My high school, along with several others, was featured in the national news for the number of suicides. My siblings and I were all lost. We were wild and for the most part unseen. And, like many Houstonians navigating the oil bust in the early 1980s, my parents were just trying to keep the lights on and postpone the inevitable loss of everything.

Regardless of how dark and hard things got, there was never any discussion of how we were doing or how we were feeling until my mom went to therapy. The more curious she became about her own life and feelings, and our lives and feelings, the worse things got. There seemed to be no stop to the endless excavating of hurt and resentment and grief. I wasn't sure if it

was worth it. But my mother, who was living on Merit cigarettes, Tab soda, and her survival instincts, saw her emotional
reckoning as a life-or-death situation. We were left wondering
if the implosion was happening because we had never recognized or questioned our pain, or if everything was falling apart
precisely because we were breaking the rules and getting too
curious about our feelings. The latter was what we had been
taught and told growing up.

But, against the odds, my mom was rising strong after a
long, slow fall that started when I was around twelve. Over the
next few years, she modeled and taught us what she was learning in therapy, and that small spark started an inextinguish-
able transformation in our family. It also led to several years of
tremendous pain and discomfort and burned down a lot of
what we knew—including my parents' marriage. While their
divorcing was the right thing to do, it was nonetheless heartbreaking for all of us.

But as poet Mizuta Masahide wrote, "Barn's burnt down /
now / I can see the moon." Eventually, the burning not only re-
vealed new light, but turned over new soil, and, with new seeds,
it brought love and renewal. If you had told me during those
fiery, dark days that eventually everything would be okay as
long as everyone kept talking about their feelings and setting
boundaries, and that one day, all four of my divorced and remar-
ried parents and in-laws would be in the hospital room cheering
as I gave birth to my children, I would have called you a liar.
What's been rebuilt is far from perfect, and there are still heart-
aches and family struggles—fights, bruised relationships, hurt
feelings, and the occasional throw-down—but the pretending
and the silence are gone. They just don't work anymore.

This experience and how it played out over the years ignited within me a spark of curiosity about emotions that has continued to grow. That spark led to my career, and it's probably why I ultimately found my own therapist (who, frustratingly and awesomely, encouraged my growing emotional curiosity). I think the willingness to engage with emotion is why I'm still married to the man I love and why I feel proud about the way we're parenting our children. The pump was primed—I learned enough about emotion to get and stay curious. And, if you question the ability of a single spark to start a revolution, think about this: Had my mom denied her emotions and disengaged from her hurt, I seriously doubt this book would exist. It often takes just a single brave person to change the trajectory of a family, or of any system, for that matter.

OFF-LOADING HURT: BARRIERS TO RECKONING WITH EMOTION

Hurt doesn't go away simply because we don't acknowledge it. In fact, left unchecked, it festers, grows, and leads to behaviors that are completely out of line with whom we want to be, and thinking that can sabotage our relationships and careers. What follows are five of the most common strategies for off-loading hurt that we think we have banished by refusing to admit it's there.

Chandeliering. My daughter, Ellen, and one of her closest friends, Lorna, play field hockey on two different teams. On a day when the field hockey planets were clearly out of alignment, both girls hurt a hand at their respective practices. Ellen came home with a black-and-blue finger that was swollen to double its size. I'm relatively calm during these situations, but that's a perk of being married to a pediatrician. After Steve pulled and pushed and felt around on Ellen's finger for a few minutes, he buddy taped it to her next finger and announced that we'd see how it was in the morning.

Not two hours later, my friend Suzanne was standing in our dining room with her daughter Lorna, who was telling us how her hand had been hit by someone's stick while Steve got ready to perform the same exam he had given Ellen. Lorna is tough and was trying her best to convince us that she was fine. You could tell she was willing her finger to be well. But the second Steve just grazed her hand, she practically jumped out of her skin. Steve looked at Suzanne and said, "It's exquisitely tender. She needs to be seen and x-rayed."

The next day I asked Steve if *exquisitely tender* is an official medical term. I had heard him use it before, and it struck me as funny—like *marvelously sore* or *fantastically achy*. He explained that it's used to describe the kind of pain that someone can't hide even if they're trying their best to be stoic. Then he said, "We also call it *chandelier pain*—like it hurts so much to the touch that people jump as high as the chandelier."

One of the outcomes of attempting to ignore emotional pain is chandeliering. We think we've packed the hurt so far down that it can't possibly resurface, yet all of a sudden, a seemingly innocuous comment sends us into a rage or sparks a crying fit. Or maybe a small mistake at work triggers a huge shame attack. Perhaps a colleague's constructive feedback hits that exquisitely tender place and we jump out of our skin.

Chandeliering is especially common and dangerous in "power-over" situations—environments where, because of power differentials, people with a higher position or status are less likely to be held accountable for flipping out or overreacting. These are places where our powerlessness and hurt get worked out. We maintain our prized stoicism in front of the people we want to impress or influence, but the second we're around people over whom we have emotional, financial, or physical power, we explode. And because it's not a side of us seen by many of the higher-ups, our version of the story is framed as truth. We see power-over chandeliering in families, churches, schools, communities, and offices. And when you mix in issues like gender, class, race, sexual orientation, and age—the combination can be lethal.

Road rage and sports are often considered socially acceptable venues for chandeliering pain. Don't get me wrong—I'm an enthusiastic sports fan, and I have a terrible habit of flipping off people under the steering wheel (so other drivers and the children in my backseat can't see). But I'm not going to lose myself in a vein-popping fury because the Longhorns are having a bad season or because you cut me off in the parking lot. I grew up around a lot of chandeliering, and I've also worked with people who pushed down emotion, then exploded. I know firsthand that uncontrolled eruptions of emotion sabotage the safety that most of us are trying to create, whether in our families or our organizations. If it happens often enough, chandeliering leads to eggshell environments— fear-based settings where everyone is on edge.

We can't pack down hurt, nor can we off-load it to someone else while maintaining our authenticity and integrity.

Most of us have been on the receiving end of one of these outbursts. Even if we have the insight to know that our boss, friend, colleague, or partner blew up at us because something tender was triggered and it's not actually about us, it still shatters trust and respect. Living, growing up, working, or worshipping on eggshells creates huge cracks in our sense of safety and self-worth. Over time, it can be experienced as trauma.

Bouncing hurt. Our ego is the part of us that cares about our status and what people think, about always being *better than* and always being right. I think of my ego as my inner hustler. It's always telling me to compare, prove, please, perfect, outperform, and compete. Our inner hustlers have very little tolerance for discomfort or self-reflection. The ego doesn't own stories or want to write new endings; it denies emotion and hates curiosity. Instead, the ego uses stories as armor and alibis. The ego has a shame-based fear of being ordinary (which is how I define narcissism). The ego says, "Feelings are for losers and weaklings." Avoiding truth and vulnerability are critical parts of the hustle.

Like all good hustlers, our egos employ crews of ruffians in case we don't comply with their demands. Anger, blame, and avoidance are the ego's bouncers. When we get too close to recognizing an experience as an emotional one, these three spring into action. It's much easier to say, "I don't give a damn," than it is to say, "I'm hurt." The ego likes blaming, finding fault, making excuses, inflicting payback, and lashing out, all of which are ultimate forms of self-protection. The ego is also a fan of avoidance—assuring the offender that we're fine, pretending that it doesn't matter, that we're impervious.

We adopt a pose of indifference or stoicism, or we deflect with humor and cynicism. *Whatever. Who cares?*

When the bouncers are successful—when anger, blame, and avoidance push away real hurt, disappointment, or pain—our egos are free to scam all they want. Often the first hustle is putting down and shaming others for their lack of "emotional control." Like all hustlers, the ego is a slick, conniving, and dangerous liar.

Numbing hurt. Numbing has been a constant in my research since the beginning. Picture emotions as having very sharp points, like thorns. When they prick us, they cause discomfort or even pain. After a while, the mere anticipation of these feelings can trigger a sense of intolerable vulnerability: We know it's coming. For many of us, the first response is not to lean in to the discomfort and feel our way through, but to make it go away. We do that by numbing the pain with whatever provides the quickest relief. We can take the edge off emotional pain with a whole bunch of stuff, including alcohol, drugs, food, sex, relationships, money, work, caretaking, gambling, affairs, religion, chaos, shopping, planning, perfectionism, constant change, and the Internet.

And just so we don't miss it in this long list of all the ways we can numb ourselves, there's always staying busy: living so hard and fast that the truths of our lives can't catch up with us. We fill every ounce of white space with something so there's no room or time for emotion to make itself known.

But no matter what we use, we can't selectively numb emotions—when we numb the dark, we also numb the light. When "taking the edge off" with a couple of glasses of red wine becomes a routine, our experiences of joy and love and trust will become duller, too. With less positive emotion in our lives, we are drawn to numbing. It's a vicious cycle, and the viciousness is as likely to be unleashed at a fancy wine-tasting party as it is with a 40 wrapped in a brown paper bag.

If we numb compulsively and chronically—it's addiction. And, as I pointed out in the TEDx talk, this is an issue. We are still the most in-debt, obese, medicated, and addicted adults in human history. Looking back over the past fourteen years of research, I've come to believe that addiction, like violence, poverty, and inequality, is one of the greatest societal challenges we face today. There is not a single person reading this right now who is not affected by addiction. You may not be the one who is or was addicted, but I guarantee that someone you love, work with, or is important in your life is struggling. It's a pandemic that's destroying families.

Stockpiling hurt. There's a quiet, insidious alternative to chandeliering, bouncing, or numbing hurt—we can stockpile it. We're not erupting with misplaced emotions or using blame to deflect our true feelings or numbing the pain. Stockpiling starts like chandeliering, with us firmly packing down the pain, but here, we just continue to amass hurt until the wisest parts of us, our bodies, decide that enough is enough. The body's message is always clear: Shut down the stockpiling or I'll shut you down. The body wins every time.

In hundreds of interviews, people have recounted how they just "kept everything inside" until they couldn't sleep or eat or they became so anxious they couldn't focus at work or grew too depressed to do anything but stay in bed. Depression and anxiety are two of the body's first reactions to stockpiles of hurt. Of course, there are organic and biochemical reasons we experience clinical depression and debilitating anxiety—causes over which we have no control—but unrecognized pain and unprocessed hurt can also lead there.

In his book *The Body Keeps the Score,* Bessel van der Kolk, a professor of psychiatry at Boston University, explores how trauma literally reshapes the brain and the body, and how interventions that enable adults to reclaim their lives must address the relationship between our emotional well-being and our bodies. There is so much wisdom in our bodies. We just need to learn how to listen and trust what we're hearing.

Hurt and the fear of high centering. If you've ever found yourself high centered in your car, you know exactly how scary and helpless it feels. Just a couple of weeks ago, I was driving with Ellen across a parking lot in San Antonio, looking for a bookstore that I had visited at least twenty times. It was ten o'clock on a Sunday morning, so the parking lot was almost empty. I became a little disoriented because the store that I knew so well was gone, as was the store next to it. My first thought was that I had pulled into the wrong shopping center, so I started looking around to orient myself. In that split second, I drove over a tall, two-foot-wide, cobblestone median strip. The sound of cement scraping against the metal undercarriage of my car was horrendous. One of the cobblestone bricks dislodged and stood straight up, pushing into the plate under my car. My front and back tires were straddling the median. I couldn't move forward and I couldn't back up. I was high centered.

One reason we deny our feelings is our fear of high centering emotionally. If I recognize my hurt or fear or anger, I'll get stuck. Once I engage even a little, I won't be able to move backward and pretend that it doesn't matter, but moving forward might open a floodgate of emotion that I can't control. I'll be stuck. Helpless. Recognizing emotion leads to feeling it. What if I recognize the emotion and it dislodges something and I can't maintain control? I don't want to cry at work or on the battlefield or when I'm with my parents. Getting high centered is the worst because we feel a total loss of control. We feel powerless.

On that day in San Antonio, I got out of my car and began pacing. Finally, a kind man pulled up and walked over. After lying on the ground and assessing the situation, he said, "You're going to need help. We can do it, we just need to think about it." After a few minutes of brainstorming, we had a plan. Ellen put the car in reverse and the man and I lifted the front end of my car just enough for the brick to fall, freeing the car. In the scheme of high centering, my car experience was easier than some of my emotional experiences of it have been.

Scraping the underbelly of our emotions when we're in a tough situation is bad enough. Getting stuck there is the definition of vulnerability and helplessness. But denying emotion is not avoiding the high curbs, it's never taking your car out of the garage. It's safe in there, but you'll never go anywhere.

Off-Loading Versus Integrating

> You may not control all the events that happen to you,
> but you can decide not to be reduced by them.
> —Maya Angelou

The opposite of off-loading is integrating. The methods outlined above represent different ways that we fail to integrate into our lives the hurt that arises in our stories of struggle. Pretending not to be hurt is choosing to become imprisoned by the dark emotion we have experienced—recognizing and feeling our way through the emotion is choosing freedom. It's seductive to think that not talking about our pain is the safest way to keep it from defining us, but ultimately the avoidance takes over our lives. The idea that "we're only as sick as our secrets" is more than an adage; there's growing empirical evidence that not owning and integrating our stories affects not just our emotional health but also our physical well-being.

THE UMBRIDGE

In relational terms, pervasive off-loading behaviors can be very unsettling to be around. They don't feel authentic. In addition to explosive tempers and contagious fear, one of the most difficult patterns to experience is what I call *The Umbridge*. It's present when light and dark are not integrated at all. There's almost something foreboding about overly sweet and accommodating ways. All that niceness feels inauthentic and a little like a ticking bomb. I named this after J. K. Rowling's character Dolores Umbridge in *Harry Potter and the Order of the Phoenix*. Umbridge wears cutesy pink suits and pillbox hats, adorns her pink office with bows and trinkets decorated with kittens, and is a fan of torturing children who misbehave. Rowling writes about her, "I have noticed more than once in life that a taste for the ineffably twee can go hand-in-hand with a distinctly uncharitable outlook on the world." She adds, "A love of all things saccharine often seems present where there is a lack of real warmth or charity." I've noticed the same thing. Too much twee emotional expression—too many claims like, "Everything is awesome," or "I just never really feel angry or upset," or "If you're just positive, you can turn that frown upside down"— often masks real pain and hurt. These behaviors are as much red flags as brooding and anger are.

Children have great radar for the emotion that lives right under the sugarcoated surface. Charlie, my fourth-grader, will sometimes say, "Be careful. I think she's a Unikitty." He's referring to the cat from *The LEGO Movie* that was all sunshine and rainbows until she snapped and turned into Super Angry Kitty. Integration is key. Being all light is as dangerous as being all dark, simply because denial of emotion is what feeds the dark.

Strategies for Reckoning with Emotion

So how do we reckon with emotion rather than off-load it? What I've learned from the research and tried to put into practice in my own life sounds way simpler than it is: Give yourself permission to feel emotion, get curious about it, pay attention to it, and practice. This work takes practice. Awkward, uncomfortable practice.

PERMISSION SLIPS

I wrote my first permission slip on a Post-it note the morning I met Oprah Winfrey for the first time and taped an episode of *Super Soul Sunday*. It said, "Permission to be excited, have fun, and be goofy." Now my jeans pockets are often stuffed with permission slips. My team and I often start difficult team meetings by writing permission slips and sharing them before we dig into our work. We're not going to recognize emotion if we don't feel like we have permission to feel emotion.

If you grew up in a family where emotion was not just permitted but encouraged, you may have an easier time giving yourself permission to feel it and recognize it. You may even think, *I don't need to do this—I'm good with emotion.* I still think it's an important step because writing down permission becomes a powerful intention to stay aware.

If you were raised in an environment where emotion was minimized, seen as weakness, invalidated, shut down, perceived as wasteful (e.g., *crying won't help*), or even punished, then giving yourself permission to feel, recognize, and explore may be a bigger challenge. You might be the first person in your life to grant yourself the permission you need to experience emotion. If you're worried that giving permission to experience and engage with emotion will turn you into something you're not or someone you don't want to become—it won't. It will, however, give you the opportunity to be your most authentic self. We are wired to be emotional beings. When that part of us is shut down, we're not whole.

PAYING ATTENTION

Every reckoning starts with giving yourself permission to engage with emotion. The next step is paying attention—taking a deep breath and becoming mindful of what we're feeling. I've been a breath holder all of my life, so the power of breathing was foreign to me and still feels a little woo-woo. I not only hold my breath when I'm nervous, anxious, working out, or mad, but also have a visceral reaction to people saying, "Take a breath, Brené," or "Just breathe." It basically makes me want to knock 'em upside the head. While holding my breath.

But over the past couple of years, breathing has become the

cornerstone of my "calm practice," which I call my don't-lose-it approach to living. Interestingly, the research partici-pants who taught me the most about breathing occupy what we would traditionally think of as opposite sides of the profes-sional continuum: yoga teachers, meditation leaders, and mindfulness practitioners on one side and soldiers, firefight-ers, first responders, and elite athletes on the other. Regardless of the teacher, though, the methods are virtually the same.

Mark Miller describes himself as a poet-warrior, a casual hero, and a student of science. He is also a Green Beret who has spent years in combat, and his descriptions of the tactical breathing techniques used by the military were incredibly helpful to me. I even taught them to my kids. In fact, in my interviews with veterans, active-duty soldiers, and first re-sponders, they were quick to tell me that they rely on these techniques to calm and center themselves in their personal lives as much as they do in crisis situations—one firefighter told me that he most recently used it while negotiating home-work with his teenage son. Here's Mark Miller's explanation of tactical breathing.

Tactical Breathing

1. Inhale deeply through your nose, expanding your stom-ach, for a count of four—one, two, three, four.

2. Hold in that breath for a count of four—one, two, three, four.

3. Slowly exhale all the air through your mouth, contract-ing your stomach, for a count of four—one, two, three, four.

4. Hold the empty breath for a count of four—one, two, three, four.

The breathing method many therapists and mindfulness practitioners teach is square or box breathing. They use it for increasing mindfulness and decreasing anxiety and stress. Take a look at how similar it is to tactical breathing.

Square or Box Breathing

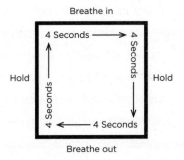

Breathing is central to practicing mindfulness. The definition of *mindfulness* that resonates most with what I've heard research participants describe is from the Greater Good Science Center at the University of California, Berkeley—one of my favorite online stomping grounds (greatergood.berkeley.edu):

Mindfulness means maintaining a moment-by-moment awareness of our thoughts, feelings, bodily sensations, and surrounding environment. Mindfulness also involves acceptance, meaning that we pay attention to our thoughts and feelings without judging them—without believing, for instance, that there's a "right" or "wrong" way to think or feel in a given moment. When we practice mindfulness, our thoughts tune in to what we're sensing in the present moment rather than rehashing the past or imagining the future.

In the Lake Travis story, what happened on the way back that was critical to the outcome was my breathing. I count strokes when I swim and normally breathe every fourth stroke. There is something about rhythmic breathing that focuses my mind and my thoughts.

When it comes to my everyday life on dry land, I struggle with being mindful. My mind is normally three miles ahead of my body, worrying about what comes next or jumping a curb three streets behind me, looking for the person who didn't give me the friendly driver's wave when I let them pull in in front of me. Living this way makes driving to the grocery store exhausting. If I'm really worked up, I can pull into the parking lot of the store and literally have no memory of how I got there.

At first, the idea of "being in the moment" scared me. I imagined that I would spend my life thinking, *Right now, the wind is blowing and I see a butterfly. Now the butterfly is gone, but the wind is still blowing. A mosquito bit me despite the blowing wind. Oh my God—make it stop! I can't do a play-by-play of every moment. I've got things to think about—work to get done.* I basically was afraid mindfulness would disrupt my flow—what the scholar Mihaly Csikszentmihalyi describes as that sacred intersection of deep enjoyment and disciplined concentration.

Then one day I noticed something in the middle of a walk. I had already found that I do my best thinking while I'm walking alone. That is when I sort and organize my thoughts. Even if I took a walk with a friend earlier, I still carve out time to walk alone. If I get stuck and it's rainy and thirty degrees outside, I walk. Well, I actually walk and talk. My neighbors constantly make fun of me because I talk to myself and swing my arms around while I'm walking our streets. I can't help it—it's my process.

But on that day I was suddenly struck by how aware I was of every single thing around me. I was completely in my work zone—my brain was on fire—but I was also keenly aware of the smell of cut grass and the color of the snapdragons my neighbor was planting. I liked the way the new socks I'd stolen from my daughter's drawer felt inside my running shoes, and I was savoring the slightly cooler weather that all Houstonians await with great anticipation. That's when I realized that mindfulness and flow are never in competition with each other. They aren't the same thing, but they share the same foundation: making the choice to pay attention.

A couple of weeks later, I returned from a productive work walk to find my son, Charlie, holding his finger and fighting back tears. He had gotten a splinter from a fence post in our backyard and needed help. Before my realization about flow and mindfulness, I would have been anxious about not being able to sit down and immediately capture all of the ideas from my walk. But on this day, I decided to simply stay present and shift my mindfulness to Charlie. While it took me a few minutes to find the tweezers and my glasses, I didn't race around the house in a panic. I got the splinter out and sat with Charlie until he was ready to go back outside.

When finally I sat down at the computer, my thoughts were all there waiting for me. My ideas and inspirations weren't something external that I tricked into following me home from the walk: They were a part of me. I was present to them and they, in turn, stayed present to me.

Newton's third law of motion states that "for every action, there is an equal and opposite reaction." I believe this law also applies to our emotional lives. For every emotion we feel, there is a response. When we feel angry, we can mindlessly lash out or shut down, or our reaction can be intentional and we can breathe, get grounded, and bring awareness to what we're really feeling and how we respond. When we're scared, we can default to the instinctual fight, flight, or freeze mode, or we can breathe and respond thoughtfully. Breath and mindfulness give us the awareness and space we need to make choices that are aligned with our values.

IN YOU MUST GO

Maybe by now you're thinking, *I don't want to do this. It seems like a lot of work. It feels too hard.* I get it. I'm with you. Just coming back to ourselves, however stunned, after falling down already demands so much of us—that should be enough. It's not. Walking into our story is the reckoning. It can feel dangerous, but "in you must go."

There's a pivotal scene in *The Empire Strikes Back* when Yoda is training Luke to be a Jedi warrior, teaching him how to honorably use the Force and how the dark side of the Force—anger, fear, and aggression—can consume him if he doesn't learn how to find calm and inner peace. In this scene, Luke and Yoda are standing in the dark swamp where they've been training when a strange look comes over Luke. He points toward a dark cave at the base of a giant tree and, looking at Yoda, he says, "There's something not right here. . . . I feel cold. Death."

Yoda explains to Luke that the cave is dangerous and strong with the dark side of the Force. Luke looks confused and afraid, but Yoda's response is simply, "In you must go."

When Luke asks what's in the cave, Yoda explains, "Only what you take with you."

As Luke straps on his weapons, Yoda hauntingly advises, "Your weapons, you will not need them."

The cave is dark and thick with vines. Steam eerily rises off the ground while a large snake winds its way over a branch and a prehistoric-looking lizard perches on a limb. As Luke slowly makes his way through the cave, he is confronted by his enemy, Darth Vader. They both draw their light sabers and Luke quickly cuts off Vader's helmeted head. The head rolls to the ground and the face guard blows off the helmet, revealing Vader's face. Only, it isn't Darth Vader's face; it's Luke's face. Luke is staring at his own head on the ground.

Walking into our stories of hurt is like walking into that cave in Yoda's swamp. It can feel dangerous and foreboding, and what we must ultimately confront is ourself. The most difficult part of our stories is often what we bring to them—what we make up about who we are and how we are perceived by others. Yes, maybe we lost our job or screwed up a project, but what makes that story so painful is what we tell ourselves about our own self-worth and value.

Owning our stories means reckoning with our feelings and rumbling with our dark emotions—our fear, anger, aggression, shame, and blame. This isn't easy, but the alternative—denying our stories and disengaging from emotion—means choosing to live our entire lives in the dark.

When we decide to own our stories and live our truth, we bring our light to the darkness.

On to the rumble.

The most
DANGEROUS STORIES
WE MAKE UP ARE THE
narratives that diminish our
INHERENT WORTHINESS.
WE MUST RECLAIM

THE TRUTH
ABOUT OUR
LOVABILITY, DIVINITY, *and*
creativity.

Five

THE RUMBLE

When you are in the middle of a story it isn't a story at all, but only a confusion; a dark roaring, a blindness, a wreckage of shattered glass and splintered wood; like a house in a whirlwind, or else a boat crushed by the icebergs or swept over the rapids, and all aboard powerless to stop it. It's only afterwards that it becomes anything like a story at all. When you are telling it, to yourself or to someone else.

—Margaret Atwood, *Alias Grace*

The reckoning is how we walk into our story; the rumble is where we own it. The goal of the rumble is to get honest about the stories we're making up about our struggles, to revisit, challenge, and reality-check these narratives as we dig into topics such as boundaries, shame, blame, resentment, heartbreak, generosity, and forgiveness. Rumbling with these topics and moving from our first responses to a deeper understanding of our thoughts, feelings, and behaviors gives birth to key learnings about who we are and how we engage with others. The rumble is where wholeheartedness is cultivated and change begins.

CONSPIRACIES AND CONFABULATIONS

The rumble begins with turning up our curiosity level and becoming aware of the story we're telling ourselves about our hurt, anger, frustration, or pain. The minute we find ourselves facedown on the arena floor, our minds go to work trying to make sense of what's happening. This story is driven by emotion and the immediate need to self-protect, which means it's most likely not accurate, well thought out, or even civil. In fact, if your very first story is any of these things, either you're an outlier or you're not being fully honest.

Remember the Thompson quote "Civilization ends at the waterline"? The rumble starts when we have the willingness, ability, and courage to cross the waterline—to wade into that first, uncivilized story we're making up. This is the beginning of Act 2.

Why is capturing this uncensored story necessary? Because embedded in this unedited narrative are the answers to three critically important questions—questions that cultivate wholeheartedness and bring deeper courage, compassion, and connection to our lives:

1. What more do I need to learn and understand about the situation?

2. What more do I need to learn and understand about the other people in the story?

3. What more do I need to learn and understand about myself?

In the absence of data, we will always make up stories. It's how we are wired. In fact, the need to make up a story, especially when we are hurt, is part of our most primitive survival wiring. Meaning making is in our biology, and our default is often to come up with a story that makes sense, feels familiar, and offers us insight into how best to self-protect. What we're trying to do in the rumble—choosing to feel uncertain and vulnerable as we rumble with the truth—is a conscious choice. A brave, conscious choice.

Robert Burton, a neurologist and novelist, explains that our brains reward us with dopamine when we recognize and complete patterns. Stories are patterns. The brain recognizes the familiar beginning-middle-end structure of a story and rewards us for clearing up the ambiguity. Unfortunately, we don't need to be accurate, just certain.

You know that wonderful sensation we experience when we connect the dots or something finally makes sense for the first time? The "*aha* moment," as Oprah calls it? Burton uses that as an example of how we might experience our brain's pattern-recognition reward. The tricky part is that the promise of that sensation can seduce us into shutting down the uncertainty and vulnerability that are often necessary for getting to the truth.

Burton writes, "Because we are compelled to make stories, we are often compelled to take incomplete stories and run with them." He goes on to say that even with a half story in our minds, "we earn a dopamine 'reward' every time it helps us understand something in our world—even if that explanation is incomplete or wrong."

For example, in the Lake Travis story, I started with a half story defined by these limited data points:

Steve and I are swimming together for the first time in decades.

I'm being unusually vulnerable and trying to connect with Steve.

He's not responding positively to my bid for connection.

The very first story I tell myself is that he's a jerk who tricked me into believing he's kind and loving over the past twenty-five years when the real truth is that he's blowing me off because I don't look great in a Speedo and my freestyle sucks.

Why is this my first story? Because "I'm not enough" is one of my go-to narratives when I'm hurt. It's the equivalent of my comfy jeans. When I am in doubt, the "never enough" explanation is often the first thing I grab. The blame story is another favorite of mine. If something goes wrong, feels bad, or leaves me feeling too exposed or vulnerable, I want to know whose fault it is. I can make up one of these meaning-making stories in a heartbeat.

What do we call a story that's based on limited real data and imagined data and blended into a coherent, emotionally satisfying version of reality? A conspiracy theory. Drawing on extensive research and history, English professor and science writer Jonathan Gottschall examines the human need for story in his book *The Storytelling Animal*. He explains that there's growing evidence that "ordinary, mentally healthy people are strikingly prone to confabulate in everyday situations." Social workers always use the term *confabulate* when talking about how dementia or a brain injury sometimes causes people to replace missing information with something false that they believe to be true. The further I got into this research, the more I agreed with Gottschall's assessment about confabulation being an everyday human issue, not just the result of specific medical conditions.

In one of my favorite studies described in *The Storytelling Animal,* a team of psychologists asked shoppers to choose a pair of socks among seven pairs and then to give their reasons for choosing that particular pair. Every shopper explained their choice based on subtle differences in color, texture, and stitching. No shopper said, "I don't know why this is my choice," or "I have no idea why I picked that one." All of them had a story that explained their decision. But here's the kicker: All of the socks were identical. Gottschall explains that all of the shoppers told stories that made their decisions seem rational. But they really weren't. He writes, "The stories were confabulations—lies, honestly told."

Many confabulations are less the result of health or memory issues and more about the interplay of emotion, behavior, and thought. Had Steve and I not resolved our problem in the lake that day, it's very likely that I would have told my sisters (whom I love, respect, and am honest with) that we had a terrible fight because Steve thought I looked like crap in my new Speedo. It would have been a confabulation. And regardless of how honestly I was conveying this untruth, it could have hurt Steve, our relationship, and me. And perhaps even my relationship with my sisters. I can just see one or both of them saying, "That doesn't sound like Steve. Are you sure?" My response probably would have been "That's perfect. Be on his side. All of you suck!" Productive, right?

We all conspire and confabulate, and sometimes the consequences appear to be negligible. But I would argue that they're not. I would argue that conspiring can become a destructive pattern over time, and sometimes a single confabulation can damage our sense of self-worth and our relationships.

The most dangerous stories we make up are the narratives that diminish our inherent worthiness. We must reclaim the truth about our lovability, divinity, and creativity.

Lovability: Many of my research participants who had gone through a painful breakup or divorce, been betrayed by a partner, or experienced a distant or uncaring relationship with a parent or family member spoke about responding to their pain with a story about being unlovable—a narrative questioning if they were worthy of being loved. This may be the most dangerous conspiracy theory of all. If there's one thing I've learned over the past thirteen years, it's this: Just because someone isn't willing or able to love us, it doesn't mean that we are unlovable.

Divinity: Research participants who shared stories of shame around religion had less in common than most people guess. No specific denomination has emerged as more shaming in my work; however, there is a strong pattern worth noting. Over half of the participants who talked about experiencing shame in their faith histories also found resilience and healing through spirituality. The majority of them changed their churches or their beliefs, but spirituality and faith remain important parts of their lives. They believed that the sources of shame arose from the earthly, man-made, human-interpreted rules or regulations and the social/community expectations of religion rather than their personal relationships with God or the divine. Our faith narratives must be protected, and we must remember that no person is ordained to judge our divinity or to write the story of our spiritual worthiness.

Creativity and ability: In *Daring Greatly,* I write, "One reason that I'm confident that shame exists in schools is simply because 85 percent of the men and women we interviewed for the shame research could recall a school incident from their childhood that was so shaming that it changed how they thought of themselves as learners. What makes this even more haunting is that approximately half of those recollections were what I refer to as creativity scars. The research participants could point to a specific incident where they were told or shown that they weren't good writers, artists, musicians, dancers, or something creative. This helps explain why the gremlins are so powerful when it comes to creativity and innovation." Like our lovability and divinity, we must care for and nurture the stories we tell ourselves about our creativity and ability. Just because we didn't measure up to some standard of achievement doesn't mean that we don't possess gifts and talents that only we can bring to the world. Just because someone failed to see the value in what we can create or achieve doesn't change its worth or ours.

Gottschall argues that conspiratorial thinking "is not limited to the stupid, the ignorant, or the crazy. It is a reflex of the storytelling mind's compulsive need for meaningful experience." He goes on to make the compelling point that ultimately, conspiracy theories are used to explain why bad things happen.

He writes, "To the conspiratorial mind, shit *never* just happens," and the complexities of human life are reduced to produce theories that are "always consoling in their simplicity."

His conclusion about conspiracy thinking on the societal level reflects some of the exact same problems at the personal and relational levels. Gottschall writes that for conspiracy theorists, "bad things do not happen because of a wildly complex swirl of abstract historical and social variables. They happen because bad men live to stalk our happiness. And you can fight, and possibly even defeat, bad men. *If* you can read the hidden story."

In my research I've found that the same can be said for the conspiracies we make up to explain that fight with our partner or the disapproving look from our boss or our child's behavior at school. We make up hidden stories that tell us who is against us and who is with us. Whom we can trust and who is not to be trusted. Conspiracy thinking is all about fear-based self-protection and our intolerance for uncertainty. When we depend on self-protecting narratives often enough, they become our default stories. And we must not forget that storytelling is a powerful integration tool. We start weaving these hidden, false stories into our lives and they eventually distort who we are and how we relate to others.

When unconscious storytelling becomes our default, we often keep tripping over the same issue, staying down when we fall, and having different versions of the same problem in our relationships—we've got the story on repeat. Burton explains that our brains like predictable storytelling. He writes, "In effect, well-oiled patterns of observation encourage our brains to compose a story that we expect to hear."

The men and women who have cultivated rising strong practices in their lives became aware of the traps in these first stories, whereas the participants who continued to struggle the most appeared to have gotten stuck in those stories. The good news is that people aren't born with an exceptional understanding of the stories they make up, nor does it just dawn on them one day. They practiced. Sometimes for years. They set out with the intention to become aware and they tried until it worked. They captured their conspiracies and confabulations.

Capturing the Conspiracies and Confabulations

To capture these first stories and to learn from them, we need to engage our second integration tool—creativity. The most effective way to foster awareness is by writing down our stories. Nothing fancy. The goal here is to write what Anne Lamott would call your "shitty first draft"—or your SFD, as I like to call it (this can stand for "stormy first draft" if you are looking for a G-rated term to teach the rising strong process to kids). Lamott's advice from her exceptional book *Bird by Bird* is exactly what we need:

> The only way I can get anything written at all is to write really, really shitty first drafts. The first draft is the child's draft, where you let it all pour out and then let it romp all over the place, knowing that no one is going to see it and that you can shape it later. You just let this childlike part of you channel whatever voices and visions come through and onto the page. If one of the

characters wants to say, "Well, so what, Mr. Poopy Pants?," you let her. No one is going to see it. If the kid wants to get into really sentimental, weepy, emotional territory, you let him. Just get it all down on paper because there may be something great in those six crazy pages that you would never have gotten to by more rational, grown-up means.

I can promise that you will meet the romping, tantrum-throwing five-year-old Brené in almost all of my first stories, like you did in the Lake Travis story. Our rational, grown-up selves are good liars. The five-year-old tyrants within us are the ones who can tell it like it is.

What you write doesn't have to be a sweeping narrative. It can be a bulleted list on a Post-it note or a simple paragraph in a journal. Just get it down. And because our goal is wholeheartedness, we need to consider our whole selves when we write our SFDs. The core (sometimes the entirety) of my SFD is normally these six sentences with maybe a few notes.

The story I'm making up:
My emotions:
My body:
My thinking:
My beliefs:
My actions:

Storytelling is also a creative endeavor, so if you have a friend or someone you trust who has the skills and patience to listen, you can talk through your SFD, but writing is always more powerful. James Pennebaker, a researcher at the University of Texas at Austin and author of *Writing to Heal,* has done some of the most important and fascinating research I've seen on the power of expressive writing in the healing process. In an interview posted on the University of Texas's website, Pennebaker explains, "Emotional upheavals touch every part of our lives. You don't just lose a job, you don't just get divorced. These things affect all aspects of who we are—our financial situation, our relationships with others, our views of ourselves, our issues of life and death. Writing helps us focus and organize the experience." Pennebaker believes that because our minds are designed to try to understand things that happen to us, translating messy, difficult experiences into language essentially makes them "graspable."

What's important to note about Pennebaker's research is the fact that he advocates limited writing, or short spurts. He's found that writing about emotional upheavals for just fifteen to twenty minutes a day on four consecutive days can decrease anxiety, rumination, and depressive symptoms and boost our immune systems.

The participants in my research did not reference a specific approach, but more than 70 percent of them did some form of short writing. Many of them worked through their emotions in letters that they knew they would never send but needed to write. One participant told me that both she and her husband wrote short letters to their nineteen-year-old son every night for one week after finding out that he had dropped out of college and was using the money they were sending him to host parties for his friends. She said, "There would have been nothing but yelling and screaming without those letters. By the time we sat down with him, we were calm and ready to hold him responsible for his decisions."

I share my own story of letter writing as an SFD in Chapter Ten, "You Got to Dance with Them That Brung You." As you'll see, working through blinding shame on paper is far less painful than working it out on a person. Pennebaker's research, combined with what I've learned in my own work, has convinced me that even brief engagements with writing can yield significant results.

When it comes to our SFDs, it's important that we don't filter the experience, polish our words, or worry about how our story makes us look (which is why writing is often safer than having a conversation). We can't get to our brave new ending if we start from an inauthentic place. So give yourself permission to wade through the sometimes-murky waters of whatever you're thinking and feeling. You can be mad, self-righteous, blaming, confused. Just don't edit and don't try to "get it right." Ninety percent of my SFDs start with "I'm feeling angry. I'm physically feeling like screaming or punching someone or crying."

Again, you can speak this process rather than write it, but there are some risks with that. Getting clear on the story that we're making up in the midst of pain is not about venting or lashing out. Your SFD is not permission to be hurtful. If you're standing across from someone and saying, "I'm making up that you're a self-centered egomaniac and everyone who works for you thinks you're an asshole"—you're on the wrong track. This process is about capturing the story you're telling yourself about your fall. This should feel vulnerable and personal. Your intention should be to embrace curiosity, awareness, and growth.

Steve and I sometimes go straight to storytelling—like we did in the lake story. But don't forget that in the lake story, I had a long swim back to sort out my confabulations and conspiracies. If we go straight to storytelling with each other or with the kids, we're very careful and respectful about how we use this tool. This first draft is a tool of inquiry and intention—not a weapon.

I normally have to walk or swim or do something that gives me the time and space I need to get clear on my SFD before I share it. About 50 percent of the research participants talked about doing something physical as a means for thinking through more complex SFDs, where they're feeling strong emotion. One participant walked down and then back up five flights of stairs at his office.

My leadership team also uses "the story I'm making up" on a regular basis. What I've noticed is that most of us have already done the romping and raging before we sit down and have the discussion. On occasion we also use it unrehearsed, but that came with practice. For example, we were recently in a brainstorming session about new ventures when I noticed that one of our team members was becoming increasingly quiet. When I asked if everything was okay, she said, "I keep asking tough questions about these ideas and I'm starting to make up that I'm being perceived as not excited or not a team player." This gave me the opportunity to redefine our objective for the session and assure the team that I expected a point of view from everyone and appreciated honesty and tough questions above all else.

Think about how much more productive that is than having someone leave the meeting angry, resentful, and confused, or having people leave questioning their contributions. As the leader of this team, I really appreciate and respect this kind of honesty. It gives me an invaluable opportunity to communicate honestly with the people I trust the most.

The SFD has changed the way we communicate. Just think about how many times you've walked away from a conflict with someone at work or read an email that pissed you off and then made up an entire story about what's happening. Of all the emails I get from leaders who are implementing my work with their teams, the vast majority talk about how getting clear on these first stories has changed the way they lead and live.

In 2014, The Daring Way launched a three-year collaboration with Team Red, White, and Blue (Team RWB) to bring what we're learning about daring and rising strong to veterans. Team RWB's mission is to enrich the lives of America's veterans by connecting them to their communities through physical and social activity. I had the opportunity to meet leaders from Team RWB during visits to West Point, the campus of the U.S. Military Academy in New York's Hudson Valley. What they taught me and what I learned through my interviews with them made invaluable contributions to the research I'm sharing with you.

Blayne Smith, a West Point graduate and former Special Forces officer, is the executive director of Team RWB. He shared this with me about his experience of rumbling with "the story we make up."

The ability to say "the story that I'm making up" is extremely helpful in a couple of ways. First, it creates the opportunity for some inner dialogue. It gives me a chance to pause and evaluate what I'm thinking and feeling before I even bring it up with another person. In some cases, that is all I need to do. At times when I need to communicate a frustration or issue, "the story that I'm making up" gives me permission to speak honestly and candidly without the fear of generating a defensive response. It is also very disarming and almost always results in a productive conversation, rather than a heated back-and-forth.

As the first paid employee of a start-up nonprofit, I've always been extremely frugal with spending. Though we have grown and now enjoy financial stability, I still maintain my old habits with the company credit card. When traveling, I rarely pay for a coffee or meal with company funds. On a recent trip to Washington, D.C., one of my teammates said he had to ask me a favor. He said, "I need you to use your company card when paying for meals on the road." When I inquired why, he responded, "Because the story that I'm making up is that whenever I use my company card to pay for a meal, you're judging me." I was floored. I hadn't even considered that. He told me that our team needed to feel comfortable when appropriately spending company dollars and that my resistance to spending made that difficult. That wasn't a major strategy issue or hotly debated company decision, but that kind of communication and honesty is a big part of what makes Team RWB a great place to work.

In addition to the cautions about not polishing your SFD, watch out for the need to be certain. Uncertainty is tricky. It moves good storytelling along—the fun of a whodunit is the mystery—but it can shut down difficult stories we are trying to capture. When it comes to the process of owning our hard stories, uncertainty can be so uncomfortable that we either walk away or race to the ending. So if you come across a part of your story that you don't understand or that makes you feel uncertain or anxious, just jot down a question mark or write yourself a note: *What the heck happened here? Total confusion. Who knows?* The important thing is not to skip it. Stay in the story until you touch every part of it.

You'll know you're being honest if you're worried that someone might see your SFD and think you're a total jerk or a nut job. Concerns like this are a good sign that you're on the right track. Don't hold back. There is no rising strong without a true accounting of the stories we make up.

RUMBLING WITH . . .

It's time to rumble. Time to unleash our curiosity. Time to poke, prod, and explore the ins and outs of our story. The first questions we ask in the rumble are sometimes the simplest:

1. What more do I need to learn and understand about the situation?

What do I know objectively?

What assumptions am I making?

2. What more do I need to learn and understand about the other people in the story?

What additional information do I need?
What questions or clarifications might help?

Now we get to the more difficult questions—the ones that take courage and practice to answer.

3. What more do I need to learn and understand about myself?

What's underneath my response?
What am I really feeling?
What part did I play?

How we rumble with our story and approach these questions depends on who we are and what we've experienced. As Yoda told Luke, what's in the cave depends on who walks into the cave. That said, some rumble topics worth investigating did consistently emerge in my interviews—issues uncovered by the participants' curiosity as they rumbled with the question of what they were feeling. Here's a list:

RUMBLING TOPICS

Grief
Vulnerability **Failure**
Forgiveness **Blame and accountability**
Disappointment, expectations, and resentment
Fear **Nostalgia** **Stereotypes and labels**
Boundaries **Perfectionism**
Identity **Trust** **Love, belonging, and heartbreak**
Regret **Need and connection** **Criticism**
Generosity **Shame**
Integrity

As you read through the chapters, you'll find that some of these topics are areas that I've researched and know well (e.g., shame, guilt, and blame), while other topics, like forgiveness and nostalgia, are subjects that put me squarely in the seat of the student. When the topics are outside my area of study, I'll introduce you to men and women who know these fields and we'll explore their work together.

THE DELTA

delta | 'del-tə | *noun* the fourth letter in the Greek alphabet—is a mathematical symbol for *difference*. A capital delta is a triangle.

The difference—the *delta*—between what we make up about our experiences and the truth we discover through the process of rumbling is where the meaning and wisdom of this experience live. The delta holds our key learnings—we just have to be willing to walk into our stories and rumble.

Even though the words *difference* and *delta* can mean the same thing, I like to use the word *delta* for two reasons, one professional and the other personal. The triangle symbol takes us back to that three-legged stool of emotion, thought, and behavior. A true rumble affects the way we feel, think, and act—our whole selves.

The personal reason is closer to my heart. The song "Delta," on Crosby, Stills & Nash's album *Daylight Again,* is one of the songs that I've turned to during the peaks and valleys of the past thirty years. I sat on the floor in my apartment in San Antonio and listened to it when I found out that Ronnie, my mother's only sibling, had been shot and killed in a random act of violence. I listened to it after my parents called my dorm room to tell me they were getting a divorce. I played it on the way to my wedding; in my parked car before walking into my dissertation defense; on the way to my first meeting with my therapist, Diana; and in the hospital when I gave birth to both of my children. The lyrics make me feel less alone—they let me see I'm not the only one navigating the "fast running rivers of choice and chance."

Thoughts
Like scattered leaves
Slowed in mid-fall
Into the streams

Of fast running rivers
Of choice and chance
And time stops here on the delta
While they dance, while they dance.

I love the child
Who steers this riverboat,
But lately he's crazy
For the deep . . .

I do love the child in me who steers my riverboat, but sometimes she is so unafraid of the dark, swift, deep water that I find myself in over my head during the rumbling part of this process. I'm so much better at being angry than I am at being hurt or disappointed or scared. This is why the rumble is so important—many of us have go-to emotions that mask what we're really feeling. Deltas are where rivers meet the sea. They're marshy, full of sediment, and forever changing. They are also rich and fertile areas of growth. This is where we need to do our work—our key learnings emerge from the delta.

In the lake story, I had to rumble with shame, blame, connection, love, trust, and generosity. The delta between the story I made up and the truth gave birth to a key learning that to this day is invaluable in our relationship: Steve and I love and trust each other, but when shame and fear visit, everything can unravel in a heartbeat if we're not willing to be vulnerable in the exact moment when we most want to self-protect. Other key learnings from the delta:

- I was reminded that shame is a liar and a story-stealer. I have to trust myself and the people I care about more than the gremlins, even if that means risking being hurt.
- I learned that one of the most vulnerable parts of loving someone is trusting that they love you back, and I need to be generous in my assumptions.
- When I played the story to the end on the swim back, I saw for the first time that many of our cold wars and arguments are predicated on bad information and that often I turn to blame when I'm scared.

As we start to integrate what we learn from the rising strong process into our lives, we get better at rumbling. In some cases, I can go from "facedown" to the delta to key learnings in five minutes. Other times, it takes me months. But if you're like me, there will always be times when we experience a completely new way of falling down, and that delta will be gaping once again, requiring more learning.

Having the courage to reckon with our emotions and to rumble with our stories is the path to writing our brave new ending and the path that leads to wholeheartedness. It's also the beginning. Understanding our fall and rise, owning our story, taking responsibility for our emotions—this is where the revolution starts. I've devoted the final chapter to the revolution.

In the meantime, the following chapters are stories that will let us examine the rising strong process in action. Each of the chapters includes additional research on the rumbling topics.

INTEGRITY IS *choosing* **COURAGE OVER COMFORT;** CHOOSING WHAT IS RIGHT *over what is* **FUN, FAST, OR EASY;** AND CHOOSING TO **PRACTICE OUR VALUES** *rather than simply* **PROFESSING THEM.**

Six

SEWER RATS AND SCOFFLAWS

RUMBLING WITH BOUNDARIES, INTEGRITY, AND GENEROSITY

knew I'd regret it the second I mumbled my halfhearted "Okay." It wasn't about the money. I have always done at least one-third of my speaking dates pro bono. That's how I support organizations or efforts that are close to my heart. But this wasn't a cause at all; I agreed to do it because the first time I'd declined their invitation, the event organizers responded with the not-so-subtle and very effective line, "We hope you haven't forgotten about the people who supported you before you were so popular."

Two of the most common messages that trigger shame in all of us are "never good enough" and "who do you think you are?" In Texas, the latter is often expressed as "you're getting way too big for your britches." Their response got me right in the britches, hence my reluctant yes. Unfortunately, it takes about ten minutes for my reluctant yes to become a resentful yes, and I was already there when one of the event organizers called to inform me that I'd be sharing a hotel room with another speaker.

After I circled around for five minutes about needing my own room but never explicitly asking for one, she finally said, "All of the speakers share rooms. They always have, and it's never been a problem. Are you saying you require something special?" *Britches. Watch the britches.*

In my family, being high maintenance was a huge shame trigger, especially for the girls. Be easy, fun, and flexible. Need a bathroom break on a road trip? We'll pull over when we don't have to cross the highway to get to the gas station. Don't like what we're having for dinner? Don't eat. Carsick? It's all in your head. Unfortunately, being low maintenance also meant not asking for what you needed and never inconveniencing anyone.

So I got really good at proving that I'm as easy as the next person. And I got really good at being resentful. The phrase "require something special" got me. "No. I'll share a room. That will be great," I replied, thinking *I hate these people. They suck and this event will suck. And my roommate will suck.*

As it turned out, the event was wonderful, the organizers taught me a valuable lesson, and my roommate changed my life. Granted, she didn't do it in an inspiring way, but the WITH GOD AS MY WITNESS, *NEVER AGAIN* kind of way works, too.

On the night before the event, I stood outside the hotel room and said a little prayer before entering. *Please, God, let me be openhearted and kind. Let me embrace this experience and be grateful for all new opportunities.*

I knocked as I used my key to crack open the door. "Hello?"

My heart sank when someone responded with a hearty

"Come on in!" *And God, please let me not be pissed that I didn't get here first to stake my claim.*

When I walked into our room, she was sitting in the corner of a love seat eating a giant cinnamon roll. Her legs were outstretched across the length of the small sofa and her hiking boots were pushing into the cushioned arm. I walked over and introduced myself, "Hi. I'm Brené." I thought my prayer might be working since I managed to refrain from saying, "Nice to meet you. Get your dirty-ass boots off the couch." I could see that she had already left a footprint on the beige fabric.

She waved her sticky hand in front of me and said, "Sorry. I've got this all over me. Otherwise I'd shake your hand." I smiled and waved back, feeling a pang of guilt about being so judgmental.

I responded in my perkiest voice, "No problem! It looks delicious."

With both hands covered in gooey icing, she was wiggling around trying to find a way to change her position without touching the sofa. Just as I was about to offer to get her a napkin, she sat straight up, put the rest of the roll in her mouth, and wiped both of her hands on the seat cushion of the couch. Then she looked at her hands and, clearly not pleased with how much frosting remained, she wiped them again, carefully avoiding the patch of upholstery where she had done the first swipe. My face must have conveyed my horror as I stood staring at the frosting-streaked cushions, because she just smiled and shrugged and said, "It's not our couch."

I was speechless. And totally grossed out. And still gripping the handle of my suitcase in one hand. Meanwhile, as I stood motionless in the middle of the room, she walked into the kitchenette, grabbed a plastic coffee cup, filled it with an inch of water, and went out onto the two-by-three-foot patio of the hotel room. Then she lit a cigarette.

Still white-knuckling my luggage, I raised my voice a little so she could hear me through the crack in the patio door. "This is a nonsmoking room. I don't think you can smoke in here."

She laughed. "They didn't say anything about the patio."

Are you kidding me?

"Seriously. The entire hotel is smoke-free," I said in my most earnest, authoritative ex-smoker voice. "Plus, the smoke is getting in the room."

She laughed again. "No big deal. We'll spray some perfume."

All right, God, I'm lowering the bar. Please don't let me kill anyone or do anything stupid. Let me keep my hate and rage on the inside. And in the name of all things holy, let there be another room available.

Three out of four isn't bad, and in hindsight, I guess it's best that the one prayer request not granted was another room being available.

I did the opening talk the next morning and left for the airport fifteen minutes after I walked offstage. As I stood at the gate waiting to board my flight, I knew something was wrong. I was taking silent issue with everyone who walked past me in the gate area. The woman in front of me was wearing too much perfume. The guy behind me was smacking his gum. The parents across from me shouldn't let their kids eat all of that candy. I stood in line ruminating about my experience at the hotel and gathering further evidence from the people around me about the disappointing state of humanity.

I couldn't get the image out of my head of my roommate

wiping the icing on the couch. But my growing irritation was a warning sign that I had come to recognize. It's one thing to be frustrated, grossed out, or even outraged by my roommate's behavior, but I was feeling something else, something closer to rage than outrage. I was stewing in self-righteousness. This is a trigger emotion for me.

After years of rumbling with this feeling, I had learned that no matter how right I think I am or how wrong someone else appears to be, self-righteousness is an off-limits emotion for me. Self-righteousness starts with the belief that I'm better than other people and it always ends with me being my very worst self and thinking, *I'm not good enough*. Even as I was standing there—knee-high in judgment—I was curious about what was happening and I knew that I wanted to get out from underneath the weight of all of the negativity I was experiencing. I called and made an appointment with my therapist, Diana, as soon as I took my seat on the plane.

When I got home later that afternoon and told Steve the story, I could tell he didn't know if he should laugh or be enraged. He went for cautious support. "The kids are at your mom's house," he said. "Do you want to go to dinner and talk some more?"

I snapped back, "What's the point? I can't eat anything that will make me feel better. I really want chicken-fried steak and mashed potatoes. I need to drown my resentment and anger in cream gravy."

He laughed. "That sounds delicious. Anything you want!" But I knew cream gravy was only a short-term fix and would break my tenuous commitment to not numb with food, so I suggested grabbing a salad at Café Express and then making a quick run to the mall to do some shopping. I can definitely suffocate rage with a pretty new sweater.

Steve reluctantly reminded me of our new budget and suggested we go for a walk after our salad. It was a bleak moment. You can't bury resentment with lettuce, and walking is for talking through feelings, not smothering them. So I stomped into the kitchen like an angry toddler, rolled some lunch meat around a cheese stick, ate it in three bites, and went to bed.

I woke up the next morning pissed off. The anger was still sharp. There was no gravy hangover to dull the senses and no new outfit in the closet to distract me from my self-righteousness. When I got to Diana's office, I didn't sit down on the couch so much as harrumph myself into it. With my arms folded tightly across my chest, I waited for Diana to say something. She just looked at me with an open face and a kind smile. Not the response I wanted.

I finally said, "Look. This wholehearted living–spiritual awakening thing is great. I'm fine with it. In fact, I like it. Except for the sewer rats and scofflaws. Those people are bullshit."

I would later learn that Diana filed this line away as one of her all-time favorite therapy session intros. I still remember exactly how I felt that morning. I remember my conviction and my restrained rage.

Diana stayed open and kind. This was our way of working together. She created a judgment-free space, and I filled it with every ounce of unfiltered emotion I could muster. Then we'd sort it out.

Without judging or attaching value, she said, "I can see you're really pissed off. Tell me about the sewer rats and scofflaws. Who are they?"

I asked her if she had seen the kids' movie *Flushed Away*. She thought for a minute, clearly scrolling through all of the movies she'd watched with her grandkids, and finally said, "No. I don't think so. What's it about?"

"It's about a great little rat named Roddy who is the pet of a wealthy young girl in London. When the family goes on vacation, he climbs out of his fancy cage and enjoys the run of the house. He dresses in a tuxedo and drives the Barbie car à la James Bond. He's British and speaks impeccable English. He watches television and plays with toys. He's super conscientious and hardworking. He keeps everything spotless and is respectful of the family's belongings. One day, while the family is still out of town, the sewer backs up. And this horrible sewer rat pops up from the kitchen sink. His big belly is hanging over his torn jeans and he's wearing a scuffed leather jacket. His feet are sticking out of his old sneakers and he has long, dirty toenails. He's a total hooligan. He burps and passes gas. He poops on the floor. He's constantly sniffing out cheese and gorging himself. He's hideous. And he trashes the family's house.

"So, Roddy, the uptown rat, tries to flush him down the toilet, but Sydney, the hooligan rat, ends up flushing Roddy instead, right into the London sewer. The rest of the story is the predictable plotline. Roddy learns to be less uptight, and he makes friends and fights a bad guy, blah, blah, blah. The point is, the sewer rat ruins everything."

Diana got the picture and asked me if I'd encountered any sewer rats lately. I launched into my story about the icing wiper, the cream-gravy denial, and our stupid budget commitment. "Just for clarification," she said, "was your roommate a sewer rat or a scofflaw?"

I had to think for a minute. "Both—she was both. And that's the worst."

Diana said she needed help understanding both terms, so I did my best to explain.

"A sewer rat doesn't care about the rules and doesn't respect other people's stuff. A scofflaw is also someone who doesn't follow the rules, but the scofflaw also makes fun of people who respect the rules. They scoff at the law. They mock people like me—rule followers. For example, my friend in college dated this guy who was the biggest scofflaw ever. One weekend we rented buggies at the beach, and there was this huge sign at the rental place that said: 'Keep your feet and hands in the buggy.' So, of course, as soon as we pulled out of the rental parking lot, he started hanging his foot over the side. I told him to stop and he laughed. 'Ooooh. Keep your feet in the buggy. Brené is the buggy police.' Ten minutes later, he crushed his ankle on a curb, and we spent five hours in the emergency room of the hospital. Everyone felt sorry for him except for me. I thought it was bullshit."

Diana's eyes widened as she listened. "I got it. I think I understand the difference. So, let's talk about your roommate. Do you think she was making fun of you?"

I could see where this was going, and I wasn't going to let this end with a discussion of how I was taking the incident too personally. I went into cross-examination mode.

"She was making fun of the rules and breaking them, even though I was conveying that they were important to me; therefore, she was making fun of what's important to me. And that's the same thing as making fun of me." *I've seen every episode of* Law and Order. *Don't jack with me.*

"I see." Diana took a deep breath and stayed quiet.

I didn't bite. I took a deep breath and stayed quiet, too. *Two can play at this.*

Diana asked, "Do you think it's possible that your roommate was doing the best she could that weekend?"

Are you kidding me? I was incensed. Totally and completely incensed. For the first time since we'd worked together, I wasn't sure I even liked Diana, and I questioned her judgment. I went completely cold. I had been flapping my arms around telling my stories, but now they were once again folded tightly across my chest, my lips pursed. I answered in my most proper voice, "No. I do not believe she was doing her best. Do you believe she was doing her best?"

With every tightening move I made, Diana seemed to unfold a little, opening her face and her body and her heart to possibility. It was making me sick.

"You know, I'm not sure. I do, however, think that in general people are doing the best they can. What do you think?"

What do I think? I think this conversation is total crap. That's what I think. I think the idea that people are doing the best they can is also crap. I can't believe I'm paying for this.

Diana interrupted my high-level reflection. "Brené, you look angry. What's going on?"

I unfolded my arms, leaned forward, and rested my forearms on my knees. I looked Diana right in the eye and asked, "Do you really believe—in your heart—that people are doing the best they can? Or . . . is that what we're supposed to believe because we are social workers? Really. Tell me the truth."

I was so close to her that there was no way I'd miss it if she flinched.

She smiled and looked toward the sky, then nodded her head.

Oh my God. You've got to be kidding me.

"Yes. Yes, I really do believe that most of us are doing the very best we can with the tools we have. I believe we can grow and get better, but I also believe that most of us are really doing our best."

"Well, that's great. Good for you. I do not."

And you and whoever you're smiling at up there should just ride your unicorns over the rainbow and leave the rest of us mere mortals to our misery and our chicken-fried steak.

Diana told me then that we were out of time, and for the first time in a long while, I was grateful to hear it. *We have nothing in common. And I'm mad. She took couch-wiper's side.*

I trudged out to my car and set off to run a few errands before heading home. Diana had floated some wild ideas by me during the course of our work together, but this was by far the most ridiculous and infuriating. Even as I stood in line at the bank, I was shaking my head and letting out exasperated breaths.

I was pulled out of my private grumbling when the woman in front of me, who had made her way to the counter, began yelling at the bank teller who was helping her. "This can't be right! I didn't make these withdrawals. I want to see a manager!"

I was only a few feet behind this woman, so I could hear and see everything. She was an older white woman, probably in her late seventies, and the young man helping her was African American and in his late twenties. The man pointed to his supervisor, who was helping another customer a couple of windows down. The supervisor was a middle-aged African American woman.

"No! I want a different supervisor!" shouted the woman at the counter. *Here we go. She's really going to wait until she gets a white supervisor? What's wrong with people?*

By this time, the supervisor had seen the commotion and made her way over. As she began escorting the woman to her office, the teller called me to the counter.

"Can I help you?" the man asked.

Clearly possessed by the demons unleashed in therapy, I blurted out, "Do you think people are doing the best they can?"

He smiled. "Did you just see what happened?"

I nodded. "I did see that. She didn't like what you were telling her and she wanted a white supervisor. It was horrible."

He raised his eyebrows and shrugged his shoulders. "Yeah. She's scared about her money," he explained.

"Yes. I heard her. But back to my question—this is the perfect example. Do you think *she's* doing the best she can?"

He thought for a moment. "Yeah. Probably. She's scared. Who knows?" Then he paused for a minute. "Are you a psychiatrist?"

He was missing the point. "No. I'm a researcher. And I can't really believe you think she's doing her best. Really?"

Completely ignoring my question, he explained that he had seen a psychiatrist when he came back from two tours in Iraq. He said his wife had had an affair with someone they both knew, and it had "done a number" on him. My question instantly felt far less important, and we talked about his experiences and my research for a couple of minutes. Aware of the growing line behind me, I thanked him and stuck my money into my purse.

As I turned to walk away, he said, "The thing is—you never know about people. That lady could have a kid on drugs stealing money from her account or a husband with Alzheimer's who's taking money and not even remembering. You just never know. People aren't themselves when they're scared. It might be all they can do."

Although I tried to dismiss Diana's idea as absurd, there was something insidious about it and I became obsessed. Over the next three weeks, I asked just more than forty people this question. I first asked a couple of colleagues and grad students, and then I reached out to some of the research participants from earlier studies. It was a simple question: *Do you think, in general, that people are doing the best they can?* By the time I finished fifteen interviews, I had saturation—clear patterns and themes had emerged that would accurately predict what I would find in the remaining interviews.

First, those who said they believe that people are doing the best they can consistently qualified their answers: "I know it sounds naïve . . ." or "You can't be sure, but I think so . . ." or "I know it sounds weird . . ." They were slow to answer and seemed almost apologetic, as if they had tried to persuade themselves otherwise, but just couldn't give up on humanity. They were also careful to explain that it didn't mean that people can't grow or change. Still, at any given time, they figured, people are normally doing the best they can with the tools they have.

Those who believe that people are not doing the best they can were unequivocal and passionate in their responses. I never once heard, "I'm not sure, but I don't think so." It was always some version of an emphatic "*No!* Absolutely not! No way!"

Unlike their "yes" counterparts, about 80 percent of these respondents used themselves as an example: "I know I'm not doing my best, so why should I assume others are?" or "I slack off all of the time," or "I don't give it 110 percent when I should." They judged their efforts in the same exacting manner that they judged the efforts of others. It was clearly important for the people answering "no" to acknowledge this parity.

I also began to see a pattern that worried me. The past research participants who answered "no" were also people who struggled with perfectionism. They were quick to point out how they're not always doing the best they could and offered examples of situations when they weren't their perfect selves. They were as hard on others as they were on themselves. Every participant who answered "yes" was in the group of people who I had identified as wholehearted—people who are willing to be vulnerable and who believe in their self-worth. They, too, offered examples of situations where they made mistakes or didn't show up as their best selves, but rather than pointing out how they could and should have done better, they explained that, while falling short, their intentions were good and they were trying. Professionally, I saw what was emerging. I didn't experience it personally, though, until I got flushed away like my friend Roddy the rat.

This happened close to the end of this experiment, when I was having dinner with a new friend. Of course, I thought it would be fun to ask her this question. We had a lot in common and I guessed that she would be a "no," like me. Our over-functioning and low tolerance for slackers were things that had drawn us to each other as potential friends. I launched into it the second we sat down. "So, here's a research question for you. Do you think that, in general, people are doing the best they can?"

She shot back a defiant and predictable negative: "Oh, hell no!"

I smiled. "Right? I totally agree."

Then she leaned over the table and began a rapid-fire explanation. "Let's take breastfeeding, for example. I'm nursing my daughter right now. Yes, it's hard. Yes, it's exhausting. Yes, I've had three infections and it feels like glass cutting into my nipple every time she latches on. But, please. Do *not* tell me about needing your body back or feeling tired or needing to supplement for work. I don't want to hear it. If you're not going to breastfeed for at least a year, you should think twice about having children. You are *not* doing the best you can, and don't you think your children deserve your best? Quitting is lazy. And if quitting really is your best, maybe your best isn't good enough."

And there I was—a chubby little sewer rat in my little battered leather jacket with my little torn jeans. I could almost smell the cheese. I was her sewer rat.

I breastfed my kids for very short periods of time, nowhere close to a year. I had the overwhelming need to explain to my new friend that I had severe hyperemesis gravidarum for the first twenty weeks of both my pregnancies, and that I did all I could do when it came to breastfeeding. I wanted to explain that pumping was so hard for me, and that I tried until I couldn't try anymore. I wanted to convince her that I love my kids as much as she loves her kids. *I wanted her to know that I did the best I could.*

But I didn't say anything, because all I could think about were the people who, when I sat in judgment, probably wanted to say to me, "You don't know me. You don't know anything about me. Please don't judge me."

By the way, I also didn't want to be backed into defending my choices as a mother. There are at least a million ways to be a great mother, and not one of them hinges on breastfeeding or any of the other hot-button issues. Great mothers know that they are worthy of love and belonging, and as a result they raise children who know they are worthy of the same things. Shaming other mothers is not one of the million ways to be a great mom.

When I got home that night, Steve was sitting in the kitchen. When he asked me how dinner went, I realized that I hadn't asked him the research question, so I told him I wanted his answer before I gave him the lowdown on dinner. He thought about it for a solid ten minutes. As a pediatrician, Steve sees the best and the worst in people. He just kept staring out the window. I could tell he was struggling with the question.

Finally, when he looked back at me, he had that same look on his face that Diana had had in her office. Steve said, "I don't know. I really don't. All I know is that my life is better when I assume that people are doing their best. It keeps me out of judgment and lets me focus on what is, and not what should or could be." His answer felt like truth to me. Not an easy truth, but truth.

One month and forty interviews later, I was back in Diana's office. I sat down on the couch, my legs folded under me and my journal in hand. Diana had her own notebook in her hand and looked over at me with her open face and kind eyes. She led with the question, "How are you?"

I started crying. "People are doing the best they can."

Diana did nothing but look at me compassionately. No gold star. No pat on the head. No "Good job, young Jedi!" Nada.

"I know what happened. I should have asked for what I needed. I should have turned down the event or, at the very least, insisted on my own room."

She looked at me, and without an ounce of irony or *I told you so,* she said, "You were doing the best you could."

The moment she said that, I thought of hearing Maya Angelou talk about how when we know better, we do better.

I then shared Steve's insights, which I thought were so wise and beautiful. "Steve says his life is better when he assumes people are doing the best they can. I think he's right. I learned some hard things about myself and about people. It's a powerful question."

"Yes," she agreed, "it is a powerful question. Want to share what you've learned? I'd love to hear."

I explained that very early on in my work I had discovered that the most compassionate people I interviewed also have the most well-defined and well-respected boundaries. It surprised me at the time, but now I get it. They assume that other people are doing the best they can, but they also ask for what they need and they don't put up with a lot of crap. I lived the opposite way: I assumed that people weren't doing their best so I judged them and constantly fought being disappointed, which was easier than setting boundaries. Boundaries are hard when you want to be liked and when you are a pleaser hell-bent on being easy, fun, and flexible.

Compassionate people ask for what they need. They say no when they need to, and when they say yes, they mean it. They're compassionate because their boundaries keep them out of resentment. When asked to speak at the event, I said yes when I wanted to say no. I put no value on my work or my needs, and the event organizers, in turn, put no value on my work or my needs.

You know the irony about speaking fees? When I do something for full fee, people are respectful and professional. When I do something pro bono because I care about the cause, people are respectful and professional. When I do something because I feel pushed, pressured, guilt-tripped, or shamed into it, I expect people to be appreciative in addition to being respectful and professional. Ninety percent of the time they are none of the above. *How can we expect people to put value on our work when we don't value ourselves enough to set and hold uncomfortable boundaries?*

I told Diana about taking the question even further with a group of clergy who serve rural families living in poverty. I described how I had asked these men and women to think of someone they find themselves judging and holding resentment toward, and to write that person's name on a piece of paper. Then I asked them to pretend with me for a minute. "What if you had it on the highest authority that the person whose name you wrote down is doing the very best that he or she can do?"

There was immediate resistance. *I don't believe it. Who is the authority?* This was easy. These were clergy! I said, "God says so." One woman burst into tears. She and her husband were sitting next to each other. They are both deacons and, without conferring, they had written down the same person's name. I asked her if she felt like sharing what she was feeling with the group.

James, the person they both referenced, was a man with six young children who lived in a trailer in the desert. Both he and his wife had long addiction histories, and Children's Services had been in and out of their lives for years. The clergy brought James and his family food, diapers, and baby formula on a regular basis, but they were convinced that he sold the goods for drinking money at least as often as he used them for his family.

In a shaky voice, she said, "If God told me that James was doing the best he can, I would do one of two things: I would continue to bring him what I could, when I could, and withhold judgment, or I would decide that giving anything directly to James is not something I can continue to do. Either way, I would need to stop being so angry, stop judging, and stop waiting for something different to happen."

Her husband put his arm around her. Fighting back his own tears, he looked at the group and said, "We're just so tired. So tired of being angry and feeling taken for granted."

Diana listened intently, and when I was done, she said, "You're right. This is hard and important work for you."

This time I felt my face and heart opening up. "Yes. It's hard. And I'm tired. But the tired I feel from doing this kind of exploration is different than the tired I feel from being pissed off and resentful all of the time. It's a good tired, not a cream-gravy tired."

THE RECKONING

That feeling of self-righteousness in the airport triggered the real reckoning for me. My "facedown" moment happened when I was standing in line thinking hateful and judgmental thoughts about every person around me and, on the surface, feeling superior. I say "on the surface" because I've studied judgment and I know we don't judge people when we feel good about ourselves. I knew something was wrong. There was a smaller reckoning when I was white-knuckling my luggage and watching my roommate walk from the icing-stained couch to the smoking patio. Like skilled poker players assess their opponents, I've studied my own tells and I know I'm knee-deep in emotion or vulnerability whenever my prayers include not wanting to hurt anyone or when I'm rehearsing really mean conversations. But ultimately my curiosity about those debilitating feelings of self-righteousness led me to make that appointment with Diana from the airplane.

THE RUMBLE

I started my SFD in my journal on the plane ride home. It was mostly bulleted points and colored-pencil doodles (and the icing wiper portrayed as the devil). My SFD was pretty straightforward (and embarrassingly approximated a temper tantrum):

- I was easy and flexible (against my will), and instead of being appreciative, the event organizers took advantage of me.

- I was good. They were bad. It wasn't fair and I didn't deserve it.

I also jotted down a basic theory on two general types of human behavior:

- Type 1—Those of us who try our very best, follow the rules, and are respectful.
- Type 2—The sewer rats and scofflaws of the world who don't try their best and who take advantage of people.

Once I got home, I added to my SFD that it's not fair that I can't eat, spend, or do what I want to comfort myself after a hard trip like that. This draft had no shortage of "not fairs."

I had to **rumble with** the shame of being high maintenance, my self-worth, blame, resentment, and perfectionism—my normal haunts. But the biggest rumble was with boundaries, self-righteousness, and integrity. The **delta** between the confabulations in my SFD and the truth was dark, wide, and swampy. I came away with these **key learnings:**

- We're all doing the best we can. The sewer-rats-and-scofflaws lens is a dangerous way to view the world because no matter how hard you're working or how many balls you can keep in the air, if you look at the world through that lens long enough, you'll eventually see yourself as a little rodent in a biker jacket.

- The trick to staying out of resentment is maintaining better boundaries—blaming others less and holding myself more accountable for asking for what I need and want.
- There is no integrity in blaming and turning to "it's not fair" and "I deserve." I need to take responsibility for my own well-being. If I believed I was not being treated fairly or not getting something I deserved, was I actually asking for it, or was I just looking for an excuse to assign blame and feel self-righteous?
- I am trying not to numb my discomfort for myself, because I think I'm worth the effort. It's not something that's happening *to me*—it's something I'm choosing *for myself*.
- This rumble taught me why self-righteousness is dangerous. Most of us buy into the myth that it's a long fall from "I'm better than you" to "I'm not good enough"—but the truth is that these are two sides of the same coin. Both are attacks on our worthiness. We don't compare when we're feeling good about ourselves; we look for what's good in others. When we practice self-compassion, we are compassionate toward others. Self-righteousness is just the armor of self-loathing.

In *Daring Greatly,* I talk about how the lyrics of Leonard Cohen's song "Hallelujah"—"Love is not a victory march, it's a cold and it's a broken hallelujah"—capture how daring greatly can feel more like freedom with a little battle fatigue than a full-on celebration. The same is true for rising strong. What I've learned from the research and my own experiences is that the rising strong process deepens our wholeheartedness, but it often feels like a good, hearty tired.

A Closer Look at Rumbling with Boundaries, Integrity, and Generosity

My formal research continues to bear out the patterns I observed when I informally asked people whether they believe others are doing the best they can. I've now asked hundreds of people the question and documented and coded their responses. I've done the exercise that I did with the deacons at twenty large conferences. Folks write down the name of someone who fills them with frustration, disappointment, and/or resentment, and then I propose that their person is doing the best he or she can. The responses have been wide-ranging. "Crap," one man said, "if he's really doing the best he can, I'm a total jerk, and I need to stop harassing him and start helping him." One woman said, "If this was true and my mother was doing the best she can, I would be grief-stricken. I'd rather be angry than sad, so it's easier to believe she's letting me down on purpose than to grieve the fact that my mother is never going to be who I need her to be."

It can be painful for organization leaders to answer this question because, as with the first comment, what often comes up is the realization that instead of prodding and pushing someone, they need to move on to the difficult task of helping them, reassigning them, or letting them go.

As miserable as resentment, disappointment, and frustration make us feel, we fool ourselves into believing that they're easier than the vulnerability of a difficult conversation. The truth is that judgment and anger take up way more emotional bandwidth for us. Beyond that, they are often shaming and disrespectful to the person who is struggling, and ultimately toxic to the entire culture.

One of the most profound responses to this exercise came out of a focus group I did with a group of leaders at West Point. One officer pushed me a little on "the accuracy of the intel" and kept asking, "You are 100 percent certain that this person is doing the best he can?"

After I answered yes two or three times, the officer took a deep breath and said, "Then move the rock."

I was confused. "What do you mean by 'move the rock'?"

He shook his head. "I have to stop kicking the rock. I need to move it. It's hurting both of us. He's not the right person for this position, and there's no amount of pushing or getting on him that's going to change that. He needs to be reassigned to a position where he can make a contribution."

This doesn't mean that we stop helping people set goals or that we stop expecting people to grow and change. It means that we stop respecting and evaluating people based on what we think they should accomplish, and start respecting them for who they are and holding them accountable for what they're actually doing. It means that we stop loving people for who they *could be* and start loving them for who they *are*. It means that sometimes when we're beating ourselves up, we need to stop and say to that harassing voice inside, "Man, I'm doing the very best I can right now."

Living BIG: Boundaries-Integrity-Generosity

Jean Kantambu Latting, a professor in my master's and doctoral program, was one of my most important mentors. She
taught leadership and organizational development (LOD). I
interned with her, did LOD research under her supervision,
and served as a teaching assistant in her LOD classes.

Whenever someone would bring up a conflict with a colleague, she would ask, "What is the hypothesis of generosity?
What is the most generous assumption you can make about
this person's intentions or what this person said?"

Based on how I was raised and my relationship with vulnerability at the time, I never thought all that highly of this
idea. I always thought it was like asking, "What's the best way
to get sucker punched in this situation?"

But now, as I started working from the new intention that
people are doing their best, I remembered Jean's question and
started applying it in my life. If someone sent me a curt email,
I would try to generously hypothesize that he was having a
crappy day, or that he's not a great email communicator, or
that maybe his actual tone didn't translate over email. Whatever the case, it wasn't about me. This was incredibly effective
and liberating—to a point. Generosity is not a free pass for
people to take advantage of us, treat us unfairly, or be purpose-
fully disrespectful and mean.

What I realized was that a generous assumption *without
boundaries* is another recipe for resentment, misunderstand-
ing, and judgment. We could all stand to be more generous,
but we also need to maintain our integrity and our boundar-

ies. I call the solution to this issue **Living BIG: Boundaries, Integrity, and Generosity.**

What boundaries do I need to put in place so I can work from a place of integrity and extend the most generous interpretations of the intentions, words, and actions of others?

Setting boundaries means getting clear on what behaviors are okay and what's not okay. Integrity is key to this commitment because it's how we set those boundaries and ultimately hold ourselves and others accountable for respecting them. I tried to find an existing definition of integrity that reflected what I saw in the data, but I couldn't. So here's my definition:

> Integrity is choosing courage over comfort; choosing what is right over what is fun, fast, or easy; and choosing to practice our values rather than simply professing them.

Living BIG is saying: "Yes, I'm going to be generous in my assumptions and intentions while standing solidly in my integrity and being very clear about what's acceptable and what's not acceptable."

In the Lake Travis story, I ultimately approached Steve with the assumption that he loved me, that there was something going on that I didn't fully understand, and that it was worth being vulnerable and putting my feelings and my fears on the table. Being honest about the stories we're making up versus just acting on our anger or self-protective impulses is a generous move. I was rooted in my integrity—choosing what I felt was brave and right over what was comfortable and easy—and

I was addressing an issue that felt like a boundary violation. It's not okay to blow me off when I am trying to reach out. Steve responded the same way. He told me the truth, held me accountable for past behavior, and stayed in his integrity. Living BIG saved us that morning. Had either one of us assumed the worst, defaulted to the easy route, or gone into self-protection or attack mode, it would be a different, albeit familiar, story.

One of the best examples of Living BIG comes from my friend Kelly Rae Roberts. Kelly Rae is an artist, teacher, and entrepreneur. Over the past five or six years, her art has exploded in popularity. If you look at her website, many of you will recognize it and say, "Oh, I love her work!"

In addition to making art, Kelly Rae runs her business, is a writer, and teaches multimedia painting courses. Interestingly, she was working as a social worker in the oncology department of a hospital when she taught herself how to paint and draw. She later followed her calling to become an artist and entrepreneur and is now generously committed to helping others do the same.

As Kelly Rae's career took off and she began licensing her work globally, she began to run into problems. Large-scale copyright infringement started happening (an unrelenting issue for many artists), and she began noticing that some of her blog followers and students from her classes were copying her art and selling it online. Kelly Rae responded to these legal breaches with one of the most powerful examples of Living BIG that I've ever seen.

She wrote a blog post titled, "What Is and Is Not Okay." The post was kind, generous, explicit, straightforward, and unflinching. Here's an edited version:

IT'S NOT OKAY

- To use one of my images as your profile photo on Facebook or any other website without an artist credit. This violates copyright law.
- To make copies of the art instructions from my book, articles, or classes and publish them to your blogs and websites. It's also not okay to reword my instructions and use them for a class you are teaching for profit, or to submit them to magazines for publication.
- To publish videos or photos on your blogs and websites showing my book, class step-by-step instructions, or painting process.

IT'S OKAY

- To be inspired. To experiment. To learn techniques and then to make them your own. The techniques shared in my book, articles, and classes are meant to be a jumping-off point for you so you can keep going, expand, grow—totally okay, and celebrated.
- To send me an email asking if you can use one of my images for any reason.
- To grab images from my website for a blog post. But you must give credit.

The entire post, which is much longer than what I'm sharing here and even includes a Frequently Asked Questions section, was framed with this message: "I hope this helps clear things up. I know that most people who have crossed the line have done so without intention. And most didn't mean any

harm whatsoever. But I think it's important that we all continue to be good stewards of the creative life and continue to
gently educate on what's appropriate and what's not, especially because breaking copyright law is very serious."

As Kelly Rae so beautifully demonstrated, boundaries are
simply our lists of what's okay and what's not okay. In fact, this
is the working definition I use for boundaries today. It's so
straightforward and it makes sense for all ages in all situations.

When we combine the courage to make clear what works
for us and what doesn't with the compassion to assume people
are doing their best, our lives change. Yes, there will be people
who violate our boundaries, and this will require that we continue to hold those people accountable. But when we're living
in our integrity, we're strengthened by the self-respect that
comes from the honoring of our boundaries, rather than being
flattened by disappointment and resentment.

One of the greatest gifts of this work is how it's changed
my parenting. Now when my kids come home from school
and talk about how someone has been unfair or how a class-
mate continually treats them badly, I have a new approach. I
still listen with empathy and ask about their part in the issue,
but now we also explore the question, *What boundaries need
to be in place so that you can stay in your integrity and make generous assumptions about this person's motivation, intentions, or
behaviors?*

Recently, my daughter and I were having this conversation
about someone acting out on social media. When I asked my
daughter how we could apply Living BIG to this situation, a
look of concern washed over her face. She said, "A generous
assumption would be that she is really hurting, not just look-

ing for attention." I agreed. We talked about how Ellen wants to maintain her integrity online and then did the tough work of making a list of what's okay and what's not okay. Finally, we discussed how she was going to set these boundaries and expectations and hold people accountable for them.

Both Ellen and Charlie have asked a lot of questions about the appropriateness of setting boundaries when someone is hurting. It's hard enough for me to get my head and heart around the relationship between boundaries and compassion, but just imagine how strange it must be for kids being raised in a culture with very few models of how boundary setting and kindness can coexist. I believe it comes down to a simple question: Can you be kind and respectful to your friend if he or she is hurting you? The answer is no, and this leads to a couple of choices: The easy solution is to be unkind and disrespectful back, or to walk away. The courageous answer is to look at this friend and say, "I care about you and I'm sorry that you're going through a hard time. But I need to talk to you about what's okay and what's not okay."

The permutations of this example are endless and stretch across every part of our lives:

"I know the holidays are hard for you. I want you to come over on Christmas Eve and be with us, but I'm not comfortable with your drinking so much that you get drunk."

"I understand that there's a lot of conflict between you and one of the other team members. This is a stressful project, and it's miserable for all of us to work under this constant tension. It's not sustainable. I need you to clean it up by next week or you'll be pulled off the team. What's your preference, and how can I support you?"

"Yes, I love you. Yes, I made bad choices when I was your age. Yes, you're still grounded."

A Note on Serial Killers, Terrorists, and Assassins

I should win the Most Likely to Be Asked About Serial Killers, Terrorists, and Assassins Award. For the past decade, when I've said that there's no convincing evidence that shame is an effective compass for moral behavior, everyone from students to journalists hits me with the question, "What about the murderers?" To which I respond, "Shame is much more likely to be the cause of destructive behavior than the cure. Guilt and empathy are the emotions that lead us to question how our actions affect other people, and both of these are severely diminished by the presence of shame."

Do I believe serial killers and terrorists are doing the best they can? Yes. And their best is dangerous, which is why I believe we should catch them, lock them up, and assess whether they can be helped. If they can't, they should stay locked up. That's how compassion and accountability work. Hold people accountable for their actions in a way that acknowledges their humanity. When we treat people like animals and expect them to emerge from prison newly minted as loving, empathic, connected people, we're kidding ourselves. Requiring accountability while also extending your compassion is not the easiest course of action, but it is the most humane and, ultimately, the safest for the community.

THE REVOLUTION

Character—the willingness to accept responsibility for one's own life—is the source from which self-respect springs.
—Joan Didion

I have moved from the self-righteousness and resentment of my SFD to a new way of looking at the world. Maria Popova, founder of the wonderfully curated website BrainPickings.org, recently shared an essay on self-respect by Joan Didion that includes the quote above. It brought so many feelings into focus for me. In my new story, I am clear on the fact that self-righteousness is a tremendous threat to self-respect. As Didion points out, I must accept responsibility for my own life and my decisions. When I was finding fault with everyone who walked by that day at the airport, my self-respect was suffering. That's why things felt so dark.

I agreed to do something for someone for the wrong reasons. I wasn't being generous or kind. I said yes to be likable and to avoid being seen as "difficult." Moving forward, I give myself permission to ask for what I need—to take care of myself. I can never be sure about the intentions of others, but I believe that assuming the best about other people can fundamentally change my life.

I now recognize that people learn how to treat us based on how they see us treating ourselves. If I don't put value on my work or my time, neither will the person I am helping. Boundaries are a function of self-respect and self-love. Even on the rare occasion when Living BIG leaves me feeling vulnerable, I'm still left standing squarely in my integrity. From there, all things are possible.

We can't
RISE
STRONG
when we're
ON THE
RUN.

Seven

THE BRAVE AND BROKENHEARTED

RUMBLING WITH EXPECTATIONS, DISAPPOINTMENT,
RESENTMENT, HEARTBREAK, CONNECTION,
GRIEF, FORGIVENESS, COMPASSION,
AND EMPATHY

Claudia reached out to me after attending a talk I gave on the rising strong research. She had recently had a difficult family experience that she was struggling to process and, she explained, several of the pieces fell into place as she listened to me speak. She generously agreed to be interviewed for the book and has allowed me to share her story.

Claudia is in her early thirties, five years into an exciting and promising career in design, newly married, and in the process of fixing up a new home in an up-and-coming neighborhood on Chicago's North Side. She is smart, kind, funny, and radiant. Claudia explained that she and her husband had decided to split up for their first Thanksgiving as a married couple so they could each spend time with their own families. They didn't have much time off from work and both were overdue for visits, so she headed for Madison, Wisconsin, while he took off for Milwaukee.

Going home for the holidays is fraught with emotion for a lot of people, and it had never been easy for Claudia. Her youngest sister, Amy, suffers from depression and alcoholism. Amy's drinking problems began in high school. She first got sober when she was eighteen, but over the next ten years, she'd bounced back and forth between relapses and further treatment. Now in her late twenties, Amy was drinking again, and this time refusing to get help. She couldn't hold down a steady job and was fighting with her parents—her only source of support. Even though they had rented an apartment in Madison for her, Amy refused to live there because it meant having to answer questions about her health and sobriety. "Holidays and family gatherings have always been tough," Claudia said. "When Amy does show up, you never know what you're in for. If she's drinking, it always ends in an altercation with my parents. When she doesn't show up, my parents' grief hangs over the house. Either way, no one talks about it. It's the elephant in the room."

One time Amy did show up, sober and on her best behavior. Claudia's then-fiancé and his family had joined them for dinner, and Claudia's father gave a rousing speech about how grateful they were to have Amy with them for the weekend. During the speech, Claudia and her other sister, Anna, exchanged glances that clearly conveyed their hurt and frustration. Amy's struggle consumed and defined their family, often making Claudia and Anna feel like there wasn't much energy or attention left for anyone else.

Amy had texted Claudia a couple of days before she arrived

in Madison, saying she was looking forward to seeing her and hoped they could get together without their parents. Thanksgiving dinner without Amy was difficult and, as Claudia had predicted, her parents were sad, but there was no conversation about Amy's absence. The night before she was to return to Chicago, Claudia and Anna went to meet Amy for dinner. "I just thought we could have one meal together," Claudia told me. "Three sisters sharing a pizza and catching up. Like a normal family." Amy texted Claudia the address where she was staying, but as Claudia and Anna approached, they began to think they'd made a mistake. The address, in a high-crime part of town, was an abandoned store. There was plywood covering the broken windows and the rotting door was slightly ajar. Claudia and Anna walked up to the door and peeked inside. When they saw a shadowy figure toward the back of the store, they looked at each other and decided to get back in the car, but before they could turn around, Amy called out, "Come in."

Fear washed over Claudia when she finally saw Amy in the dim light of the small apartment upstairs, where she was staying. She looked worse than ever. She was dirty, disheveled, and had dark circles under her eyes. The room was full of trash, and as they stood there staring at Amy, a mouse ran across the floor. Claudia was overwhelmed by pain at the sight of Amy and her suffering. Claudia explained to me, "Five years ago I would have asked myself when I saw Amy, *Is she drunk or sober?* But this far into her disease, she doesn't have to be drunk for you to know she's suffering. Even when she's sober you can tell she's sick."

Anna was also overwhelmed by her sister's appearance, but unlike Claudia, she wasn't speechless. Echoing words they'd heard their father say many times, Anna shouted, "What's wrong with you? How can you live like this? Jesus! Pull yourself together!" The whole scene was traumatic.

Amy became agitated and insisted that Anna leave right away. After a few minutes of negotiating, Anna caught a cab home. Claudia stayed with Amy and for the next two hours Amy unloaded on Claudia, who did her best to listen while Amy told her how miserable she was and complained about their parents' unfair treatment and expectations. Claudia was overcome with grief and guilt—grief for her sister and guilt for thinking, *How long do I have to stay here listening to this? When can I leave? How soon can I get back to the life I've worked so hard to build in Chicago?* Claudia told me, "Initially I thought my face-down moment was sitting in that terrible place across from my sister, who was as bad off as I've ever seen her, but it wasn't. I wasn't curious about what I was feeling, I just wanted to stop feeling it. I didn't want to know more. I wanted to get out of there and back to Chicago."

At one point Amy said to Claudia, "You're the only one in the family who really understands me. I know you can help me. You can make everything better. I'll come live with you in Chicago. You can take care of me." Claudia instantly felt guilt, but also panic. She told Amy that she could and would stay more connected and would help her, but moving in with her wouldn't work. Amy's struggle had started when the girls were all teenagers. Claudia's entire family life had been hijacked by Amy's addiction. Claudia wasn't willing to jeopardize her marriage and her life. After another hour of conversation, Claudia left and drove back to her parents' house.

She knew her parents would be waiting up when she got

home, hoping for a full report. But Claudia couldn't bring herself to talk about it. It was too hard, too awful. They asked, but she said nothing. The three of them sat in silence and watched TV for an hour. Claudia was so glad she was leaving the next morning.

On the quick flight from Madison to Chicago, Claudia convinced herself that the best way to get on with her life was to leave this painful experience behind her. She wasn't even going to share what had happened with her husband. "I'm so tired of being that person," she told me. "The one with the crazy family—the one that, instead of having the kind of Thanksgiving dinner you see in the movies, visits her alcoholic sister in a rodent-infested abandoned store."

As Claudia rode the train home from the airport, a fistfight broke out in the aisle between the seats. All of a sudden two large men were going at it—punching, shoving, and pulling hair. The train was full of families carrying shopping bags stuffed with post–Thanksgiving Day bargains. Some of the people on the train were yelling, "Stop! There are children here! Stop fighting!" The two men were still fighting when the train finally reached the next station. The passengers all made beelines for the platform, many of them calling for the police as they pushed their way past the brawling men.

THE RECKONING

Already feeling tender from her experiences with her family, Claudia was shaken by the fight on the train. "It affected me in a powerful way," she said. "I know it sounds crazy, but there was something almost metaphysical about it. It was as if the universe were telling me that I can't run from a conflict, because it will just follow me.

"This was my reckoning. Something about this violent fight . . . I think this was my facedown moment. I didn't know what I was feeling or why, but I knew that something was happening here, something I had to understand better."

Claudia decided she would tell her husband about her visit and Amy's situation. He was grateful that she shared it with him and they agreed that they wouldn't keep difficult things like that from each other. Claudia told me that her initial impulse not to tell her husband was part of her SFD.

"The story I made up starts with the questions I ask every year as the holidays approach: *Why can't I just go home and have a normal visit? Is it too much to ask to just grab some pizza with my sisters over the Thanksgiving holiday?* The experience is always disappointing at best, and intensely painful at worst. I resent that it's always so hard. Also, I make up that if I spend more time with Amy and try to support her and love her, I'll get sucked in and somehow end up taking care of her for the rest of our lives. And I know what that looks like. She's almost thirty years old. Short of having her committed, what can I do if she refuses to get help? I know I can't take care of her. On the other hand, if I don't take care of her or I limit my time with her, I'm a bad sister. I also make up that if we don't talk about what's happening, it's easier. And, if I don't talk about it with my husband, I can keep it away from the life I've built. There's also the fear that if I do talk about it with my husband, he'll think something is wrong with me and my family."

THE RUMBLE

When I asked Claudia where she was in the process, she said, "I'm definitely still in Act 2. I know I need to rumble with my expectations about time with my family. I don't know why I keep thinking that things might somehow be different the next time I go home. It's always hard and I keep experiencing the same disappointment over and over. I'm not even sure where I came up with the idea that 'normal' holidays exist for anyone. But at the same time, it's hard to give up my fantasy of a 'normal' family, and to accept that visits with my sister will always be difficult. Just getting clear on how I'm setting myself up to go in is a big start."

Claudia explained, "I'm also rumbling with connection. It was hard to talk about what happened with my husband. When I finally told him the part about coming home and watching TV in silence with my parents rather than discussing what had happened with Amy, he pointed out how disconnected the three of us were, and how that only makes things worse. I know that's true. We don't know how to talk about it in my family. I think my whole family is rumbling with heartbreak and we're afraid that opening up that discussion will mean being overcome with sadness. But not talking about it isn't working either."

As Claudia thought more about the new story she wants to write, she said, "What I do know for sure is that I love my sisters and my parents. I can't worry about 'being the person with the crazy family.' I know so many people who have a parent or sibling suffering with mental illness or addiction, or both. I need to work on owning this story. Moving away and limiting my time at home doesn't change the fact that this is part of my life. I'm also rumbling with boundaries. Sacrificing my life won't make Amy better. I can be a good sister and still set boundaries around my life. I need to figure out how to do that. I'm still rumbling."

Claudia then shared one of the most powerful insights about the process that I've ever heard: "It's so hard to be face-down on the arena floor, but if you open your eyes when you're down there and take a minute to look around, you get a completely new perspective on the world. You see things that you don't see when you're standing tall. You see more struggle—more conflict and suffering. It can make you more compassionate if you open your eyes and look around while you're down there."

I'm grateful for Claudia's willingness to let me share this story for several reasons. First, it takes courage to share a story that's still in process—to say, "I'm still in the rumble, still trying to figure out what's true and what's not." Sometimes SFDs are written over the course of years; it may take a long time to challenge and reality-check our narratives. Second, I've never met a single person who hasn't had to rumble with expectations, disappointment, and resentment. It's a standing rumble for most of us.

Third, we all experience different kinds of heartbreak over the course of our lives, but the heartbreak associated with addiction and mental, behavioral, and physical health struggles is not something we talk about enough. We need to have more conversations about the protracted heartbreak that stems from feeling helpless as we watch someone we love suffer, even as that suffering pulls us down. Last, our silence about grief serves no one. We can't heal if we can't grieve; we can't forgive if we can't grieve. We run from grief because loss scares us, yet our hearts reach toward grief because the broken parts want to mend. C. S. Lewis wrote, "No one ever told me that grief felt so like fear." We can't rise strong when we're on the run.

Rumbling with Disappointment, Expectations, and Resentment

Often stories of falling are threaded with sadness, frustration, or anger, describing something that, for some reason, just didn't turn out the way we hoped it would. We need to examine our story for phrases like, "I had my heart set on it," or "I counted on this happening," or "I just thought. . . ." If expressions like these show up, we might be struggling with disappointment. Here is what you need to know about disappointment: *Disappointment is unmet expectations, and the more significant the expectations, the more significant the disappointment.*

The way to address this is to be up-front about our expectations by taking the time to reality-check what we're expecting and why. Expectations often coast along under our radar, making themselves known only after they have bombed something we had high hopes for into rubble. I call these *stealth expectations*. Claudia recognized her stealth expectations when it came to going home for a visit with her family—for example, the idea that she should be able to have a "normal" night out with her sisters over pizza. If your story is full of question marks—places where you have scribbled "Huh?" or "What just happened?" or "Was that too much to ask?"—it is likely a story of stealth expectations and the disappointment they have produced.

As Anne Lamott said, "Expectations are resentments waiting to happen." We have the tendency to visualize an entire scenario or conversation or outcome, and when things don't go the way we'd imagined, disappointment can become resentment. This often happens when our expectations are based on outcomes we can't control, like what other people think, what they feel, or how they're going to react.

It's going to be a great holiday! My sister-in-law is going to love her gift and be so impressed with dinner.

I can't wait to share my project ideas with the team tomorrow. They're going to be blown away.

For Steve and me, stealth expectations, disappointment, and resentment have been the sources of some of our most difficult arguments. About five years ago, we noticed a pattern where one of us would slip into resentment after a weekend of trying to jointly juggle our family's hectic soccer–birthday party–sleepover–school project–church schedules along with our own personal plans. It's so much easier when we are flying solo—but how on earth could it be easier for Steve to hold down the fort when I'm out of town? Why is it simpler for me to navigate a busy weekend when he's on call and at the hospital for hours on end? Our arguments after weekends together always ended with one of us feeling resentment and going into blaming mode: *You're not helpful. You don't add anything. You just make it harder.* So painful.

I finally said to Steve, "I'm tired of this argument about it being easier without the other one here. It totally hurts my feelings. I feel like I don't belong here. Something about the story we're telling ourselves is not true. I don't believe it." So we started rumbling on the stories behind these arguments. It took a lot of trial and error—and several near meltdowns—until Steve finally said, "When it's just me with the kids, I have no expectations for getting my own stuff done. I give up my to-do list." It was that simple.

This fight was all about stealth expectations. When I'm on my own for a weekend with the kids, I clear the expectations deck. When Steve and I are both home, we set all kinds of wild expectations about getting stuff done. What we never do is make those expectations explicit. We just tend to blame each other for our disappointment when they're not realized. Now, before weekends, vacations, or even busy school or work weeks, we talk about expectations.

That doesn't mean stealth expectations no longer trip me up. In 2014, we were packing for spring break at Disney World when Steve, who was looking in my bag, said, "Should we reality-check expectations for the week?"

I gave him a tight-lipped smile, my that-is-so-sweet-but-I've-got-this grin, and replied, "No. I think we're good, babe."

Steve pointed to the three novels I had stuffed into my carry-on bag and said, "Tell me about those."

As I started to explain how I wanted to sleep late, relax, and read three good mysteries over the course of our week away, I suddenly heard what I was saying. Who was I kidding? We were going to be at Disney World with five kids for seven days! The only thing I'd be reading was the sign that says, "You must be this tall to ride." Sure enough, we were out the door by eight o'clock every morning of that vacation and I didn't read a thing, but we had a great time—once I had reality-checked my expectations.

I've heard people say that disappointment is like a paper

cut—painful, but not long lasting. I do believe we can heal disappointment, but it's important not to underestimate the damage it inflicts on our spirit. I recently watched the magnificent Japanese animated film *Spirited Away*, written and directed by Hayao Miyazaki. There's a scene in the film where a young boy named Haku, who has taken the form of a dragon, is being attacked by a relentless swarm of birds. The attackers are actually origami birds, and they cut into Haku, leaving him battered and bloodied. Disappointments may be like paper cuts, but if those cuts are deep enough or if there are enough of them, they can leave us seriously wounded.

Rumbling with disappointment, resentment, and expectations is essential. These experiences permeate every aspect of our personal and professional lives. A lifetime of unexplored disappointments can make us bitter, and stored-up resentment is toxic. Nelson Mandela wrote, "Resentment is like drinking poison and then hoping it will kill your enemies." Wholeheartedness requires being conscious of the litany of expectations that hum along below the surface so we can reality-check our thinking. This process can lead to stronger and deeper relationships and connections.

Rumbling with Love, Belonging, and Heartbreak

Heartbreak is more than just a particularly hard form of disappointment or failure. It hurts in an entirely different way because heartbreak is always connected to love and belonging. Over time, the more I've thought about heartbreak and love, the more clearly I've realized how vulnerable we are when we

love anyone. The brokenhearted are the bravest among us—
they dared to love.

When I ran this idea by my dear friend and mentor Joe
Reynolds—an Episcopal priest and one of the wisest people I
know—he was quiet for a while, then said, "Yes. I do think
heartbreak is about love. I just want to think about it some
more." A couple of days later, he sent me a letter sharing his
thoughts, and later he gave me permission to include it here.

Heartbreak is an altogether different thing. Disappointment doesn't grow into heartbreak, nor does failure.
Heartbreak comes from the loss of love or the perceived
loss of love. My heart can be broken only by someone (or
something, like my dog, though a part of me really believes my dog is a person) to whom I have given my heart.
There may be expectations, both met and unmet, in a
relationship that ends in heartbreak, but disappointment is not the cause of the heartbreak. There may be
failures within the relationship—indeed, there certainly
will be, for we are imperfect vessels to hold the love of
another person—but the failures didn't cause the heartbreak. Heartbreak is what happens when love is lost.

Heartbreak can come from being rejected by the one
you love. The pain is more intense when you thought
the other person loved you, but the expectation of returned love isn't necessary for heartbreak. Unrequited
love can be heartbreaking.

The death of a loved one is heartbreaking. I didn't
expect them to live forever, and death is nobody's fault

regardless of smoking, bad diets, no exercise, or whatever. But my heart is broken anyway. A related heartbreak is the death of something unique, maybe even essential, in someone I love. I didn't want my children to stay children all their lives, but at times the loss of innocence was heartbreaking.

The loss of love doesn't have to be permanent to be heartbreaking. Moving away from a loved one can break your heart. Change in another person I love may be a good thing. It may be significant personal growth, and I may be happy about it and proud of it. It can also change our relationship and break my heart.

The list goes on. There is a plethora of ways in which a heart can be broken. . . . The common denominator is the loss of love or the perceived loss of love.

To love with any level of intensity and honesty is to become vulnerable. I used to tell couples getting married that the only thing I could tell them with certainty was that they would hurt each other. To love is to know the loss of love. Heartbreak is unavoidable unless we choose not to love at all. A lot of people do just that.

The message in Joe's beautiful letter is the first thing to know if you are rumbling with heartbreak in your story: "Heartbreak is what happens when love is lost." As Joe points out and as Claudia's story illustrates, the loss of love doesn't have to be permanent or even tangible—it can be love that's been lost to suffering, to addiction, or to any struggle that takes away our capacity to practice love and to receive it.

There are two reasons why most of us are slow to acknowledge that what we're feeling is heartbreak. The first is that we normally associate heartbreak with romantic love. This limiting idea keeps us from fully owning our stories. The greatest heartbreaks of my life include the loss of what I knew as my family after my parents' divorce, watching my mom's pain after my uncle was killed, loving someone struggling with trauma and addiction issues, and losing my grandmother—first to Alzheimer's and then to death. The second reason we don't acknowledge heartbreak is its association with one of the most difficult emotions in the human experience: grief. *If what I'm experiencing is heartbreak, then grieving is inevitable.*

Rumbling with Grief

As someone who has spent close to fifteen years studying the emotional landscape of the human experience, I can tell you that grief is perhaps the emotion we fear the most. As individuals, we're afraid of the darkness grief brings. As a society, we have pathologized it and turned it into something to cure or get over. Owning our stories of heartbreak is a tremendous challenge when we live in a culture that tells us to deny our grief.

There are many helpful books about the nature of grief and the grieving process. Many of these resources are based on research, but some of the most profoundly healing books are memoirs by people who have courageously shared their own stories. I have a full list of both in the library on my website (brenebrown.com). What I want to share here is what I've learned about grief from the research. Specifically, the three most foundational elements of grief that emerged from my studies: loss, longing, and feeling lost.

Loss—While death and separation are tangible losses associated with grief, some of the participants described losses that are more difficult to identify or describe. These included the loss of normality, the loss of what could be, the loss of what we thought we knew or understood about something or someone.

Grief seems to create losses within us that reach beyond our awareness—we feel as if we're missing something that was invisible and unknown to us while we had it, but is now painfully gone. In the moving novel *The Fault in Our Stars,* John Green captures one of those secret losses that accompanies grief. "The pleasure of remembering had been taken from me, because there was no longer anyone to remember with. It felt like losing your co-rememberer meant losing the memory itself, as if the things we'd done were less real and important than they had been hours before." This quote grabbed me because until I read it, I wasn't able to articulate one of the losses that I still feel from my parents' divorce: funny memories shared with both of my parents. I know the events still happened, but my parents and I are no longer "co-rememberers" in the way we once were.

For Claudia, the fact that her sister's addiction and depression consume her family means that buried within her heartbreak is the loss of her parents—the feeling that her relationship with them is diminished or overshadowed by their preoccupation with her sister. Holidays and family gatherings are good if Amy is doing okay, and they're undercut by sadness and anger if she's a no-show or arrives clearly impaired. It's easy to understand why parents focus on the child who is struggling, especially when the other children seem to be doing well, but over the years I've heard many participants in my research talk about the feelings of grief and loss they experience in similar situations.

Longing—Related to loss is longing. Longing is not conscious wanting; it's an involuntary yearning for wholeness, for understanding, for meaning, for the opportunity to regain or even simply touch what we've lost. Longing is a vital and important part of grief, yet many of us feel we need to keep our longings to ourselves for fear we will be misunderstood, perceived as engaging in magical or unrealistic thinking, or lacking in fortitude and resilience.

This insight helped me make sense of something I've experienced a dozen times but never articulated, even to Steve. When you drive into San Antonio from Houston on I-10, you pass the exit for my grandmother's house. Sometimes when I see the exit, I feel a pull inside me to get off the highway and go to her house just to sit in the backyard with her and drink iced tea. I want to touch her face and smell her house. The yearning is so physical and strong that I can actually smell the flowers in her yard and taste the tea. It's not rational. She's not there. And yet it still takes my breath away.

I once heard a friend say that grief is like surfing. Sometimes you feel steady and you're able to ride the waves, and other times the surf comes crashing down on you, pushing you so far underwater that you're sure you'll drown. Those moments of longing can have the same effect as upwellings of grief—they come out of nowhere and can be triggered by something you didn't even know mattered.

Feeling lost—Grief requires us to reorient ourselves to every part of our physical, emotional, and social worlds. When we imagine the need to do this, most of us picture the painful struggle to adjust to a tangible change, such as someone dying or moving away. But again, this is a very limited view of grief. On several occasions during her story, Claudia described feeling frozen—not knowing what to do, what to say, or how to behave. In the midst of her pain, she sat in silence with her parents, watching TV. Another good example of this is the couple who talked to me about navigating the grief they were experiencing after their oldest child left for college. "Everything was off," the father told me. "Nothing felt normal. I wasn't sure where to park my car at our house. He had his car with him, but I still left his space open. Setting the table for dinner was strange; walking down the hall past his room felt painful—we were completely lost and at the same time happy for him and proud of his accomplishments. We didn't know if we should laugh or cry. We've done a lot of both."

The more difficult it is for us to articulate our experiences of loss, longing, and feeling lost to the people around us, the more disconnected and alone we feel. Of the coping strategies my research participants have shared with me, writing down experiences of heartbreak and grief have emerged as the most helpful in making clear to themselves what they were feeling so they could articulate it to others. Some participants did this as part of their work with helping professionals; others did it on their own. Either way, the participants talked about the need to write freely, without having to explain or justify their feelings. It was these interviews that led me to look more closely at the idea of writing SFDs as part of the rising strong process.

Rumbling with Forgiveness

I've been engaged in a full professional rumble with the concept of forgiveness for ten years. It has been glaringly absent from my work and all of my books. Why? Because I couldn't get to saturation—I couldn't find a meaningful pattern in all of my data.

I got very close before I wrote *The Gifts,* but right as the book was going to press, I did three interviews, and what I learned during those interviews fell completely outside the pattern. Ordinarily, that would be fine: Most research methodologies allow for what we call outliers. If there are one or two small exceptions in the data, that's okay as long as the majority fall within the pattern. In grounded theory, though, there can be no outliers. Every story matters, and for your hypothesis to be valid, all your categories and properties must fit, be relevant, and resonate with your data. If something doesn't work, you're not there yet. It's incredibly frustrating, but sticking to this principle hasn't failed me yet.

Then, several years ago, I was at church listening to Joe talk about forgiveness. He was sharing his experience of counseling a couple who were on the brink of divorce after the woman discovered that her husband was having an affair. They were both devastated by the potential end of their marriage, but she couldn't forgive him for betraying her, and he couldn't seem to forgive himself, either. Joe looked up and said, "In order for forgiveness to happen, something has to die. If you make a choice to forgive, you have to face into the pain. You simply have to hurt."

I instantly buried my head in my hands. It was as if someone had finally put the right sequence of numbers into a giant combination lock that I had been carrying around for years. The tumblers started turning and falling into place. Everything was clicking. That was the piece that was missing. Forgiveness is so difficult because it involves death and grief. I had been looking for patterns in people extending generosity and love, but not in people feeling grief. At that moment it struck me: Given the dark fears we feel when we experience loss, nothing is more generous and loving than the willingness to embrace grief in order to forgive. To be forgiven is to be loved.

The death or ending that forgiveness necessitates comes in many shapes and forms. We may need to bury our expectations or dreams. We may need to relinquish the power that comes with "being right" or put to rest the idea that we can do what's in our hearts and still retain the support or approval of others. Joe explained, "Whatever it is, it all has to go. It isn't good enough to box it up and set it aside. It has to die. It has to be grieved. That is a high price indeed. Sometimes, it's just too much."

I spent the next couple of years revisiting the data through this new lens of forgiveness, this time including *an ending* and the grief associated with that ending. I recoded and reworked my research, did more interviewing, and read through the literature. I wasn't surprised to find a growing number of empirical studies showing that forgiveness positively correlates with emotional, mental, and physical well-being. A strong and clear pattern was emerging. This pattern would be confirmed when I read *The Book of Forgiving: The Fourfold Path for Healing Ourselves and Our World,* by Archbishop Desmond Tutu and his daughter, the Reverend Mpho Tutu.

Archbishop Tutu served as the chair of South Africa's Truth and Reconciliation Commission, and Reverend Mpho Tutu, an Episcopal priest, is the executive director of the Desmond & Leah Tutu Legacy Foundation. *The Book of Forgiving* is one of the most important books I've ever read. I honestly did not have the words to adequately describe it to people after I finished it. It not only confirmed what I had learned about forgiveness from Joe, but also supported everything I've learned about vulnerability, shame, courage, and the power of story. The book outlines a forgiveness practice that includes telling the story, naming the hurt, granting forgiveness, and renewing or releasing the relationship. Archbishop Tutu writes:

> To forgive is not just to be altruistic. It is the best form of self-interest. It is also a process that does not exclude hatred and anger. These emotions are all part of being human. You should never hate yourself for hating others who do terrible things: The depth of your love is shown by the extent of your anger.
>
> However, when I talk of forgiveness, I mean the belief that you can come out the other side a better person. A better person than the one being consumed by anger and hatred. Remaining in that state locks you in a state of victimhood, making you almost dependent on

the perpetrator. If you can find it in yourself to forgive, then you are no longer chained to the perpetrator. You can move on, and you can even help the perpetrator to become a better person, too.

So, forgiveness is not forgetting or walking away from accountability or condoning a hurtful act; it's the process of taking back and healing our lives so we can truly live. What the Tutus found in their work on forgiveness validates not just the importance of naming our experiences and owning our stories but also how rumbling with a process can lead to clarity, wisdom, and self-love. So often we want easy and quick answers to complex struggles. We question our own bravery, and in the face of fear, we back down too early.

As Claudia works through her rising strong process in her dealings with her family, it's likely that she will need to rumble with forgiveness. I've never met anyone—personally or professionally—who didn't have to rumble with forgiveness. That includes self-forgiveness, too. Within families and in other close relationships, we love each other and we hurt each other. The question becomes, *What has to end or die so we can experience a rebirth in our relationships?*

In one of my most difficult rumbles with self-forgiveness, I had to kill off the idea that being a shame researcher and knowing the pain inflicted by shame somehow exempted me from ever shaming other people. It seems counterintuitive, but my belief that I knew better than to shame someone sometimes left me blind to hurt I caused and unaware of when I needed to make amends. That myth had to die, and I had to forgive myself for setting unattainable and, ultimately, damaging expectations.

One of my most powerful experiences of forgiveness happened when I finally stopped running from the grief I felt about my family falling apart and started walking toward forgiveness. This process led to some of the toughest but most important "deaths" of my life. I had to bury my idealized version of my parents and see them instead as people with struggles and limitations, with their own difficult histories and heartbreaks. As the oldest child, I tried to protect my siblings by keeping them as far away as I could from the front lines, which meant that I saw most of it up close. And what I saw then was rage and blame. But what I now recognize is the amount of pain, hurt, fear, and shame that my parents must have been feeling beneath that rage and blame.

Back then, there was nowhere for my parents to turn and nothing they could do with that negative emotion. No one talked about that kind of stuff. There were no movies or television shows or national conversations about what was really happening within families. I can't imagine the pressure of losing everything, trying to keep a family of six afloat, while having no support or permission to be afraid or vulnerable. My parents were raised in families where talking about emotions was way down at the bottom of the list of things needed for survival. There was no space for talking about emotions. Instead, it was just grind on . . . more of the same . . . push harder . . . yell louder.

The death of the idealized versions of our parents, teachers, and mentors—a stage in the hero's journey—is always scary because it means that we're now responsible for our own learning and growth. That death is also beautiful because it makes room for new relationships—more honest connections be-tween authentic adults who are doing the best they can. Of course, these new connections require emotional and physical safety. We can't be vulnerable and open with people who are hurting us.

The birth of this new relationship with my parents also forced me to bury the idea that if you're smart or talented enough, you can shield your family from your pain. If you are struggling, your partner and children are also in the struggle. And that's okay as long as we acknowledge the hurt, provide everyone with a safe space in which to talk about it, and don't pretend that we can compartmentalize pain. Struggle hap-pens. We give our children a gift when we teach them that falls are inevitable and allow them to participate in a loving, sup-ported rising strong process.

Rumbling with Compassion and Empathy

What Claudia told me about the importance of seeing the world from the floor of the arena is central to the concept of compassion. The definition of compassion that most accu-rately reflects what I've learned from the research is from American Buddhist nun Pema Chödrön. In her book *The Places That Scare You,* Chödrön writes:

> When we practice generating compassion, we can ex-pect to experience our fear of pain. Compassion prac-tice is daring. It involves learning to relax and allow ourselves to move gently toward what scares us. . . . In cultivating compassion we draw from the wholeness of

our experience—our suffering, our empathy, as well as our cruelty and terror. It has to be this way. Compassion is not a relationship between the healer and the wounded. It's a relationship between equals. Only when we know our own darkness well can we be present with the darkness of others. Compassion becomes real when we recognize our shared humanity.

Although Claudia is still in her rumble, she has told me that her experience is helping her to be more compassionate toward herself and more empathic toward others. By getting to know her own darkness, she is learning how to feel compassion for the darkness of others. The most compassionate people I've met and interviewed are people who not only have spent time facedown in the arena, but also were brave enough to open their eyes to the suffering of others lying there with them.

There are many debates about the differences between compassion, empathy, and sympathy. Relying on my data, this is what I've come to believe:

Compassion: Recognizing the light and dark in our shared humanity, we commit to practicing loving-kindness with ourselves and others in the face of suffering.

Empathy: The most powerful tool of compassion, empathy is an emotional skill that allows us to respond to others in a meaningful, caring way. Empathy is the ability to understand what someone is experiencing and to reflect back that understanding. It's important to note here that empathy is *understanding what someone is feeling,* not feeling it for them. If someone is feeling lonely, empathy doesn't require us to feel lonely, too, only to reach back into our own experience with loneliness so we can understand and connect. We can fake empathy, but when we do, it's not healing or connecting. The prerequisite for real empathy is compassion. We can only respond empathically if we are willing to be present to someone's pain. Empathy is the antidote to shame and it is the heart of connection.

Sympathy: Rather than being a tool for connection, sympathy emerged in the data as a form of disconnection. Sympathy is removed: When someone says, "I feel sorry for you" or "That must be terrible," they are standing at a safe distance. Rather than conveying the powerful "me too" of empathy, it communicates "not me," and then adds, "But I do feel for you." Sympathy is more likely to be a shame trigger than something that heals shame.

THE REVOLUTION

As Claudia continues to rumble with her story and discover her own delta and key learnings, I hope she will remember that choosing curiosity and connection rather than walking away or shutting down, while painful, is choosing courage. It's also the path to cultivating compassion, connection, and forgiveness. The brokenhearted are indeed the bravest among us—they dared to love, and they dared to forgive.

C. S. Lewis captured this so beautifully in one of my favorite quotes of all time:

To love at all is to be vulnerable. Love anything and your

heart will certainly be wrung and possibly be broken. If you want to make sure of keeping it intact, you must give it to no one, not even an animal. Wrap it carefully round with hobbies and little luxuries; avoid all entanglements. Lock it up safe in the casket or coffin of your selfishness. But in that casket, safe, dark, motionless, airless, it will change. It will not be broken; it will become unbreakable, impenetrable, irredeemable. To love is to be vulnerable.

CONNECTION

DOESN'T EXIST

without

GIVING AND RECEIVING.

WE NEED TO GIVE

and we need to

NEED.

Eight

EASY MARK

RUMBLING WITH NEED, CONNECTION,
JUDGMENT, SELF-WORTH, PRIVILEGE,
AND ASKING FOR HELP

April

I called Amanda the minute I read about the lecture in the paper. "Anne Lamott is coming to town! It must be a sign!"

My friend and former graduate student Amanda shares my enthusiasm for Anne's work, and we made plans to go hear her speak. Amanda is one of the smartest people I know, and she never shies away from a good theological throw-down. To this day, she and I carry on a constant, sometimes heated, but always loving debate about the nature of faith. Amanda, who comes from an evangelical background, was at that time beginning to explore other expressions of faith. Steve and I were wrestling with the idea of going back to church for the same reason many people do—we had young children and wanted them to at least have a foundation from which to make their own choices.

Steve and I are both grateful that we grew up in families with strong spiritual foundations, but at some point we felt betrayed by religion and we left. Neither one of us could really articulate how we felt until I heard Lamott referencing Paul Tillich and telling the audience, "The opposite of faith is not doubt—it's certainty." Steve and I didn't leave religion because we stopped believing in God. Religion left us when it started putting politics and certainty before love and mystery.

As we took our seats in the high school auditorium before the lecture began, a jazz quartet began to play and pictures of homeless men and women faded in and out on a large screen. The event was a fundraiser for Lord of the Streets, an Episcopal church in Houston dedicated to serving the homeless. After a few minutes, Father Murray Powell walked onstage to talk about the work being done at Lord of the Streets before he introduced Lamott. One line in particular from his remarks cracked me wide open. He said, "When you look away from a homeless person, you diminish their humanity and your own."

When you hear something like that, you don't have to fully understand it to know that it's true. I know Father Murray well enough now to know it wasn't his intention, but the second he spoke those words, I felt the flush of shame. I suddenly thought, *He's talking to me. I look away.*

As a researcher who has spent years studying the power of connection, I should understand better than anyone the human need to be seen. Yet I look away, even when I roll down the window and hand someone on the street a bottle of water and a PowerBar, or maybe a dollar bill. I might flash a quick smile, but I don't make eye contact. And worse, I had no idea why. It's not that I'm afraid of seeing pain or hurt: I've worked at agencies for child protection and with victims of domestic violence and never looked away. I've sat across from violent offenders and grieving parents and not blinked. Why was seeing someone living on the street so hard for me?

As I lay in bed that night, my curiosity showed up, as it often does, as a prayer. Specifically, I prayed for help in understanding why, despite knowing as much as I do about the importance of connection, I turn away so predictably. I woke up the next morning half expecting to have the answer. I even stayed still with my eyes closed, waiting for whatever insight might have come in the night to register. Nothing.

Father Murray moved me to tears and I prayed hard for understanding, but this time understanding was going to take nine months of curiosity, prayer, and rumbling. Rather than a single moment of insight, I experienced a collection of holy and unholy moments that would eventually bring me face-to-face with one of my greatest fears and, in the process, teach me exactly what Saint Teresa of Ávila meant when she said, "There are more tears shed over answered prayers than over unanswered prayers."

June

There's nothing better than the warm embrace of belonging—that feeling you get when you're a part of something you love or believe in. And there's no tangible sign of belonging greater than seeing your name and picture on an official membership roster. After a two-decade hiatus from organized religion and a yearlong search for the right community, Steve and I had finally found a great church for our family. Early one Saturday morning, we were embracing our big decision to join by having our family picture taken for the church directory. I woke up early, got myself ready, made breakfast, and put a good spit shine on the kids. For a moment in the car that morning, I felt pure joy. We were together. We were laughing. At one point all four of us, even Charlie, who was just two years old then, were singing along to Alison Krauss's "Down to the River to Pray."

As we pulled up in front of the grand cathedral, the sun was shining through the spires and down onto the courtyard. I felt a huge sense of pride about belonging to a church that had such an impressive 150-year history in downtown Houston— a sacred place that was deeply spiritual, unapologetically questioning, and passionately committed to serving the homeless. I loved knowing that the very first members of our new church were spirited men and women who had left the United States to build a new nation—the Republic of Texas. As Steve parked, I stared out the car window, thinking: *This is my church. I'm a part of this history and community, just like the men and women who attended this church when they were running cattle down Texas Street.*

I was also excited because now we had a place to give back to—a place to make contributions to our community and to teach our children how to do the same.

As soon as we parked the car, the kids jumped out and headed toward the fountain in the courtyard. I called after them, "Don't get wet! Don't put your hands in the fountain!

No dirty hands! It's picture day!" Steve shook his head as if to say, *Good luck.*

As we walked past the front entrance and toward the side door, I noticed a stack of newspapers and a few pieces of trash under the awning. *This is my church. That litter won't do.* I walked over and grabbed the loose trash in one hand and some folded newspapers in the other and walked toward a city trash can.

With every step I took, a terrible smell wafted from the trash. Reflexively, I held up the trash in my left hand and took a whiff. Nothing. Maybe stale french fries. Then, with my right hand, I lifted the folded newspapers toward my face. Just as the smell made its way inside my nose, my mind calculated the weight, density, and feel of the stacked newspapers that were folded strangely into a triangle, forming a nearly perfect pocket.

"Oh my God! It's poop! Steve, help! It's poop! Oh my God! Holy shit! Someone pooped in here." I raced toward the trash can, shouting. I threw everything in and shook my empty hands over the trash can, trying to fling the germs off. Steve was literally bent over, laughing hysterically.

"It's not funny. Why are you laughing? Oh my God! Holy shit, I'm so grossed out!"

Steve struggled to get the words out: "Stop saying it. Oh, I can't take it. It's so funny."

Infuriated, I snapped back, "What's funny? There's nothing funny!"

Steve stopped laughing just long enough to say, "*Holy shit.* Get it? *Holy shit.*" Then he started laughing again.

I rolled my eyes and made a beeline for the restroom. After the fourth surgeon's-scrub-in washing, I realized it was sort of funny. When I walked out, Steve was waiting for me with a repentant look on his face that was quickly replaced by another burst of uncontrollable laughter.

For the next few months, I thought about that stack of newspapers every time I saw a homeless person, which is, unfortunately, pretty much every day in urban Houston. I thought about the indignity of having no place to go to the bathroom except a stack of newspapers in the entryway of a downtown church. I thought about the homeless people I had worked with in my career as a social worker, and how many of them were veterans, and how most struggled with trauma, addiction, and mental illness. I also thought about the dread that still washed over me whenever I got caught at a stoplight and found myself right next to someone asking for help.

I still wasn't really looking—not in a meaningful way—and the newspaper incident made me wonder if it was related to my sense that I was not helping other people enough. My go-to response to discomfort is often *Do more! Help more! Give more!* Maybe I could look people in the eye if I didn't feel so much shame about not helping. So, I ramped up my volunteering and stocked my car with Gatorade and granola bars.

But it wasn't working. Something was still getting in the way of seeing the humanity outside my car window.

September

Exactly three months after picture day at church, I was in Whole Foods picking up lunch for myself and a friend who was recovering from surgery. As I did a reconnaissance lap around the salad and hot-food bars, I noticed a man watching me. He was a middle-aged white guy in a flannel shirt, dirty jeans, and mud-caked boots. He wore a cap pulled so low over his face that it almost covered his eyes. He looked as if he worked in construction. I probably wouldn't have noticed him, except that he was standing in one place, shifting his weight from foot to foot and studying the hot food.

We made eye contact, and I flashed a quick, uncomfortable smile and looked away. Strangely, he grabbed a flip phone from his pocket and started talking. As someone who has deployed the phone decoy trick in awkward situations, I knew what he was doing—there wasn't anyone on the other end. My suspicions were confirmed when he stuffed the phone back in his pocket in midsentence as soon as I walked to the other side of the hot-food bar.

I filled a container with lentil soup for my friend. As I headed for the salad bar, I glanced up at the construction guy. Something seemed off. Every time I lowered my head to see under the sneeze shield and steal a glance at him, he looked away. When I caught him watching me, I looked away.

I was pouring salad dressing into a little paper cup when I saw a commotion from the corner of my eye. The man had run up to the hot-food bar and, with both cupped hands, scooped up pot roast, gravy, and roasted vegetables and then made a break for the front door. The only other person nearby just stood there, holding her basket with one hand and covering her open mouth with the other.

An employee ran over and asked what had happened. I explained, and he shook his head, quickly grabbed the large metal pan holding the remaining pot roast, and hurried back to the kitchen. I stared, unable to move.

What the hell had *happened? Did the man find a safe place to sit and eat his food, or did he just eat it as he ran? I should have smiled at him. Why did I look away when he looked at me? Maybe he was trying to tell me something. I could have bought him a real lunch. In a container. With a fork. Had the food burned his hands? No one should have to do that for a meal.*

That was when I started wondering if my discomfort was less about not helping enough and more about privilege. Maybe I wasn't looking folks in the eye because I'm uncomfortable with my own privilege. I make more money now. My car starts every day. We don't get our lights turned off anymore. I'm not picking up extra bartending shifts to make the rent. No one looks at me at Whole Foods and wonders what I'm up to.

I've had the great honor of teaching courses on race, class, and gender at the University of Houston—one of the most racially and ethnically diverse research institutions in the United States. I've learned enough about privilege to know that we're at our most dangerous when we think we've learned everything we need to know about it. That's when you stop paying attention to injustice. And make no mistake, not paying attention because you're not the one getting harassed or fired or pulled over or underpaid is the definition of privilege. *Maybe looking away is about privilege. I need to think harder and longer about my choices and recognize that choosing whom I see and whom I don't see is one of the most hurtful functions of privilege.*

Acknowledging privilege and taking action on injustice require constant vigilance. But no matter how conscious I tried to stay, privilege wasn't the only thing getting in my way. The rumble continued.

January

Several months later, on a cold January afternoon, I received one of those calls—the kind that brings time to a standstill and, without warning, violently reorganizes everything. It was my sister Ashley. "Something's wrong with Mom! She passed out in my driveway. Something is wrong."

I'm someone who chronically and compulsively rehearses tragedy, assuming that I then will be prepared when it comes. Or that it might never come because I'm ready for it. After all, I did my part: I sacrificed joy in the moment of feeling it to forestall future pain. Now I want what I'm owed: less hurt, less fear, less panic. But trading joy for less vulnerability is a deal with the devil. And the devil never pays up. So all I felt in the moment as I listened to my sister's voice was sheer terror. *Nothing can happen to my mom. I won't survive it.*

Thirty minutes after that call, I was at the emergency room with Steve and Ashley. We were huddled together, waiting for someone to tell us what was happening to our mother behind the heavy automated doors. There was no doubt in my mind that it was serious. The room beyond those doors was filled with too much commotion, plus it was written all over Steve's face. The good news in these situations is that Steve's a doctor, so he can translate what's happening. The bad news is that I've been looking into his eyes for twenty-five years, and I know when he's scared or worried.

No one can come through those doors with that look on her face.

I refuse to let anyone come through those doors with that look on her face. I refuse to accept that outcome. I can't do it.

Finally, a nurse walked out and, without breaking her stride, said something to Steve about my mom getting a heart catheter. Steve was explaining to us how a heart catheter works when the doctor came out. My mom's heart had stopped. The electrical system that controls her heartbeat had shut down, and the default condition was a very low heart rate. They were moving her to the cardiac intensive care unit.

This made no sense to me at all. My mom was healthy. She was young and active, she worked full-time, and she lived on black beans and spinach.

The doctor explained that they had scheduled her for surgery the next morning and that it would be a couple of hours before we could see her. We stayed at the hospital and waited. My other sister, Barrett (Ashley's identical twin), arrived from Amarillo, and my brother was on standby in San Francisco.

Slowly, and outside of my awareness, my physical stance became more resolute. I don't know if it was in response to my own pain or to seeing my younger sisters in such deep fear, but my teeth clenched, my jaw hardened, and my eyes narrowed with focus. The tears stopped, my hunched shoulders straightened, and the armor began to lock into place. In a series of barely perceptible movements choreographed by history, my arms slid around my sisters' shoulders and I grew taller. I became the protector—just as I had when I gathered everyone in my room while our parents fought. The same protector who intervened with my parents when I thought one of my sisters or my brother was in trouble. This is my role. Co-parent. While

I'm in it, I am fierce. I am the protector. And, unfortunately, I am the worst damn over-functioner you've ever seen.

In Harriet Lerner's book *The Dance of Connection,* she explains that we all have patterned ways of managing anxiety—some of us over-function and others under-function. Over-functioners tend to move quickly to advise, rescue, take over, micromanage, and basically get in other people's business rather than looking inward. Under-functioners tend to get less competent under stress: They invite others to take over and often become the focus of worry or concern. On the outside, over-functioners appear to be tough and in control, and under-functioners can seem irresponsible or fragile. Many of these behaviors are learned and line up with the roles we play in our families. It's not uncommon for firstborns to be over-functioners, as is certainly the case for me.

When we were finally allowed to see our mom, my sisters did their best, but they were barely holding it together. I, on the other hand, was unflinching. "What do you need from home?" I asked her. "What can I do? Who do I need to call from the office? What needs to be done at home?" Over-functioner to over-functioner, my mother and I came up with a long to-do list. When the doctor came in, he reached across my mother to shake hands with my stepfather, but I intercepted the handshake, introduced myself, and began drilling him for information. My stepfather took a step back and let me run the show.

Afterward, we regrouped on the first floor of the hospital. The sprawling lobby at Houston Methodist Hospital is beautiful—huge fresh flower arrangements sit atop perfectly appointed tables, sculptures stand in the halls, and there's even a grand piano. It's wonderful, but weird. Every time I walk through it, I struggle to reconcile what feels like the lobby of a fancy hotel with all of the wheelchairs and people in scrubs.

Standing beside the piano, I pulled out the list my mother and I had made and began to delegate the assignments.

"Ashley, can you go to Mom's house and get all of her medicines? Put them all in a bag, including her vitamins. Barrett, I need you to call Jason and give him an update. We also need to get Mom some lightweight cotton pajamas."

As I wrote down my sisters' initials next to each item, I began getting nervous about the dwindling number of items left. Mom wanted a few things from the store, but that wasn't enough to keep me busy.

"You know what? Let me get Mom's medicines. I know where she keeps all of that stuff. And Barrett—I should call Jason. He's scared and it will be a tough conversation. It's hard to be far away. I also know where to get some pajamas that button up the front."

I studied the list and nodded my head, proud of my decision to reclaim the chores. *Yes. This is much better. It's best if I do all of these things.* In the brief moment it took me to change the initials and make new notes on the to-do list, my sisters had stepped back from our circle and were whispering to each other. When I finally looked up and saw them, they were holding hands and looking straight at me.

"What? What's wrong? What is it?" I impatiently asked.

Ashley said, "You are over-functioning."

Barrett quickly jumped in. "We can help. We know what to do."

My body abruptly went limp, and as I dropped the list on

the floor, I fell into the chair behind me and started sobbing. I was inconsolable. People customarily cry in the waiting rooms upstairs, but not in the fancy lobby. I'm sure I was making a scene, but I couldn't stop. My sisters had pierced my armor. It was as if forty years of *doing* instead of *feeling* had caught up with me. Ashley and Barrett were also crying, but they held me and told me that we were going to be okay and that we were going to take care of one another and Mom. My stepfather, David, who had been watching this whole show for the past hour (and the past twenty years), kissed us on the heads, accepted my apology for being so rude in the hospital room, and took off with the list.

Once again, my mom's own history of rising strong was at play. Her choices and the work she had done on her own life didn't just spark my curiosity, they also transformed my sisters and my brother. Mom buys important books like Harriet Lerner's *The Dance of Connection* in bulk and gives us all copies. It's not subtle, but it's effective. My sisters and I were able to have this honest rumble because Mom had made sure we were exposed to ideas and information that were not available to her as a young woman.

Looking at these responses through a vulnerability lens, it's easy to see that both ways of functioning are forms of armor—learned behaviors for getting out from under fear and uncertainty.

Over-functioning: *I won't feel, I will do. I don't need help, I help.*

Under-functioning: *I won't function, I will fall apart. I don't help, I need help.*

My mom's surgery the next morning was successful, and by the afternoon we were sitting with her in her hospital room. Someone brought in a pamphlet that explained her new pacemaker. The cover of the brochure featured a silver-haired couple in matching pastel sweaters riding bicycles. My sisters and I did an entire shtick about her new life of bicycling and wearing sweaters. We all laughed until we cried. Then we got kicked out. They told us to come back in an hour, so we decided to walk across the street to grab dinner at a fast-food Mexican restaurant.

It was already dark outside, and even though Houston's Texas Medical Center complex, where Mom's hospital was located, is the largest of its kind in the world, there's not much pedestrian traffic at night. So we stayed aware of our surroundings as we crossed the street. Inside the restaurant, Ashley and I were at the counter ordering when we heard Barrett's raised voice. I turned around to see a man wrapped in a blanket being pushed out of the restaurant and onto the sidewalk by a restaurant employee. In the scuffle, he had been accidentally shoved into Barrett, and she had yelled, "What are you doing?" to the employee. It was all over in less than a minute. It was confusing and upset all of us, especially Barrett. We tried to eat our food, but all the emotion of the day, combined with what had just happened, left us queasy. We left the restaurant and started walking back to the hospital.

When we crossed the street and got closer to the hospital, we saw the man in the blanket again. He was African American, probably in his late twenties or early thirties. His face and hair were dust streaked, and you could almost see a little cloud around him. He had the face of someone who had been hit a lot. After spending several years working in the domestic violence field, I recognized that look. Getting hit in the face repeatedly over time changes a person's bone structure.

I tried to approach him to see if we could buy him dinner or help in some way. For a brief moment our eyes met before he hurried away. What I saw in his eyes communicated something so painful that I could barely even register it. His eyes seemed to say, *This was not supposed to happen. This is not supposed to be my story.* I started crying again, asking my sisters, "How does this happen to a man like that? How do we let this happen?"

We were physically and mentally exhausted. We went back to the hospital and spent another thirty minutes with Mom until we were asked to leave for the night.

The next morning, I arrived at the hospital early. I smiled as the automatic glass doors slid open because the grand lobby was filled with music. And not just any music—someone was playing a resounding version of "Memory" from Andrew Lloyd Webber's *Cats* on the grand piano. As I rounded the corner in front of the valet parking desk, I caught a glimpse of the piano player. I couldn't believe what I saw. It was the homeless man from the night before. His blanket was spread over the piano seat, and his hands were moving across the keys. Desperate to validate what I was seeing, I turned toward the woman sitting at the desk and blurted out, "Oh my God. I saw him last night. I think he's homeless."

She replied, "Yeah. He only knows a couple of songs. He plays them over and over until the security guys kick him out."

"But I don't understand. Where does he go? Who is he?" I asked.

She continued to process the valet tickets. "I don't know, sweetie. He's been coming here for about a year."

Just then the music stopped. The security guards were telling the man to gather up his stuff, after which they walked him outside. I was still in shock when I got to my mom's room. She was sitting up and eating. She had her color back and she was in a talkative mood.

"You look like you just saw a ghost," she said.

"It's worse than that," I explained. "I'm seeing real people, and I know they're trying to teach me something, but I don't know what it is."

I told her the story about the church trash, the guy at Whole Foods, and the piano player. She put down her fork, leaned back, and asked, "Can I tell you a story about your grandmother?" I curled myself into a ball at the foot of her bed and listened.

When my mom was in grade school, her family lived half a block from the railroad tracks in San Antonio. There was a viaduct—a small, arched brick bridge that the train crossed—right at the end of their street. The grassy side of the small hill leading up to the tracks was covered with bushes and plants, providing the perfect place for "hobos" to jump from the boxcars.

My grandmother kept five metal plates, five metal glasses, and five metal forks in a dishpan under the sink. She always cooked more food than the family could eat, and according to my mom, hobos would knock on their door on a pretty regular basis and ask for dinner. The men sat on the front porch or on the porch swing, and Me-Ma served their meals on her special dishes. When they were done eating, Me-Ma would boil the dishes and store them back under the sink until the next group arrived.

When I asked my mom how it worked—why Me-Ma trusted them and why they trusted her—she said, "We were marked." The hobos used a system of markings on the curbs of the neighborhood to indicate who was safe and who wasn't, who might feed them and who wouldn't. I later found out that this may have been the origin of the term *easy mark*.

My mom explained that Me-Ma trusted them for two reasons: The first was that the woman across the street had a brother who returned from World War II and became a hobo. So, Me-Ma never thought of them as "the other" because she knew hobos personally and, more important, because she considered herself "the other," too. She had lived through poverty, domestic violence, divorce, and her own alcoholism (she quit drinking when I was born). She didn't judge.

Second, Me-Ma had no problem with need. "She wasn't afraid of people in need because she wasn't afraid of needing others," my mom explained. "She didn't mind extending kindness to others, because she herself relied on the kindness of others."

My mom and I didn't need to unpack the emotion behind that story. We both understood exactly what Me-Ma had that we didn't: the capacity to receive. My mom and I aren't good at asking for or receiving help. We are givers. Me-Ma loved receiving. She got excited when friends dropped off fresh-baked pies or when I offered to take her to the movies. She didn't mind asking for help when she needed it. It also went without saying that at the end of Me-Ma's life, when dementia had ravaged her mind, the kindness of others kept her alive and safe.

When I got home that night, Steve and the kids were at a soccer game. I sat on the couch in the dark and thought about Me-Ma and one of the most difficult experiences of my life. Her son Ronnie's death exacerbated Me-Ma's mental and emotional decline. One of her neighbors called my mom to tell her that she was concerned about Me-Ma, who had been walking up and down the block wearing nothing but a long coat and cowboy boots, knocking on doors, and asking the neighbors if they had heard about Ronnie dying.

It was becoming increasingly dangerous to leave her alone. Between fears about her roaming the neighborhood, leaving lit cigarettes in ashtrays, and using the gas stove, we knew it was time. My mom, who was living in Houston, was scrambling to find the right facility. I was living in San Antonio at the time and trying to help as much as possible. Me-Ma would occasionally stay at my apartment, but anytime we took her out of her house, she'd become disoriented and anxious. Even before Steve and I were married, he'd sit with her some evenings so I could go to work.

During one of my final visits to her house before she moved to an assisted living facility in Houston, I noticed that Me-Ma had stopped bathing. She wasn't clean. I drew her a bath and got out a clean towel. She just stood there and smiled at me.

"Take a bath, Me-Ma. I'll be right out here. When you're done, I'll make us dinner."

She just smiled and raised her hands above her head. She wanted me to undress her. I pulled off her shirt, kissed her on the forehead, and stepped out of the bathroom, hoping she would take it from there. I was twenty-nine years old and terrified.

I don't know if I can do this. I've never even seen her without her clothes on. I don't know how to bathe someone. Get your shit together, Brené! This is Me-Ma. She's bathed you a thousand times.

So I walked back into the bathroom, undressed my grandmother, and sat her down in the old pink porcelain tub. She smiled and relaxed as I lathered her up and rinsed her off. When she leaned back and closed her eyes, I just held her hand. Of course, the dementia made her less inhibited and even childlike at times, but it wasn't her failing mind that made her unashamed; it was her huge, giving heart. She knew the truth: *We don't have to do all of it alone. We were never meant to.*

As I thought back to that moment in Me-Ma's bathroom, I knew exactly why I looked away. I was so afraid of my own need that I couldn't look need in the eye.

THE RECKONING

This story is a great example of how the rising strong process can stretch out over months, even years. The reason I call rising strong a practice is that had I not stayed curious after each one of these experiences, the rumble would have fallen apart. If I hadn't connected these separate incidents by the common discomfort each one provoked in me, I'd be no closer to understanding a key piece of how I engage with the world and the people around me.

While there were several moments in this story that took my breath away, my reckoning happened at the Anne Lamott lecture. My facedown moment was hearing Father Murray articulate so powerfully how the choice not to see someone fundamentally diminishes our shared humanity. I'm not even sure I was conscious of that behavior before he spoke those words. It was a quiet moment: I didn't flinch or cry or get angry. You wouldn't have noticed me falling if you were watching me, but I felt it. And I was committed to understanding more before I left the auditorium that evening.

Maybe part of the metaphorical power of Roosevelt's quote—"The credit belongs to the man who is actually in the arena, whose face is marred by dust and sweat and blood"—is that it's possible to feel our faces marred with dust and sweat and blood when the arena is an emotional smackdown rather than a physical one. I felt beat-up on the way home from the lecture. Father Murray shined a light into a dark, unexplored corner of my behavior, and I knew that what I saw had to change.

THE RUMBLE

My SFD started as self-talk in the car on the way home from the lecture, and it became the subject of a conversation with Steve when he walked in the door that night. I ultimately jotted down this in my journal:

I'm not helping other people enough.

I feel shame about how much I have and how little I do, so I can't look the folks I should be helping in the eye.

DO MORE!!!

In this case, my SFD wasn't based on traditional confabulations—explanations that offered me self-protection and pointed blame toward someone or something else—but it was equally troublesome because it was made up of half-truths. I really do need to make sure that I'm giving and helping. I absolutely need to stay uncomfortably aware of my privilege. But after six months and three powerful experiences in which I had to confront my discomfort, I realized that the real reason I look away is not my fear of helping others, but my fear of needing help.

My rumbles with shame, judgment, privilege, connection, need, fear, and self-worth taught me that it wasn't the pain or the hurt that made me look away. It was my own need. Act 2 is all about trying to find a comfortable way to solve the problem until those options are exhausted and you have to walk straight into discomfort—"the lowest of the low." Helping and giving are comfortable for me. I wanted to solve this issue by doing more of what I already do. When I look back at this rising strong example now, I think about how often we all try to solve problems by doing more of what's not working—just doing it harder, grinding it out longer. We'll do anything to avoid the lowest of the low—self-examination.

And, as it turns out, I'm not so sure I was great at giving. How can we be truly comfortable and generous in the face of someone's need when we're repelled by our own? Wholeheartedness is as much about receiving as it is about giving. The delta did not mean rewriting my story completely, but rather adding and integrating new key learnings into an existing story I'd been telling myself that was misleading and incomplete. This meant looking back at my history.

From a young age, I learned how to earn love, gold stars, and praise by being the helper. It was the role I played in my family, with my friends, and even with a few of my early boy-friends. After a while, helping became less about gold stars and more about my identity. Helping was the most value I brought to a relationship. If I couldn't help or, God forbid, if I had to ask for help, what value did I bring?

Over the years, I think I unconsciously developed a value system that helped me make sense of my role—a way to look at giving and receiving that made me feel better and soothed the pain of not allowing myself to ask for help. The axiom of that dangerous system was simple: Helping is courageous and com-passionate, and a sign that you have it together. Asking for help is a sign of weakness. What grew out of this way of living was even more faulty thinking: If I'm not feeling brave or gen-erous enough, I'm not helping enough.

The key learnings from this rumble totally challenged this system:

- When you judge yourself for needing help, you judge those you are helping. When you attach value to giving help, you attach value to needing help.
- The danger of tying your self-worth to being a helper is feel-ing shame when you have to ask for help.
- Offering help is courageous and compassionate, but so is asking for help.

THE REVOLUTION

May you always do for others and let others do for
you.

—Bob Dylan

I love this lyric from Dylan. It's such a beautiful wish because
so many of us are good at giving help, but not at receiving it.
Giving help can occasionally feel vulnerable; asking for help
always means risking vulnerability. This is critical to understand because we can't make it through the rising strong process without help and support. We all will need people we can
turn to for help when we are rumbling with the more confusing parts of our stories. I turn to the people I trust most, like
Steve, my sisters, and my mother, for insight into the process.
I've also leaned heavily on my therapist, Diana.

In my work with the Daring Way leadership groups, we talk
about what it means to trust people. We ask leaders to identify
two or three specific behaviors that allow them to trust others.
Two of the top answers that always emerge are:

- I trust people who will ask for help or support.
- If someone asks me for help, I'm more likely to trust
  them because they're willing to be vulnerable and honest with me.

This exercise gets interesting when leaders, in turn, talk about
how reluctant they are to ask for help and support. How many
times do we implore the people who work for us to ask for help
when they need it? But experience shows that simply asking

them to do this probably won't correlate strongly with how often they actually ask for help. We found a better correlation between the number of times we modeled what asking for help looks like and how comfortable folks are with asking for help. Both giving and receiving help must be part of the culture, and we as leaders need to model both if we are committed to innovation and growth.

In *The Gifts of Imperfection,* I define connection as "the energy that exists between people when they feel seen, heard, and valued; when they can give and receive without judgment; and when they derive sustenance and strength from the relationship." Connection doesn't exist without giving and receiving. We need to give and we need to need. This is true at work and at home.

In a culture of scarcity and perfectionism, asking for help can be shaming if we're not raised to understand how seeking help is human and foundational to connection. We can encourage our children to ask for help; however, if they don't see us reaching out for support and modeling that behavior, they will instead attach value to never needing help. We also send strong messages to the people around us, including our children, friends, and employees, when they ask for help, and in return, we treat them differently—as if they are now less reliable, competent, or productive.

The bottom line is that we need each other. And not just the civilized, proper, convenient kind of need. Not one of us gets through this life without expressing desperate, messy, and uncivilized need. The kind we are reminded of when we come face-to-face with someone who is in a deep struggle.

Dependence starts when we're born and lasts until we die.

We accept our dependence as babies, and ultimately, with varying levels of resistance, we accept help as we get to the end of our lives. But in the middle of our lives, we mistakenly fall prey to the myth that successful people are those who *help rather than need,* and broken people *need rather than help.* Given enough resources, we can even pay for help and create the mirage that we are completely self-sufficient. But the truth is that no amount of money, influence, resources, or determination will change our physical, emotional, and spiritual dependence on others. Not at the beginning of our lives, not in the messy middle, and not at the end.

For most of us, being an "easy mark" has come to mean being a chump or a sucker or a pushover—shaming identities that are associated with weakness and a lack of street smarts. For the strangers who broke bread at my grandmother's house, the mark was a sign of courage and compassion. For my grandmother, generosity and giving were not the opposite of receiving: They were parts of the compact between human beings.

REGRET IS A
TOUGH
but fair teacher.
TO LIVE WITHOUT REGRET
IS TO BELIEVE YOU HAVE
NOTHING TO LEARN
no amends to make, and
NO OPPORTUNITY *to be*
BRAVER
WITH YOUR LIFE.

Nine

COMPOSTING FAILURE

RUMBLING WITH FEAR, SHAME,
PERFECTIONISM, BLAME, ACCOUNTABILITY,
TRUST, FAILURE, AND REGRET

ndrew is known around his office as a listener, a thinker, an expert in strategy, and the keeper of culture. He's the guy who doesn't say much, but when he does, everyone listens. His point of view is sought by colleagues throughout the successful advertising agency where he's worked for twelve years, especially when it comes to estimating costs and putting together bids for pitches. One colleague said, "Andrew is the reason it all works. His word is gold and everyone trusts him."

Andrew was part of a small group of senior leaders that I met with to discuss early versions of the rising strong process. After we met, Andrew, like Claudia, reached out to me to share what he described as a painful failure at work. I'm grateful that he allowed me to interview him and his two colleagues about his experience. I recognized so much of myself in his story, and I think you might, too.

In most advertising agencies, teams respond to proposals from potential clients by creating pitches that include their creative concepts and the estimated cost of executing them. This is notoriously stressful work, with fierce competition among ad agencies for clients and frequent tension between a company's creative and business teams. The creatives strive to wow the clients, while the business team has to make sure the project nets a profit. One of Andrew's primary responsibilities is overseeing the financial estimates and approving the final budget that accompanies every bid—basically, telling the prospective client, "We can do it for this much money."

Because Andrew has always framed the tension between art and money as necessary and valuable to the process, he is highly respected and liked by both sides of the organization. A colleague from the creative side said, "If Andrew tells me that we need to bring down expenses to make it work, I know he's thought about it, and I know he understands what he's asking me to do. I do it." One of Andrew's direct reports said, "I'm learning from him and I trust him 100 percent. He's one of the most thorough people I know. And he's a straight shooter."

The trust and influence that Andrew has earned over the years have also positioned him as the unofficial watchdog of the company culture. He accepted that there would naturally be tension between colleagues from time to time, but he had little tolerance for gossip, favoritism, and back-channel negotiations. Even in heated arguments, which there were plenty of, he was always up-front, respectful, and appreciative. This set the tone for the entire agency.

When I asked Andrew how he got so good at his job, he said, "There's certainly a skill set when it comes to interpreting the creative piece and the management piece in terms of time and materials, but the real key is knowing yourself. You have to know where the quicksand is—everyone has their own sinkholes." When I asked Andrew for examples of "sinkholes," he gave me what he thought were the five most common ones:

1. Emotional blinders—I'm so emotionally invested in working with this client that I'm blind to the fact that our bid is too low for the scope of the work.

2. The loss leader—I'm convinced that a big discount on this project, even if we lose money, will lead to future work that will be more profitable and eventually offset this loss.

3. Uncharted territory—I'm going after business in a category I have no experience in. *I don't know what I don't know.*

4. Win at any cost—I'm addicted to the thrill of the win. Another variation: My self-worth is tied to how much business I bring in.

5. Defensive pricing—I have to protect my turf with an existing client by making it difficult for a competitor to match my price, even if we take a loss.

As I wrote these down, I couldn't help but notice their application to everyday life. I told Andrew that I'd never in my life put together a bid, but I'd spent plenty of time in similar sinkholes, like getting sucked in emotionally, living in the future, thinking in the short term, wanting to win, and being defensive. We laughed for a bit before Andrew got more serious and said, "But sometimes the greatest threat is keeping your head down and staying so focused on dodging the sinkholes that you lose sight of where you're going and why." This is his story.

Everyone at Andrew's agency was ecstatic when they were asked to pitch a huge ad campaign for a well-known and influential brand. The proposal was especially exciting because the brand's needs intersected very well with the agency's strengths. The creative team was grateful for the big-budget opportunity to showcase their work and hoped to add the high-profile company to their individual portfolios. The business team saw the tremendous revenue potential in this new strategic partnership. Within hours, the atmosphere in the office was electric. People were calling home to let their families know they'd be spending long hours in the office over the next two weeks. This pitch would require all hands on deck.

Andrew wasn't quite as excited as the rest of the team. Everyone was already stretched thin. They had just the right number of projects in various places on the design and production timeline. Adding another—especially one of this size—could tip the balance. He also had mixed feelings about the client, who had a reputation in the industry for treating partners poorly. One of his good friends, a colleague who worked in a related field, had once described the client as a bully. Andrew was mulling over these concerns when Manuel, a senior member of the creative team, showed up in his office.

"We've got this," Manuel said. "People are psyched about the project, and we can do it." His enthusiasm was contagious, and Andrew didn't want his doubts to squelch the team's passion, so he jumped in. "I know. We *can* do this." Andrew was generally measured in his responses, but he also liked a challenge and wasn't immune to the growing energy.

For the next couple of weeks, Andrew worked long hours

with the team to develop their pitch for the first round of selection. Managing internal relationships and building team cohesion during that period felt like a full-time job. When people are stretched, their coping skills start to fray. A mere twenty-four hours after Andrew spoke the words *We can do this,* the account manager and the creative director stood in front of him, having it out with each other.

Despite the fatigue and tough group dynamics, the entire agency came together to celebrate when they found out they had made it to the second round of the selection process. The win felt like a balm for the frazzled, emotionally and physically exhausted team.

But Andrew was still worried about the burden the heavy workload was placing on everyone, and he continued to have some nagging concerns about the client's reputation. Still, he was invested now, so he pushed down his uneasiness and joined in the celebration.

The second round of the process required Andrew and the pitch team to fly to the Midwest for a face-to-face meeting with the company's branding team. In Andrew's words, "This is where things went south.

"For almost an hour, I watched our team put heart and soul into explaining our ideas and concepts," he said. "Meanwhile, the entire branding team sat there typing away on their laptops, rarely, if ever, looking up. We're used to some degree of inattention during these meetings, but it was obvious that these side conversations weren't even related to our pitch." Two people on the branding team then asked questions that had been addressed in the presentation, confirming that they had been too busy emailing or doing whatever it was on their laptops to even pay attention. After a third member of the branding team made an inappropriate and disrespectful comment to the presenter, Andrew told me, "I did nothing."

He looked at me. "Within minutes of that meeting ending, I thought to myself, *I am a screwup. I am a failure. I let them down and they will no longer trust me.* It was absolutely a facedown moment for me. My team had worked sixty-plus hours a week for two months only to be completely dismissed by a group of people I had known, in advance, had the capacity and propensity to do that. Why hadn't I done something to prevent this? How would they ever trust me again?"

Nobody talked much on the car ride to the airport or on the plane ride home. The team members were deflated and angry, and absolutely exhausted. The long hours had taken a toll on their health and their relationships both inside and outside of work. Andrew said, "The only thought in my head during the entire trip back was, *I'm a screwup. I didn't protect my people. I didn't do my job. I'm a screwup. I failed. I've lost their trust.* The tape was on a constant loop in my head.

"When I woke up the next morning, my first thought was, *I'm a failure and a screwup.* My second thought was, *I need to get out of this. I need to make this work. I need an easy fix. Who else is to blame? Who else was responsible for this mess?* Then it hit me. *I'm hustling. Not only that, I'm underneath a rock. I need to get out from underneath this rock first. I can't make any good decisions from under here.* I thought of your work and realized, *Shit, I know this rock is shame.* I called a friend who is also familiar with your work and told him the story. I told him that I couldn't get past the voice saying *I'm a screwup.* I couldn't get past how much I had let everyone down, including myself. I couldn't get past losing their trust."

Andrew told me that making that call to his friend was incredibly difficult, but the rising strong talk was still fresh in his mind, and he realized he was in it. He added wryly, "I was willing to give it a shot—desperate times call for desperate measures." His friend's reply was, "I get it. And I think you might have screwed up. But you make a hundred judgment calls every day. Do you think you're going to make the right call every time? Does making a bad call make you a failure?"

He went on to ask Andrew what he would say to someone who worked for him if she had made a similar mistake. Andrew replied automatically, "That's different. Making mistakes is a part of the process."

After hearing himself say that, Andrew sighed. "No mistakes allowed," he said to his friend. "This is my perfectionism talking, isn't it?"

"Maybe so," his friend replied. "That's probably why you called me. This is my stuff, too."

Andrew described the feeling that came over him during that conversation as relief. "It was so helpful to recognize that rock as shame and to make the choice to get out from underneath it. It doesn't mean that what's ahead is going to be easy, but it does mean that I can stop hustling. I can start making decisions that are in line with my values. At this point in my career, I need to know how to own my mistakes and set things right."

When Andrew got to work that day, he was greeted by a team that was still emotionally spent, but also completely confused. Despite their reading of the pitch meeting as a disaster, it turned out that they, along with one other agency, had made it to the final round. No one knew how to react. That's when Andrew called a meeting to decide their next move.

"I have to tell you," he said, "when we decided to take on this project, I was so focused on proving that we can do this that I forgot to ask the most important question: Should we do it? We were stretched to the max before we started, and I knew this client was potentially a bad fit for us. It was my job to step back and ask questions, and I didn't. I screwed up. I made a mistake, and I apologize. I hope I can regain your trust."

The room was quiet until Manuel finally responded, "Thank you for saying that. I do trust you. What happens next?"

Andrew told them that given the time everyone had put in, and the money and resources invested by the agency, they needed to decide as a team if they should continue or not. His vote, he said, was to walk away. Manuel seconded Andrew's vote and looked toward Cynthia, the account manager. The tension between Manuel and Cynthia was no secret, and everyone in the room knew that Cynthia could probably tell you, to the penny, what the aggressive pitching process had cost the agency over the past two months. Cynthia leaned forward in her chair and said, "I saw the way they treated Manuel yesterday. I vote *hell no*." The rest of the team agreed, and the vote was unanimous.

In addition to the financial consequences, Andrew knew that fallout was likely in the advertising community. It's highly unusual to get that far in a pitch process and pull out. But this was a risk that he, the team, and the agency's owners were willing to take. During the call to the client explaining their decision, Andrew did not blame the decision on the poor behavior of the company's branding team, but instead took responsibility for not accurately assessing the fit and timing. Several months later, he received a call from a leader in the company's branding division asking about his team's experience. Andrew had the sense that the brand was trying to understand its growing reputation as a difficult partner. This time he told her more directly what he thought about the culture clash and the behaviors he found to be unprofessional.

Andrew and his colleagues told me that something changed the day they decided not to pursue the pitch. Andrew attributed it to Manuel and Cynthia coming together to protect the team. His colleagues agreed about the power of that moment, but they also said that Andrew's willingness to own his mistake and apologize shifted something in the spirit of the place. The one thing they could say emphatically was that the levels of trust, respect, and pride within the team skyrocketed after that experience. Andrew said, "We worked together. We fell together. We climbed up together. That changes people."

THE RECKONING

Andrew's facedown-in-the-arena moment was very clear to him. It came with the pain and guilt he felt over not intervening as he watched his talented team being treated with disrespect while they were presenting work that was important to them. His curiosity was less about *What is this feeling?* and more about *What am I going to do now?*

THE RUMBLE

Andrew laughed when he told me that he thinks he has the shortest SFD in history—a single three-word sentence: *I'm a screwup.* When I asked him what the rumble had been like to let him get from *I'm a screwup* to *I screwed up,* he said, "I had to take on shame, blame, fear, perfectionism, accountability, trust, and failure, for sure. I can give other people a break, but I'm hard on myself. Self-trust was a big part of it for me."

Rumbling with Shame and Perfectionism

The difference between shame and guilt lies in the way we talk to ourselves. Shame is a focus on self, while guilt is a focus on behavior. This is not just semantics. There's a huge difference between *I screwed up* (guilt) and *I am a screwup* (shame). The former is acceptance of our imperfect humanity. The latter is basically an indictment of our very existence.

It's always helpful to remember that when perfectionism is driving, shame is riding shotgun. Perfectionism is not healthy striving. It is not asking, *How can I be my best self?* Instead, it's asking, *What will people think?* When looking at our own stories, we can benefit from wondering: *Did something happen in this story that left me feeling like my cover was blown, revealing that I'm really not what I want people to think I am? Did my pretend/please/perfect/ perform/prove house of cards come tumbling down?* For those of us who struggle with perfectionism, it's not difficult to find ourselves in a situation similar to Andrew's, one where we look back and think, *I got sucked into proving I could, rather than stepping back and asking if I should—or if I really even wanted to.*

Another one of shame's sidekicks is comparison. I have a picture over my desk of the pool where I swim that reminds me to keep comparison in check. Under the picture I wrote, "Stay in your own lane. Comparison kills creativity and joy." For me, swimming is the trifecta of health—meditation, therapy, and exercise—but only when I stay in my own lane, focused on my breathing and my stroke. Problems begin when I happen to sync up with the swimmer next to me and we push off the wall at the same time, because I always start comparing and competing. A couple of months ago, I did it to the point where I almost reinjured my rotator cuff. Believe me, comparison sucks the creativity and joy right out of life.

If our story includes shame, perfectionism, or comparison and we're left feeling isolated or "less than," we need to employ two completely counterintuitive strategies. We need to:

1. Talk to ourselves in the same way we'd talk to someone we love.

Yes, you made a mistake. You're human.

You don't have to do it like anyone else does.

Fixing it and making amends will help. Self-loathing will not.

2. Reach out to someone we trust—a person who has earned the right to hear our story and who has the capacity to respond with empathy.

The second strategy is especially effective because shame can't survive being spoken. It thrives on secrecy, silence, and judgment. If we can share our experience of shame with someone who responds with empathy, shame can't survive. We share our stories—even our SFDs—to get clear on what we're feeling and what triggered those feelings, allowing us to build a deeper, more meaningful connection with both ourselves and our trusted friends.

Andrew reached out to a friend, shared his struggle, got an empathic response, and was encouraged to give himself the same grace he so willingly offered others. There are a million ways this story could have gone bad, and only one way to turn it around: Address the shame.

Rumbling with Blame and Accountability

In research terms, we think about blame as a form of anger used to discharge discomfort or pain. The shame-blame combo is so common because we're desperate to get out from underneath the pain of shame, and we see blame as a quick fix. If, for example, I suddenly realize that I missed an important conference call earlier, sometimes in a split second I'm discharging that frustration by yelling at my child or my student or my employee. I always say, "When we're in shame, we're not fit for human consumption. And we're especially dangerous around people over whom we have some power."

It doesn't have to be something big—blame works to discharge mild discomfort, too. You're late for work and you can't find that shirt you want to wear, so you yell at your partner for hanging the dry cleaning in the wrong place in the closet. It doesn't have to make sense either. It just has to give us some sense of relief and control. In fact, for most of us who rely on blaming and finding fault, the need for control is so strong that we'd rather have something be *our* fault than succumb to the bumper-sticker wisdom of "shit happens." If stuff just happens, how do I control that? Fault-finding fools us into believing that someone is always to blame, hence, controlling the outcome is possible. But blame is as corrosive as it is unproductive.

I always know that I need to rumble with blame when there's a kid-self in my SFD waving her arms wildly and saying with righteous fury, "It's all their fault!" Or if I'm looking for the person, unfairness, or annoyance that tripped me up and landed me facedown. In Andrew's case, one of the first thoughts that came to mind when he was hustling under the rock was, *Who's to blame?* I imagine most of us have had the experience of trying to blame and hustle our way out of the pain of *I'm a screwup*.

The difference between accountability and blame is very similar to the difference between guilt and shame. Guilt gets a bad rap, but the emotional discomfort of guilt can be a powerful and healthy motivator for change. Of course, feeling guilty about something over which we have no control or something that isn't our responsibility is not helpful, and more times than not, what we think is guilt is really shame and the fear of not being enough.

Like guilt, accountability is often motivated by wanting to live in alignment with our values. Accountability is holding ourselves or someone else responsible for specific actions and their specific consequences. Blame, on the other hand, is simply a quick, broad-brush way to off-load anger, fear, shame, or discomfort. We think we'll feel better after pointing a finger at someone or something, but nothing changes. Instead, blame kills relationships and organizational cultures. It's toxic. It's also a go-to reaction for many of us.

Accountability is a prerequisite for strong relationships and cultures. It requires authenticity, action, and the courage to apologize and make amends. Rumbling with accountability is a hard and time-consuming process. It also requires vulnerability. We have to own our feelings and reconcile our behaviors and choices with our values. Andrew demonstrated both vulnerability and courage when he stood in front of his team and said, "I screwed up, and I'm sorry."

Rumbling with Trust

Trust—in ourselves and in others—is often the first casualty in a fall, and stories of shattered trust can render us speechless with hurt or send us into a defensive silence. Maybe someone betrayed us or let us down, or our own judgment led us astray. *How could I have been so stupid and naïve? Did I miss the warning signs?* If I've learned anything in my research, it's that trust can't be hot-wired, whether it's between two friends or within a work team; it's grown in a process that takes place over the course of a relationship.

Several of the Daring Way facilitators referred me to Charles Feltman's *The Thin Book of Trust*. While the book focuses on building trust at work, I found Feltman's definitions of *trust* and *distrust* to fit powerfully with my own findings. Feltman describes *trust* as "choosing to risk making something you value vulnerable to another person's actions," and he describes *distrust* as deciding that "what is important to me is not safe with this person in this situation (or any situation)."

When rumbling with our stories about losing trust, we need to be able to identify exactly where the breach lies and to speak to it. As Feltman writes, "It isn't surprising people seldom talk directly about distrust. If it requires you to use words like 'sneaky, mean, or liar' to tell someone you don't trust him or her, you're probably going to think twice about it." The ability to point to specific behaviors rather than just using the word *trust* can also help us rumble with our stories of falling. The more specific we can be, the more likely it is that we can create change.

In my research, seven elements of trust emerged as useful in both trusting others and trusting ourselves. I came up with an acronym—*BRAVING*—for the elements. It also serves as a checklist when I'm rumbling with trust issues with the people in my life. As Feltman so wisely suggests, breaking down the attributes of trust into specific behaviors allows us to more clearly identify and address breaches of trust. I love the BRAVING checklist because it reminds me that trusting myself or other people is a vulnerable and courageous process.

Boundaries—You respect my boundaries, and when you're not clear about what's okay and not okay, you ask. You're willing to say no.

Reliability—You do what you say you'll do. At work, this means staying aware of your competencies and limitations so you don't overpromise and are able to deliver on commitments and balance competing priorities.

Accountability—You own your mistakes, apologize, and make amends.

Vault—You don't share information or experiences that are not yours to share. I need to know that my confidences are kept, and that you're not sharing

with me any information about other people that
should be confidential.

Integrity—You choose courage over comfort. You
choose what is right over what is fun, fast, or easy.
And you choose to practice your values rather than
simply professing them.

Nonjudgment—I can ask for what I need, and you can
ask for what you need. We can talk about how we
feel without judgment.

Generosity—You extend the most generous interpreta-
tion possible to the intentions, words, and actions
of others.

Self-trust is often a casualty of failure. In many of the interviews about professional and personal failure, the research
participant would say, "I don't know if I can trust myself again"
or "I've lost faith in my own judgment." If you reread this
checklist and change the pronouns, you'll see that BRAVING
also works as a powerful tool for assessing our level of self-trust.

B—Did I respect my own boundaries? Was I clear about
what's okay and what's not okay?

R—Was I reliable? Did I do what I said I was going
to do?

A—Did I hold myself accountable?

V—Did I respect the vault and share appropriately?

I—Did I act from my integrity?

N—Did I ask for what I needed? Was I nonjudgmental
about needing help?

G—Was I generous toward myself?

If you hold up Andrew's choices and behaviors against any one of these elements of trust, you'll see that mistakes don't bankrupt trust in the way that violations of personal account-ability, integrity, or values can. Trust and mistakes can coexist, and often do, as long as we make amends, stay aligned with our values, and confront shame and blame head-on.

Rumbling with Failure

Part of the tape that was playing on a loop in Andrew's head was, *I am a failure. Failure* is a slippery word because we use it to describe a wide range of experiences—from risky efforts that didn't pan out or ideas that were never launched to painful, life-altering losses. Whatever the experience, failure feels like a lost opportunity, like something that can't be redone or un-done. Regardless of the context or magnitude, failure brings with it the sense that we've lost some of our personal power.

Many of us have a negative, almost stomach-clenching re-action to the word *power*. I think this is because we automati-cally conflate *power* and *power over*. But the type of power I'm talking about is more in line with Martin Luther King, Jr.'s definition of it: the ability to achieve our purpose and to effect change.

Experiencing failure often leads to feeling powerless simply because we didn't achieve our purpose and/or effect the change we wanted to see. The connection between failure and power-lessness is important, because all of my years of research lead me to argue that we are most dangerous to ourselves and to the people around us when we feel powerless. Powerlessness leads to fear and desperation. Look behind an act of violence, from bullying to terrorism, and you will often find a frantic attempt to escape powerlessness.

The feelings of powerlessness that often accompany failure start with those all-too-familiar "could have" or "should have" self-inventories. And our fear grows in tandem with the strength of our belief that an opening has been forever closed. Pervasive feelings of powerlessness eventually lead to despair. My favorite definition of despair comes from author and pastor Rob Bell: Despair is a spiritual condition. It's the belief that tomorrow will be just like today. My heart stopped when I heard him say this. *Man. I know what it feels like to be under that rock and to believe, with all of my heart, that there's no way out and that I'll be in that exact same spot tomorrow.* For me, that feeling is absolutely a spiritual crisis.

In my work, I've found that moving out of powerlessness, and even despair, requires hope. Hope is not an emotion: It's a cognitive process—a thought process made up of what researcher C. R. Snyder called the trilogy of "goals, pathways, and agency." Hope happens when we can set goals, have the tenacity and perseverance to pursue those goals, and believe in our own abilities to act. Snyder also found that hope is learned. When boundaries, consistency, and support are in place, children learn it from their parents. But even if we didn't get it as kids, we can still learn hope as adults. It's just tougher when we're older because we have to resist and unlearn old habits, like the tendency to give up when things get tough.

Hope is a function of struggle. If we're never allowed to fall or face adversity as children, we are denied the opportunity to develop the tenacity and sense of agency we need to be hopeful. One of the greatest gifts my parents gave me was hope.

When I fell, failed, or screwed up, they did not run to the rescue. They supported me, but they always expected me to figure it out. They placed high value on grit and moxie, and this has served me well—especially in my career as a writer.

I wrote my first book in 2002. The title was *Hairy Toes and Sexy Rice: Women, Shame, and the Media.* The title was based on two stories from my own life, set twenty-five years apart. The "hairy toes" part was the story of my first experience with shame and body image. When I was eight years old, I found a little peach fuzz on my big toe and spent months quietly scouring the pages of *Seventeen* and *Young Miss* magazines, trying to figure out if I was normal. Nothing. Any close-ups of a model's feet showed toes that were totally bald. Convinced that I was the only girl in the world with hair on her toes, I did the only two things I could think of: I bought more of the things I saw in the magazine ads, like Noxzema and Bonne Bell lip gloss, and I hid my toes. This is how my love affair with clogs started.

"Sexy rice" referred to a television commercial popular between 1999 and 2000. Once, after a long day of teaching, I was looking forward to a little alone time before Steve and my then one-year-old daughter got home. Once the bra-off, hair-up, TV-on ritual was complete, I sank into the couch and was contemplating what to fix for dinner when something on the television caught my eye. A beautiful woman in a silk teddy and a gorgeous, beefy guy were panting, groping each other, and sliding down the front of a Sub-Zero refrigerator. Every couple of seconds, the lovers would pause to take turns spoon-feeding each other. *Damn, I think that's rice,* I thought. Finally, in the very last shot, the camera panned to a bowl of rice and a familiar logo appeared on the screen. I rolled my eyes and thought, *That was so stupid.*

Next I started thinking, *Do they think people actually do that? I bet guys would love that—to come home and have dinner spoon-fed to them as they have sex against the fridge.* Then, as the advertising gods intended, I started feeling a little sad about my own mundane dinner plans . . . and the sweats I was wearing . . . and the sandwiches we would probably eat . . . and the half conversations we would have while we played with Ellen . . . and the baby weight that I couldn't lose . . . and the inevitability of falling asleep during the news.

So, I used these experiences to title my first book, about the research I was conducting on women and shame. I spent six months trying to find an agent, at the end of which all I had to show for my efforts was a huge file of impersonal rejection letters. My last hope was a writers' conference in Austin where, for the price of a ticket, I could have a ten-minute audience with a real live editor from New York City. I was scared, excited, and hopeful. My ten-minute meeting was with an editor from a house known for publishing serious nonfiction. I immediately liked the look of him. He had disheveled hair, he was wearing chunky weird glasses, and he seemed a bit tortured. In my mind, those things made him legit. "What do you have for me?" he asked as I sat down.

Surprisingly, I wasn't nervous at all as I started to deliver the lines I had rehearsed for days. He propped his chin on his fist and frowned as I told him about my book. "Do you have anything with you?" he asked. I pulled out a proposal complete with a cover letter addressed to him. He grabbed some pages and began reading. After a few minutes, he told me he thought I had something important and valuable here, but he hated the title. Then he said, "There's nothing funny about shame. Don't lighten up the subject. Nietzsche said, 'What do you consider the most humane? To spare someone shame. What is the seal of liberation? To no longer be ashamed in front of oneself.' Be serious. You have the credentials."

I started to tell him that I disagreed, that being serious about shame and recognizing the importance of humor and laughter to healing aren't mutually exclusive, but then my time ran out. He quickly gave me the name and number of an agent. As I walked out of the room, his parting words were, "I really hate the humor. I hate the title. No funny stories. Remember Nietzsche!" The door closed behind me.

I was under the rock. Rather than trying to crawl out, I took his advice, changed the title to *Women and Shame,* and got rid of some of my funny stories. I couldn't bear to strip all the laughter out of the book, but looking back, I know now I took out way more than I should have and I wasn't being true to myself. His agent friend turned down my proposal, and over the next year I sent forty more query letters to agents and publishers. All I got in return were form letters that said some version of "As titillating as a book about shame written by an academic sounds, we're not interested." So I borrowed money from my parents, and in 2004 I self-published *Women and Shame.* Self-publishing was relatively new back then, and it was expensive and clunky. I had to store the books myself, and Steve and I did most of the shipping with the help of my friend Charles. I even sold books out of my trunk at events.

One day a faculty colleague stopped me in the elevator and

said, "I read your book. It's really powerful. I'm going to order it and add it to my syllabus. Who is your publisher?"

I stalled for a minute, then said, "I published it myself."

He stepped out of the elevator and, as he held the door open with his hand, turned back to me and said, "I really can't add a vanity-published book to my syllabus."

I couldn't breathe. The weight of that rock literally took my breath away. I immediately pictured myself hawking my book on the corner, wearing one of those coin-changer belts. I was so full of shame that at one very low point, when a woman pulled out her checkbook and asked to whom she should write her check, I actually said, "Make it out to the publisher" as I held up the book and pretended to read the name of the publisher off the spine, as if it wasn't me.

Six months later, though, the book caught on with mental health professionals and began selling like hotcakes. I even convinced a large distributor to help me get it into a few Barnes & Noble stores. Then, on one very magical evening, I met one of my great heroes, the psychologist and author Harriet Lerner. One thing led to the next, and within three months I had an agent and a book deal for *Women and Shame*. I couldn't believe it!

The reworked book was titled *I Thought It Was Just Me,* and it came out in February 2007. Steve and I were psyched, and our parents were ready to hold down the fort and help with the kids while I traveled to media outlets and did the book tour. I maxed out one of our credit cards buying new clothes. I practiced my *Today* show interview every morning in the mirror. It was GO TIME.

Go, go, go.

Now.

It's go time!

Nothing. The phone rang once on publication day. It was the bank informing us that we had overlooked a student loan payment and owed a late fee. I was devastated. The phone didn't ring the next day, or the next. And there I sat, with my closet full of new outfits and a Post-it note I'd named Katie Couric stuck on my bathroom mirror.

In a moment of desperation, I scrambled to put together a book reading in Chicago, where I was already doing a lecture for mental health professionals. It was the coldest February day on record. Five people came to the reading. One woman was drunk, and two of them were there because they thought I was a mystery writer.

Six months after the book came out, I got a call from the publisher asking if I wanted to buy copies at a great low price. At first I was excited. But then I learned that they were offering me the opportunity to buy hundreds of books. "This isn't a good thing, Brené," the publisher said. "Your book is being re-maindered. The sales are too low to keep it in our warehouse. That's valuable real estate, and if we're not moving books, they have to go."

"I don't understand," I replied. "What does *remaindered* even mean?" I sat on the floor in my kitchen and listened to him explain the process of moving books from the warehouses to the bargain bins. Any leftover books are sent to the pulping machines.

I'm being composted, I thought. It was a devastating failure for me. Five years of work gone in six months. I felt it all—the powerlessness and the despair and the shame. After I spent three weeks in shame-fueled blaming of others and berating myself for everything I should and could have done, Steve helped me out from under that rock. As I would learn, the hardest part of coming out from hiding is facing the painful work of rumbling with the real story. And the real story was that I had set myself up for failure.

I swore that if I ever had the opportunity to publish a book again, I'd do it differently. I wasn't going to get dressed up in my new outfit and wait for someone to knock on my door and ask me about my work. I'd put on my shit-kickers and start knocking on doors myself.

I've published four books now, and I still feel scared and exposed and vulnerable as I prepare to share a new idea with the world. I still flinch a little when I turn to my community and say, "I'm trying this, and I would love your support!" But I try to remind myself that, on the flip side, I love it when someone is genuinely excited about his or her work. I've also learned in all of my rumbles that if you don't put value on your work, no one is going to do that for you.

I've rumbled with failure and shame enough over the past decade to know this: You can do everything right. You can cheer yourself on, have all the support you can find in place, and be 100 percent ready to go, and still fail. It happens to writers, artists, entrepreneurs, health professionals, teachers—you name it. But if you can look back during your rumble and see that you didn't hold back—that you were *all in*—you will feel very different than someone who didn't fully show up. You may have to deal with the failure, but you won't have to wrestle with the same level of shame that we experience when our efforts were halfhearted.

And, in addition to assessing the level of our effort, our experience of failure is also shaped by how well we lived out our values: *Were we all in and were we true to ourselves?* When you're rumbling with failure and it's clear that the choices you made along the way were not in alignment with your values, you have to grapple not only with the fallout of failing but also with the feeling that you betrayed yourself. Andrew had to reconcile his decision to push down his concerns and uneasiness about the new project and his choice to stay quiet during the meeting with what he believed in his heart. I had to rumble with the consequence of silencing my instincts on the best ways to approach the topic of shame and to successfully get a book out into the world.

I knew the most effective way for me (maybe not for everyone, but certainly for me) to talk about shame was to use everyday stories—even a few funny or absurd ones, like sexy rice—to illustrate how we fall prey to ridiculous and unattainable messages about perfection. But I took that Nietzsche advice and ran it through my *not good enough* processor until it morphed into, *Grow up. Be serious and stop clowning around.* I also knew how to sell books—coin-changer belt and all. Sadly, at the time a new academic, I ran the "vanity publishing" comment through the same gremlin processor and redefined a *proper and sophisticated author* as one who distanced herself from the unsavory ordeal of promoting and selling the book.

When I look back at these two experiences today, I know that both were potential facedown-in-the-arena moments—ones that if they happened today, I hope would lead me to acknowledge my self-doubt and shame.

I'm grateful for the advice from the editor, but it doesn't mean I need to accept it unquestioningly.

Damn! That vanity-publishing comment was hurtful and probably meant to be shaming, but his view of my efforts doesn't need to dictate how I see myself. But I didn't have the information or experience that I have today, so rather than getting curious about the hurt I was feeling, I silenced my pain by codifying the expert advice. Choosing to place greater value on what the experts thought than on what I was feeling or what I knew about my own work made the composting conversation (which was ultimately my facedown moment) far more painful.

In both instances, I walked away from the two values that guide my life—my faith and my commitment to be brave. My faith calls me to practice love over fear, and in this experience I let fear trample all over self-love. I made every decision with the mindset *What will people think?* rather than *I am enough.* That is as unholy as it gets for me. Courage calls for me to show up and be seen, and in this instance, I literally hid at home and waited for someone else to show up and do the work, including the publisher and the book-buying public. Of all the things I regret from this experience, the biggest one is betraying my own values and being so unkind to myself. But, as you'll see in the next section, I'm a student of regret, and she's a tough but fair teacher whose lessons on empathy and compassion are critical pieces of wholehearted living.

Rumbling with Regret

If there is one thing failure has taught me, it is the value of regret. Regret is one of the most powerful emotional reminders that change and growth are necessary. In fact, I've come to believe that regret is a kind of package deal: A function of empathy, it's a call to courage and a path toward wisdom. Like all emotions, regret can be used constructively or destructively, but the wholesale dismissal of regret is wrongheaded and dangerous. "No regrets" doesn't mean living with courage, it means living without reflection. To live without regret is to believe you have nothing to learn, no amends to make, and no opportunity to be braver with your life.

A friend of mine who knew I was studying regret in my data sent me a picture of a tough-looking kid who had NO RAGRETS tattooed across his chest. I later found out that the image was from the film *We're the Millers*. It's such a perfect metaphor for what I've learned: If you have no regrets, or you intentionally set out to live without regrets, I think you're missing the very value of regret.

One of the truest things I've ever heard about regret came from George Saunders's 2013 commencement address at Syracuse University. He talked about how when he was a child, a young girl was teased at his school and, although he didn't tease her and even defended her a little, he still thought about it. He said, "So here's something I know to be true, although it's a little corny, and I don't quite know what to do with it.

"What I regret most in my life are *failures of kindness*.

"Those moments when another human being was there, in front of me, suffering, and I responded . . . sensibly. Reservedly. Mildly."

During a research focus group at West Point, I asked a group of officers, many of whom had lost troop members during combat, about the word *regret* and how it fit into their combat experiences. One officer said, "I wouldn't say *regret*. It's different. I have profound grief about the losses. I made all of the calls to the parents myself. I would trade places with any of my soldiers in a minute if I could. But I can't. And I've been over it one thousand times. I believe I was doing the best I could with the intelligence we had. Do I wish there was a different outcome? Every minute of the day."

Wondering if maybe he subscribed to the "no regrets" school of thought, I asked if he had any regrets at all. He responded with a story remarkably similar to the one Saunders included in his speech. "Yes. When I was in high school, there was a girl who was different. She had special needs and every now and then she would eat lunch in the cafeteria with us. She had a crush on me and my friends gave me a hard time about it. When she asked to sit with me once, I told her she couldn't. I deeply regret that. I could have done something different at that moment, and I didn't. I deeply regret it."

I believe that what we regret most are our failures of courage, whether it's the courage to be kinder, to show up, to say how we feel, to set boundaries, to be good to ourselves. For that reason, regret can be the birthplace of empathy. When I think of the times when I wasn't being kind or generous— when I chose being liked over defending someone or something that deserved defending—I feel deep regret, but I've also learned something: Regret is what taught me that living outside of my values is not tenable for me. Regrets about not taking chances have made me braver. Regrets about shaming or blaming people I care about have made me more thoughtful. Sometimes the most uncomfortable learning is the most powerful.

THE REVOLUTION

In the introduction, I wrote, "People who wade into discomfort and vulnerability and tell the truth about their stories are the real badasses." I think this is why I appreciate Andrew's story so much. In my book, he's a total badass. Here's a person who didn't have to own anything—a leader who could have shifted the blame to his own team or to the brand's disrespectful team. But instead, he had the courage to feel pain, to recognize that he was feeling shame, to reach out and be vulnerable with a friend, to own his part, and to stand in front of his team and be accountable.

The delta between *I am a screwup* and *I screwed up* may look small, but in fact it's huge. Many of us will spend our entire lives trying to slog through the shame swampland to get to a place where we can give ourselves permission to both be imperfect and to believe we are enough.

While composting may be a terrible fate for a book, it's a powerful metaphor for failure. Having the courage to own our mistakes, screwups, and failures and to embed the key learnings from these rumbles in our lives, our families, and our organizations yields the exact same results as adding nutrient-rich humus to soil: It brings growth and new vitality. In her book *The Rise,* Sarah Lewis writes, "The word *failure* is imperfect. Once we begin to transform it, it ceases to be that any longer. The term is always slipping off the edges of our vision, not simply because it's hard to see without wincing, but because once we are ready to talk about it, we often call the event something else—a learning experience, a trial, a reinvention—no longer the static concept of failure." Failure can become nourishment if we are willing to get curious, show up vulnerable and human, and put rising strong into practice.

We can't be brave
IN THE BIG WORLD
WITHOUT AT LEAST
one small safe space to
WORK THROUGH *our*
FEARS AND FALLS.

Ten

YOU GOT TO DANCE WITH THEM THAT BRUNG YOU

RUMBLING WITH SHAME, IDENTITY, CRITICISM, AND NOSTALGIA

I had a visceral reaction when Andrew compared shame to being under a rock. I knew exactly what he was talking about when he described the folly of trying to make decisions while in that impossibly dark, heavy, suffocating place. When we experience shame, we are hijacked by the limbic part of the brain that limits our options to "flight, fight, or freeze." Those survival responses rarely leave room for thought, which is why most of us desperately shift around under the rock, looking for reflexive relief by hiding, blaming or lashing out, or by people pleasing.

I was also inspired by Andrew's willingness to do the bruising work of getting out from under the rock before he took action. That not only requires self-awareness and a strong reckoning with emotion, but also being ready and willing to rumble, even when, like Andrew, we recognize that climbing out will leave us more exposed and, ultimately, require more courage. Most of us have developed ways of off-loading or numbing the pain, so when Andrew and I reconnected so he could review his story for this book, I told him that I was in awe of his awareness. He attributed it to learning about shame and being able to recognize when he's in it.

His rock analogy also reminded me of two things. The first was the description of Act 2 that Darla, the producer from Pixar, shared with me: *The protagonist looks for every comfortable way to solve the problem. By the climax, he learns what it's really going to take to solve the problem. This act includes the "lowest of the low."* The second was a particular time in my life when I was trying to operate from a place of shame. It's the perfect cautionary tale about the dangers of under-the-rock decision making. I want to share it with you for several reasons. The first is that although we can't go back and change history, we can benefit from thinking about some of our past falls and viewing them through the lens of the rising strong practice. In this case, I was able to look back and see exactly where shame and fear ran roughshod over my curiosity.

This story also illustrates how writing can be an extremely powerful tool for uncovering the story we're making up. When I'm in the whirlwind of high emotion, writing my SFD in the form of a letter, or even fantasizing about what I'd like to say to someone, can help me get clear on the story I'm making up. As I mentioned in Chapter Three, "Owning Our Stories," the value of writing and storytelling came up in the research, but it wasn't until I thought about this particular story that I connected it to myself. It's nice to know there's some constructive use for all those conversations and revenge schemes I rehearse in my head when I'm lying in bed at night.

This story is a great reminder of the power of engaging with a therapist or coach, or being part of a support group that gives us the space to explore our emotions and experiences without judgment. My therapist, Diana, retired at the end of our work together (*I know, don't say it*). Since then I've had a hard time finding a safe place to do this work. I worked with a leadership coach concerning a very specific work crisis, and that was invaluable, but in writing this story for the book, I've realized that I could use more consistent support. I believe we all need that. It's unfair to ask our partners to hold space for the thrashing about that is a necessary part of the reckoning and the rumble, especially when they're part of the story. The same is true for our colleagues.

Over the past two years, I've been surprised and heartened by the number of leaders I've encountered who either work closely with a therapist or coach, or are part of a small group of other leaders who meet specifically to support each other in working through tough emotional issues. I'm reminded, in particular, of a group of eight Dallas CEOs who invited me to join them last year for one of their regular support gatherings. For years, this group has come together to share and work through the exact kind of issues I'm talking about in this book—what it takes to be authentic, to be all in, and to fall and get back up. In fact, each of the members had written his story using Joseph Campbell's hero's journey as a framework.

The evening I met with them, several of the men shared their journeys. It was transformative. The stories were full of courage, heartbreak, wild success, and devastating personal and professional failures. With that group, they had created what I call "a safe container"—a place where people can share experiences honestly, knowing that what they share will be respected and kept in confidence. The story I'm about to tell reminded me of why we all need this kind of support: *We can't be brave in the big world without at least one small safe space to work through our fears and falls.*

LONG VOWELS AND SHORT FUSES

Part of my email-sorting process is to review the sender and subject lines of each message before opening it. Blindly clicking on emails is like opening the front door without looking through the peephole: It can be dangerous. On this particular day several years ago, one name sent up a flare as I scrolled down the list, though at first I couldn't quite put my finger on why.

I read the name over and over as I tried to match it with the places and groups that make up my life: The university? The church? The kids' schools? The neighborhood? Speaking events? Nothing. I pushed my chair back a little bit and read the name out loud. When it finally came to me, I rolled my eyes so hard I'm surprised they're not still lodged in the back of my head.

The email was from a woman whom we'll call Pamela. It has the same number of syllables as her actual name, which is important for no real reason except that even the way she said her name bugged me: "Pam-ah-la," as if I were two years old and just now learning to "use my words."

I'd met Pamela several weeks earlier, after a talk I gave at a fundraising event and luncheon. I first saw her when I was standing in the lunch buffet line right after the lecture. I have pretty set boundaries for eating at my speaking events. I don't eat in public before I speak. This means that if I'm invited to speak at a luncheon, I'm going to eat before I arrive and just drink water while I'm waiting to be introduced. I'm too nervous to eat, and there's no good way to pick pepper out of your teeth when you're sitting at a table next to the stage and surrounded by hundreds of people watching you.

I also don't like to eat after events very often because I'm extremely introverted. People who don't know me always assume that I'm an extrovert, while the people who do know me would describe my severe introversion as one of my defining characteristics. Being onstage is comfortable for me because it's my work, but put me in the middle of a cocktail party and you'll find me with a frozen smile, wishing I could curl up under a table in the fetal position. On this particular day, I was joining a small group of college students for a thirty-minute lunch after I spoke. This seemed completely doable: I love talking to students. It feels like home to me.

As I stood in the buffet line, I spotted Pamela right away. I wasn't sure what she was telling the people who stood between us, but I could see that she was picking them off one by one, moving ever closer to me. Finally, when there were only two people left standing between us, I heard her tell the woman behind me, "I'm sorry. I need to talk to Dr. Brown about event issues."

When I finally turned around, she was literally six inches away. With some awkward squeezing, she drew her wrist up against her chest and stuck out her hand for a quick introduction handshake. I backed up as much as I could, but there was still only about a foot between us. I raised my eyebrows in a kind of greeting and said, "Hello, I'm Brené. Nice to meet you." There was no way in hell that I was going to attempt a handshake in the minuscule space between us.

By this time we were about three people away from the food. I turned around so we were both facing forward and spoke to her over my shoulder. "So, are you on the event team? Everything turned out really well."

"Oh, no," she replied. "I'm here representing a large chain of organizations. I wanted to talk to you about the possibility of doing some events for us. I attend events, like a scout, looking for talented speakers."

I was a little annoyed at her subterfuge, but I managed to stay civil. In the three minutes it took to make our way from the silverware, past the chicken salad, and to the cans of soda at the end of the table, I learned these three things from Pamela:

1. She hates where she works because her bosses are always telling her that her job would be the first to go if there was downsizing.

2. She isn't really trained in mental health, but she's seen so many presentations that she could do it better than most of the people who do it for a living.

3. Her dream is eventually to stop scouting for speakers and become a speaker herself.

As we walked away from the buffet, plates and drinks in hand, I turned to her and said, "Well, it was nice to meet you," then kept walking. I sat down at a table that was reserved for our group. It was empty except for purses and event programs that students had left to save their spaces. I purposely sat down in an unsaved seat sandwiched between two saved seats so I could give those students my attention. Following resolutely behind me, Pamela set her plate down next to my plate and moved someone's jacket and event program to free the seat.

Before I could say anything, she was beside me. I watched her eyes grow small and her jaw tighten. "My bosses send me around to find good speakers. I could speak circles around most people. Of course, I can't tell them that. They want credentialed people. Like a list of letters behind your name makes you a good speaker. But I can't ever challenge them because they'll remind me that I'm expendable. I'm tempted to tell them I can't find any decent speakers and offer my services. They're too stupid and concerned about money to recognize talent that's right in front of them."

By now the students had returned to the table. The student whose belongings had been moved looked confused for a second and then sat down. Pamela practically leaped out of her seat upon their arrival. Taking in the table, she squealed, "Look! Look! We get to have lunch with the speaker! Isn't she just fabulous? She's *just precious*!"

Listening to her, I still sensed the bitterness and fear in her words. She was working hard to fake excitement for the newcomers, but I wondered how long she could keep that anger and resentment at bay. I wasn't sure why she was so angry, but it was clear that she was. I stayed for thirty minutes, trying to keep focused on the students, before I rose from my seat. The students looked at me with understanding and a little bit of nervous desperation at being left with this woman. Pamela stared up at me with barely cloaked contempt. It would have been so easy to say, "Thanks for ruining my lunch, you nut job," but that would have been bad manners. I just said, "Please excuse me, I need to pack for my flight."

The memories of meeting Pamela were enough to convince me to wait awhile before opening her email. I read a few other emails, made myself a cup of coffee, sat back down at my computer, and clicked.

> Dr. Brown,
> I have told my boss Sheryl that I highly recommend you based on the fact that most conference attendees seemed to enjoy your presentation. You will probably hear from her in the next couple of weeks.
>
> Just a bit of friendly feedback: If you're going to position yourself as an expert and scholar in your area, I think it's important that you pronounce your colleagues' names correctly. When you quoted Pema Chödrön, you said, "PEE-ma CHO-dron." The correct pronunciation is Pim-a Chod-ron.
>
> Sincerely,
> Pamela

The words were perfectly clear on the computer screen, but in my head they started to dance around, getting all jumbled up with my fear. *Had I made a fool of myself?* Her intent linked up with my shame and made it impossible for me to keep it all straight. Within a matter of seconds, I had turned "If you're going to position yourself as an expert and scholar" into "Stop pretending that you're an expert and a scholar." I felt like a scared middle-schooler.

I found myself completely hijacked by "that moment"— a moment that I have described to tens of thousands of people. I wrote the book on that moment, literally. It is the moment when shame crashes over you with such force that you go into do-or-die survival mode.

Ironically, I always warn people—especially mental health professionals—not to be seduced into believing that they can manage these moments simply because they've learned how they work. We call shame the master emotion for a reason.

Had I been able to whisper in my own ear as I sat there staring at this email and fighting off the pain of feeling like an exposed impostor, I would have told myself: *This is the moment. Don't do anything. Don't say anything. Just breathe and feel your way through it. Don't hide out. Don't suck up. Don't fight back. Don't talk, type, or make contact with anyone until you get back on your emotional feet. You'll be okay.*

Unfortunately, I couldn't whisper those assurances to myself. Mispronouncing Pema Chödrön's name had hit all of my shame triggers related to "never being good enough." Rather than sounding like a refined academic, I imagined that I had sounded just like Minnie Pearl on *Hee Haw:* "Howwwdeeeee! Let's give a warm welcome to our little Buddhist friend, Sister PEE-ma CHO-dron!" *Cue the banjos.*

My heart raced and rage coursed through my veins with such force that my entire body was shaking. I sat rigid in my chair. My eyes were ablaze. The heat was unbearable, and I became convinced that sitting still for too long would result in Houston's first case of spontaneous human combustion. I finally pounded my fist on the computer table. "Oh, that pinch-faced, passive-aggressive shithead!" I yelled. I pulled in as much air as I could through my nose and pushed it out of my mouth. Again. Again. A cool calm returned to my body. Not the kinder, gentler type of calm that I teach people about, but the kind of calm that comes before calculated cruelty.

I shut down my email program and opened up Microsoft Word. I would craft my response in Word first so I could make sure there were no spelling or grammatical errors. Nothing dulls the edge of an otherwise lethal weapon like a *their* that should be a *there* or an *effect* that should be an *affect*.

I opened up a new document and, just like Charlie Daniels sings in "The Devil Went Down to Georgia," fire flew from my fingertips:

> *The devil opened up his case*
> *And he said, I'll start this show,*
> *And fire flew from his fingertips*
> *As he rosined up his bow.*
>
> *Then he pulled the bow across the strings*
> *And it made an evil hiss,*
> *And a band of demons joined in*
> *And it sounded something like this.*

With every keystroke, I felt better. I wrote and edited and wrote and edited. When I was done, I copied the letter and pasted it into an email addressed to Pamela. Just one millisecond before I hit "Send," I panicked. I was flooded with uncertainty. It's hard to fight fire with fire without backup. I needed support and a tiny smidgen of approval.

In addition to perfecting and performing, I am an expert pollster. When in doubt, survey! So, in call after call to friends, I explained the situation and asked for advice. After five calls, it was unanimous: (1) She was indeed a pinch-faced, passive-aggressive, wannabe shithead, and (2) I should *not* send the email. Two of my friends thought it wasn't worth it because it would jeopardize my chance of speaking for this large national organization; one friend told me that she avoided conflict at all cost and advised the same for me; and my other two friends thought it was just a bad use of my time and energy.

I still wasn't sure. My email response was magnificent. It's so hard to let go of that kind of craftsmanship. Plus, I had the opportunity to hurt someone who'd hurt me—those opportunities don't come around every day. I finally printed copies of Pamela's email and my email, and stuck them both in my purse. I had an appointment with Diana the next day. She could help me decide.

I plopped down on Diana's sofa, pulled out the emails, and said, "I need your help. I'm going crazy." We both chuckled, then I clarified, "No, really. I have a specific crazy thing—not a general going-crazy thing."

I set the whole thing up for Diana. I told her about how Pamela had cut the line, the lunch, everything. Then I read the email from Pamela aloud. Diana grimaced. I acknowledged her frown by saying, "Pretty shitty, right?"

Diana said, "Yes. Totally shitty."

I told her that I thought Pamela was a pinch-faced, passive-aggressive shithead and that all of my friends thought so, too. Diana hit me back with a look that said, *Not interested in your survey results*. Diana wasn't too supportive of my living my life according to polls.

"Okay, anyway . . . are you ready for my response?"

Diana said, "Ready."

I unfolded my reply and read:

Dear Pamela,

I received your email regarding future event collaborations. I'm copying Sheryl, your boss, on this email as it pertains to both of you.

I have some serious concerns about working with your organization. During our lunch in Miami, you told me that your bosses are "stupid and only concerned about money." I'm not sure if this is an accurate representation of your organizational environment or was merely an inappropriate expression of your frustration regarding your current work situation. Either way, I found these comments to be very unprofessional, especially coming from someone who was publicly representing such a well-respected organization.

Secondly, I understand your desire to become a speaker; however, I was alarmed when you mentioned that you're considering telling your superiors that you were unable to find a suitable speaker in the hopes that they would invite you to speak. While I agree with your statement that credentials are not a prerequisite for being an effective speaker, I do hope you understand the credentialing requirements of lectures done for continuing education and training. Regardless of your talents, to position yourself as a mental health professional would have serious ethical implications for your organization.

Again, I appreciate your recommendation to Sheryl; however, before I can commit to speaking on behalf of your organization, I'll need some clarification regarding the concerns outlined in this email.

Best,

Brené Brown,

PhD, LMSW

I was pleased as punch. I felt as if I doubled in size as I read that letter. I felt all proud and puffy, like a third-grader reading a teacher's commendation to her mother.

Diana said, "Wow. You cc'd her boss. Going for total annihilation, huh?"

I smiled. "Like my dad says, 'You mess with the bull, you get the horns.'"

Diana was still for a moment, then responded, "So, tell me . . . when you picture Pamela reading this email, what is she feeling? How do you want her to feel when she reads this, knowing that her boss has a copy of it?"

Creasing the printouts, I wondered where to start. I'm sure on an unconscious level I knew how I wanted her to feel—I'm sure it's what drove me. I thought about it for a minute, then told Diana, "I want her to feel small. I want her to feel 'found out.' I want her to feel scared, like she's been caught. I want her to squirm . . . I want . . ."

A wave of heat made its way up from my chest until my entire face felt as if it were melting. This time it wasn't the fire of rage: It was the slow burn of truth. A terrible silence filled the air, and the room started to do what it always does whenever a painful insight is washing over me—it became unbearably stuffy. I felt unbearably small.

To make matters worse, Diana started doing the weird face thing that she always did when she had to sit silently while truth washed over me. Her eyes winced, she pursed her mouth a little bit, and she took on the look of a mother watching her infant get a shot. I knew the look—I had worn it many times, as a mother, a teacher, and a social worker.

Her face said, *I don't like this either, but it's why we're here. Just hang on. I can't stop the hurt, but I'm right here to help you feel your way through it.*

I set my printouts down on the couch. Then I kicked off my flip-flops, pulled my knees up to my chest, wrapped my arms around my legs, and rested my forehead on my knees. I sat very still.

"Oh God. I can't believe this. This is terrible." I slowly repeated what I had just said. "I want her to feel small and stupid and found out. I want her to feel ashamed and afraid and not good enough. I want her to feel like an impostor who's been caught."

Diana still said nothing. A kind, nonjudgmental, nurturing nothing. She had a way of helping me believe in normal-crazy. Like, however crazy we may be, we're all the same, and the only danger of normal-crazy is not knowing what you're doing and why you're doing it. I never felt ashamed with her. Ever.

I didn't lift my head when I said, "This makes perfect sense, but I hate it. This is such bullshit."

Diana always knew exactly what to say: nothing.

My forehead still resting on my knees, I realized that I needed to say it out loud. A decade of studying shame had taught me the value of doing the one thing that felt the scariest and most counterintuitive—I had to speak shame. I had to say this out loud: "I have such shame about mispronouncing words and things like that. I feel stupid and small and found out and ashamed and afraid and like an impostor and like someone who got caught pretending to be smart."

There was just a whole bunch more quiet after that. Of *course* I wanted Pamela to feel like an impostor who'd been exposed—that's exactly how I felt. *I'll never write enough books or earn enough degrees to meet the standard I set up for "smart"— the* New Yorker *smart, the Ivy League smart, the anywhere-but- where-I'm-from smart.* No credentials or letters behind my name can change the fact that I am a fifth-generation Texan with imperfect grammar, the tendency to cuss too much when I'm tired or fired up, and an ongoing struggle to police my long vowels and colloquialisms.

As I sat there in the uncomfortable silence, the first visual that crept into my mind was that dreadful scene in *The Silence of the Lambs* when Hannibal Lecter exposes Jodie Foster's character, FBI agent Clarice Starling: "You're so-o-o ambitious, aren't you? You know what you look like to me, with your good bag and your cheap shoes? You look like a rube. A well-scrubbed, hustling rube, with a little taste. Good nutrition's given you some length of bone, but you're not more than one generation from poor white trash, are you, Agent Starling? And that accent you've tried so desperately to shed—pure West

Virginia. What does your father do? Is he a coal miner? Does he stink of the lamp?"

I wanted Diana to say something—to make it better. I wanted her to chase down Hannibal Lecter and all of my gremlins and make them go away. But she would never jump in and interfere with the critically important process of my actually feeling something. My work with her was about letting all of the hard-fought knowledge that I kept stored in my head seep down into my very protected heart. I needed space to let that happen, and if there's one thing Diana could do, it was hold space. She could hold the space I needed to feel. She could hold whatever space I needed to cuss and thrash around and hate people. She could hold the space I needed to be exhausted and imperfect and angry. She's an extraordinary space holder.

When I finally put my feet back on the floor and looked up, I said, "This is painful. So much worse than pissed off. So much more painful than anger."

Diana said, "Yes. This is harder than pissed off."

Then we were quiet for another long stretch of time.

Finally, I looked at her and said, "So, is writing a pissed-off letter a pretty reliable tool? If you figure out how you want to make someone feel, can you always use that to understand how you're feeling?"

By this point in our relationship, Diana was keenly aware of my love of formulas and tools. She said, "Every situation is different, but I think it could be a very helpful way for you to explore what you're feeling—especially when you're in 'mess with the bull' mode."

THE RECKONING

I'm pretty sure that having fire flying from my fingertips and fearing spontaneous combustion are solid physiological markers of emotion. My first facedown-in-the-arena moment in this story happened when I read Pamela's email. However, not having a rising strong practice back then, I chose getting even over getting curious. My second facedown moment happened on Diana's couch when I realized that my letter was a hurtful attempt to shift shame from myself to Pamela. Mercifully, with Diana's help, I chose curiosity this time.

To be honest, choosing curiosity when I'm in shame is something that I'll need to stay mindful of for the rest of my life. I shared this story with my dad and told him that we needed to come up with a new bull saying. Thank your lucky stars that you weren't on that call. I get my predilection for metaphors from him, and we spent thirty minutes talking about bulls tearing through emotional china shops and staying atop shame bulls for eight seconds to qualify for the rodeo. We finally gave up trying to be clever in favor of something straightforward. "How about: 'When you mess with the bull, the bull is going into time-out for thirty minutes,'" I said. My dad's response tells you everything you need to know about us: "Well, Sis, it doesn't have quite the ring or the gravitas, but if you can wrestle that bull into the barn while you sort out your emotions, you'll save yourself some serious heartache."

THE RUMBLE

To get to the delta and the key learnings, I had to rumble with shame, identity, criticism, and nostalgia. One reason for this is the complexity of shame resilience. In my earlier books, I talk about the four elements of shame resilience that had emerged in my research. Men and women with high levels of shame resilience:

1. Understand shame and recognize what messages and expectations trigger shame for them.

2. Practice critical awareness by reality-checking the messages and expectations that tell us that being imperfect means being inadequate.

3. Reach out and share their stories with people they trust.

4. Speak shame—they use the word *shame,* they talk about how they're feeling, and they ask for what they need.

In the process of reality-checking the messages that fuel shame, we often have to dig into identity, labels, and stereotypes. We also have to explore whether the expectations are rooted, as they often are, in nostalgia or the perilous practice of comparing a current struggle with an edited version of "the way things used to be."

Rumbling with Identity

> I dearly love the state of Texas, but I consider that a
> harmless perversion on my part, and discuss it only
> with consenting adults.
>
> —Molly Ivins

Integration is the soul of rising strong. We have to be whole to be wholehearted. To embrace and love who we are, we have to reclaim and reconnect with the parts of ourselves we've orphaned over the years. We have to call back home all of those parts of ourselves that we have abandoned. Carl Jung called this individuation.

In his book *Finding Meaning in the Second Half of Life,* Jungian analyst James Hollis writes, "Perhaps Jung's most compelling contribution is the idea of *individuation,* that is, the lifelong project of becoming more nearly the whole person we were meant to be—what the gods intended, not the parents, or the tribe, or, especially, the easily intimidated or the inflated ego. While revering the mystery of others, our individuation summons each of us to stand in the presence of our own mystery, and become more fully responsible for who we are in this journey we call our life."

One of the greatest challenges of becoming myself has been acknowledging that I'm not who I thought I was supposed to be or who I always pictured myself being. From the time I was in ninth grade, I wanted out of my Texan identity. I wanted to be just like Annie Hall. I dreamed of the day I could be a sophisticated New York intellectual with a loft in SoHo and a weekly appointment with an expensive analyst. I wanted to be erudite, stylish, and fashionably complicated.

Well, as it turns out, I've got more in common with Annie Oakley than I do with Annie Hall. I'm a cusser from a long maternal line of cussers. I call the refrigerator the *icebox* and the countertops *drainboards*. I grew up hunting deer and shooting skeet. I don't understand why everyone doesn't use the words *tump* and *fixin'* and *y'all*. They're efficient. (Why waste time saying "turn and dump" when you can just say, "Kids! Be careful! Y'all are fixin' to tump those glasses over.") Besides, *y'all* is much more gender friendly than *you guys*. And, as Pamela pointed out, I can run my vowels long and hard.

I once received an email asking me to reconsider my "violent animal sayings." Given my total squeamishness and low tolerance for violence, I was shocked. However, while sharing a parenting story with a large audience, I apparently said something like, "I couldn't get the kids dressed, and I was running around the house like a chicken with its head cut off. Finally, when Charlie wouldn't raise his hands up so I could slip on his shirt, I said, 'Skin a rabbit right this minute! We're late for school. I mean business.'" I'll admit this sounds pretty gross. But honestly, you don't even notice it when you're raised hearing this stuff. It's not as if you're actually envisioning a skinned rabbit or a headless chicken.

Sometimes I get nice emails, too. Nothing praising my amazing scholarly stage presence or my diction, but nice emails nonetheless. Like the time in Boise when my microphone fell off its stand for the twentieth time and, out of total frustration, I shouted, "Well, shit fire and save matches!" in front of 1,500 people. I got a sweet email from a woman who wrote, "It made me cry when you said that. I hadn't heard anyone say that since my granny died."

Slowly but surely, I've let go of the images of me in Manhattan and started trying to embrace the real me. If I stand in the "presence of my own mystery," I see a girl who:

Was born in San Antonio.
Was educated at the University of Texas at Austin.

Was married at a hundred-year-old honky-tonk on
    Cibilo Creek.
Teaches at the University of Houston.
Gave birth to two children in the Texas Medical
    Center.
Is raising a family in Houston.
Plays in the Texas Hill Country.
Spends summers fishing in Galveston.
And is having a lifelong love affair with this great state.

But I also see the shadows that stretch over the hills and valleys of my life and this state. As I continued to dig into my Texas roots in an effort to integrate and become the one whole person I was meant to be, I learned something very powerful about the connection between my annihilation acumen and my upbringing. There's a reason that our state motto is "Don't Mess with Texas."

From the time we're old enough to stand, most girls raised in this state are taught the opposite of integration. We're raised to compartmentalize. We are raised to be tough and tender, but never at the same time. I was schooled on important matters like when to wear white shoes, how to set a table, and why upstanding families use only white meat in their chicken salad. But I was also taught how to spit, shoot a gun, and throw a Hail Mary pass on third-and-ten.

We're taught how to be tough and sweet, and, of equal importance, we're taught *when* to be tough and *when* to be sweet. As we get older, the consequences of being tough and independent when you're supposed to be tender and helpless increase in severity. For young girls, the penalties range from a stern look to descriptors like "tomboy" or "headstrong." But as we get older, the consequences for being too assertive or independent take on a darker nature—shame, ridicule, blame, and judgment.

Most of us were too young and having too much fun to notice when we crossed the fine line into "behavior not becoming of a lady"—actions that call for a painful penalty. Now, as a woman and a mother of both a daughter and a son, I can tell you exactly when it happens. It happens on the day girls start spitting farther, shooting better, and completing more passes than the boys. When that day comes, we start to get the message—in subtle and not-so-subtle ways—that it's best that we start focusing on staying thin, minding our manners, and not being so smart or speaking out so much in class that we call attention to our intellect. This is a pivotal day for boys, too. This is the moment when they're introduced to the white horse. Emotional stoicism and self-control are rewarded, and displays of emotion are punished. Vulnerability is now weakness. Anger becomes an acceptable substitute for fear, which is forbidden.

I don't think there's any question that while also serving to keep existing power structures in place, the rules punish both men and women. And it's not just men who discourage integration and enforce the rules; it's the women, too. While there are many women fighting for a different way of life, there is still a powerful core group of sisters who have pledged their allegiance to a system where tender and tough are so driven apart from their natural coexistence that each one metastasizes into a dangerous version of itself. Tender turns into ass kissing and people pleasing. Tough turns into neck wringing and bad mouthing.

These are the roles and behaviors that many of us were raised to adopt, even if they don't reflect who we are deep down inside. Gender politics is a lot like dancing. If you've ever seen a couple cutting a rug to a fast Texas polka, you get the picture. Gender itself is a combination of highly choreographed steps and well-rehearsed compromises. No matter who is calling the dance, it takes two to two-step. And while the music and the moves may differ by location or background, the underlying rhythms are pretty much the same. From Long Island to Silicon Valley, a fear of being perceived as weak forces men into pretending they are never afraid, lonely, confused, vulnerable, or wrong; and an extreme fear of being perceived as cold-hearted, imperfect, high maintenance, or hostile forces women to pretend they're never exhausted, ambitious, pissed off, or even hungry.

Rumbling with Nostalgia

Nostalgia sounds relatively harmless, even like something to indulge in with a modicum of comfort, until we examine the two Greek root words that form *nostalgia: nostos,* meaning "returning home," and *algos,* meaning "pain." Romanticizing our history to relieve pain is seductive. But it's also dangerous. In fact, in the case of my own family, the seduction of nostalgia bordered on lethal.

When you're raised by a wild pack of storytellers the way I was, nostalgia is the currency of the realm. A certain poetry is assigned to those hard-living and fun-loving characters whose stories of mayhem and mischief were legendary in our family. No matter how many times we heard the tales, we loved them, and we loved knowing that a little outlaw blood coursed through our veins. But the truth cut right through the nostalgia of those stories one afternoon when I sat down to work on one of the last projects in my master's program—a family genogram.

A genogram is a tool that behavioral health professionals use to visually map out a client's relationships and history. Genograms utilize complex symbols and lines to represent health histories and the social-emotional relationships between family members. I love maps and I love relationships—so I gladly got out my paper, sharpened my colored pencils, and called my mom to talk with her about our family history. Two hours later, I was staring at a map that could have been titled, "Hardscrabble, Texas. Population: Brené's Family."

Looking at that map, I realized that much of what had been dressed up as hard living was really addiction and mental health issues. Yes, there were wonderful folkloric stories of struggle, triumph, and rebellion, but there was also story after story of trauma and loss. I remember at one point in our conversation saying, "Jesus, Mom. This is scary. What the hell?" Her reply was, "I know. I lived a lot of it."

I graduated two weeks later, on May 11, 1996. I stopped drinking and smoking and went to my first Alcoholics Anonymous meeting on May 12, 1996. I wasn't sure if I was an alcoholic, but I had been plenty wild in my teens and twenties, and I did *not* want to become a hard-living character in someone else's yarn or another casualty of addiction on someone's genogram.

In *The Gifts of Imperfection,* I tell the story of not quite fit-ting in at AA and being told by my first sponsor that she thought I had the "pupu platter of addictions"—not too much of any one thing, but enough of each one to be concerned. She suggested that it would be best if I covered all my bases and just quit drinking, smoking, co-parenting my siblings, and comfort eating. I took her advice, and let's just say it freed up a lot of time. I haven't had a drink or a cigarette in almost twenty years. I'm doing much better with the family stuff, and I'm taking the food—my real drug of choice—one day at a time, as they say.

Over the past two decades, I've learned that what I really need is a Vulnerability Anonymous meeting—a gathering place for people who like to numb the feelings that come with not having control, swimming in uncertainty, or cringing from emotional exposure. When I wiped the nostalgia off my history to uncover the real trauma behind many of those stories, I began to understand why we didn't talk about emotions growing up. **Of all the things trauma takes away from us, the worst is our willingness, or even our ability, to be vulnerable. There's a reclaiming that has to happen.**

Sometimes, the deep love we feel for our parents or the sense of loyalty to our family often create a mythology that gets in the way of our efforts to look past nostalgia and toward truth. We don't want to betray anyone—we don't want to be the first to get curious and ask questions or challenge the stories. We ask ourselves, *How can I love and protect my family if I'm rumbling with these hard truths?* For me, the answer to that question is another question: *How can I love and protect my family if I'm* not *rumbling with these hard truths?*

We know that genetics loads the gun and environment

pulls the trigger. In order to teach our children about rising strong, we first need to teach them the truth about their history. I've told both of my kids, "Drinking may not be the same for you as it is for your friends. Here's what you need to know and understand." I also don't frame my own wild stories as war stories from "the good old days." Yes, I have wonderful family memories and stories of crazy adventures that I love to share, but when it comes to addiction, medical histories, and mental health, I believe that nostalgia is deadly.

Stephanie Coontz, author of *The Way We Never Were: American Families and the Nostalgia Trap,* puts her finger on some real dangers of nostalgia. She writes, "There's nothing wrong with celebrating the good things in our past. But memories, like witnesses, do not always tell the truth, the whole truth, and nothing but the truth. We need to cross-examine them, recognizing and accepting the inconsistencies and gaps in those that make us proud and happy as well as those that cause us pain."

Coontz suggests that the best way to reality-check our nostalgic ideas is to uncover and examine the tradeoffs and contradictions that are often deeply buried in all of our memories. As an example, Coontz writes:

I have interviewed many white people who have fond memories of their lives in the 1950s and early 1960s. The ones who never cross-examined those memories to get at the complexities were the ones most hostile to the civil rights and the women's movements, which they saw as destroying the harmonious world they remembered. But others could see that their own good experiences were in some ways dependent on unjust social arrangements, or on bad experiences for others. Some white people recognized that their happy memories of childhood included a black housekeeper who was always available to them because she couldn't be available to her children.

Coontz is careful to point out that the people who rumbled with their nostalgia didn't feel guilt or shame about their good memories—instead, their digging made them more adaptable to change. She concludes, "Both as individuals and as a society, we must learn to view the past in three dimensions before we can move into the fourth dimension of the future."

There is a line in director Paolo Sorrentino's gorgeous and haunting film *The Great Beauty* that illuminates the pain often underlying nostalgia. One of the main characters, a man reconciling his past while longing for love and relevance in his present life, asks, "What's wrong with feeling nostalgic? It's the only distraction left for those who have no faith in the future." Nostalgia can be a dangerous distraction, and it can underpin a feeling of resignation or hopelessness after a fall. In the rising strong process, looking back is done in the service of moving forward with an integrated and whole heart.

Rumbling with Criticism

To avoid criticism say nothing, do nothing, be nothing.
—Aristotle

All criticism is not created equal and certainly doesn't have the same intention behind it. When I think about Aristotle, I picture a group of philosophers gathered in a grove of olive trees for discussions about knowledge and meaning. I think of criticism as reasoned, logical, and respectful challenges among men and women with a shared passion for expanding thought and discovering truth. Strictly emotional and personal arguments were seen as the antithesis of knowledge-building. Criticism was a social conversation between people who all risked owning and sharing their ideas for the sake of building knowledge. For criticism to be useful, you have to have some skin in the game.

Today when we think about criticism, we picture mean-spirited, hurtful personal jabs made by anonymous users on Twitter. Personal emotional attacks made by people not engaged in problem-solving have zero value in building or creating anything—they're only an attempt to tear down and invalidate what others are attempting to build, with no meaningful contribution to replace what has been destroyed. This pervasive type of criticism—what I call cheap-seat criticism (or chicken-shit shots)—is why Roosevelt's quote "It is not the critic who counts" resonates so strongly with people. For those of us trying to live in the arena—trying to show up and be seen when there's no guaranteed outcome—cheap-seat criticism is dangerous. Here's why:

1. It hurts. The really cruel things people say about us are painful. Cheap-seat folks are season-ticket holders in the arena. They're good at what they do and they can hit us right where it hurts: our shame triggers. For women, they'll go after appearance, body image, mothering, and anything else that could dent be-perfect-and-make-everyone-happy expectations. For me, they'll go straight for the jugular—any appearance of weakness or failure. This is dangerous because after a few hits, we start playing smaller and smaller, making ourselves harder targets. We're more difficult to hit when we're small, but we're also less likely to make a contribution.

2. It doesn't hurt. We turn to the old standby, "I don't give a shit what anyone thinks." We stop caring or, at the very least, we start pretending that we don't care. This is also dangerous. Not caring what people think is its own hustle. The armor we have to wear to make *not caring* a reality is heavy, uncomfortable, and quickly obsolete. If you look at the history of armor (as any history-loving vulnerability researcher would) you see a forever-escalating story of weapons and fighting styles. You cover every inch of your body with plate armor? Okay, we'll start fighting with a tapered sword that can penetrate the small gaps. You cover those gaps? We'll use maces that can cause injury *through* your armor. Not caring what people think is a hustle, and it's not winnable.

3. When cheap-seat criticism becomes the loudest, most prevalent type of criticism we encounter, it pushes out the idea that thoughtful criticism and feedback can be and often are useful. We stop teaching people how to offer constructive, helpful feedback and critiques, and, in order to save ourselves, we shut down all incoming data. We start to exist in echo chambers where nothing we do or say is challenged. This is also dangerous.

When we stop caring what people think, we lose our capacity for connection. But when we are defined by what people think, we lose the courage to be vulnerable. The solution is getting totally clear on the people whose opinions actually matter. On a one-inch-by-one-inch square of paper, I want you to write down the names of the people who really matter. This is a sacred little space. If you have more names than can fit on a square this size, you need to edit. These should be the people who love you not despite your imperfections and vulnerabilities, but because of them. When you're facedown in the arena, these are the folks who will pick you up and confirm that the fall totally sucked, then remind you that you're brave and they'll be there to dust you off the next time. You should also include the people who are brave enough to say "I disagree" or "I think you're wrong," and who will question you when they see you acting outside of your values.

I carry my square in my wallet. That way when I'm trying to hack into the back end of Amazon to find the IP address of the jerk who left the hurtful review about me and not the book, I can catch myself. *Yes, this hurts. But he's not on my list.* When I'm struggling to make a difficult decision, rather than closing my eyes and trying to imagine how the cheap seats will respond, I go to someone on my list who will hold me accountable to my own standards.

THE REVOLUTION

I was full of shame and fear after reading Pamela's email that day. But the real pain came from comparing my SFD to what I learned from my rumbles and from realizing that the rock hadn't been rolled on top of me—I had crawled under a rock of my own making. My key learnings were:

1. I was holding on to an idea of intellectual stature that defined *smart* as everything I was not and as everything my history would prevent me from ever being. I basically defined *smart* as "the opposite of me and where I'm from." Toni Morrison wrote, "Definitions belong to the definers, not the defined," and I learned that I must redefine what I believe is valuable and make sure I'm included within that definition.

2. I came to love who I am and where I'm from. Yes, some of it is hard and broken and rough around the edges, but much of it is beautiful and strong. Most important, all of it made me who I am.

3. I realized that I am capable of engaging in the exact same behaviors I consider unethical and hurtful. Yes, I received a crappy, mean-spirited email, but my own capacity for cruelty was a source of greater pain than what the sender inflicted with her email. Being curious aligns with my values. Being mean is outside of my integrity.

I have a vivid memory of being a teenager and sitting with Me-Ma and her friend Louise, listening to the two of them argue about which pair of dancers on *The Lawrence Welk Show* was the best. *Lawrence Welk* was a big-band variety show that Me-Ma and I loved to watch on Saturday nights. Most nights, we'd try to learn the steps of the new routines, dancing through the house together in our pajamas and cowboy boots. I'd lead and Me-Ma would laugh. Me-Ma had won her share of polka contests, and she believed that there was no finer dance team than Bobby and Cissy—the most famous of Welk's dancers. She was convinced that they were a "real-life couple," and according to Me-Ma, "nothing beats a polka danced by people in love."

Supper that night was one of the standbys at my grandmother's house: chipped beef on toast and canned green beans
chased down with cold iced tea served in tall brown plastic
glasses from the Ace restaurant supply store. At the end of the
meal, Me-Ma brought out a speckled blue melamine plate of
orange petit fours from Johnson's Bakery—hands down the
best bakery on the south side of San Antonio.

Curly, Me-Ma's husband, was a few feet away in his recliner
in the living room. He was a forklift driver at Pearl Brewery,
and he didn't have much to say beyond weather updates and
random comments on the intersection of his schedule and the
TV lineup. "Time for *Gunsmoke*," he'd say. "Waiting for *Hee
Haw*." "Early shift tomorrow—won't make Carson tonight." As
Me-Ma, Louise, and I were chatting at the kitchen table, he
was smoking a cigarette and chuckling along with Hoss and
Little Joe trading barbs on *Bonanza*, while holding a small tran-
sistor radio in his lap. It was set to KBUC, the classic country
station. The radio volume was turned down low enough for
him to hear the TV, but loud enough so he didn't miss any
weather alerts.

In a hushed voice, my grandmother leaned across the table
and started telling me and Louise a story about how earlier in
the week Curly had tried to pull a stack of lawn chairs out
of the back shed after he heard a critter scurrying around behind the push mower. Between fits of laughter and one long
drag on her cigarette, she whispered, "It was hotter than hell
out there, and the mosquitoes were big enough to saddle. But I
couldn't go in the house. I just stood there staring at him while
he yanked at those chairs to get at whatever was inside. It was
like watching someone wrestling a greased pig in the dark.

When that big ol' possum finally showed itself and ran out of the shed, he threw those damn lawn chairs straight up in the air and took off like a ruptured duck."

I laughed until I couldn't breathe. The story was funny, but what was even better was the fact that Me-Ma and Louise were both literally knee-slappers. They'd push their chairs back from the table and slap their knees over and over until they had slapped every ounce of funny from a joke. In the midst of completely falling out, I vaguely remember thinking, *Who says these things? Who talks like this?*

Little did I know then that the answer to that question would eventually be *Me—I talk like that.* But now I know why. Not only was I was raised on these sayings, they're strangely accurate, too. I can't think of a better way to describe what it feels like to try and get your head and heart around *who you are* and *where you come from* than wrestling a greased pig in the dark. Our identities are always changing and growing, they're not meant to be pinned down. Our histories are never all good or all bad, and running from the past is the surest way to be defined by it. That's when it owns us. The key is bringing light to the darkness—developing awareness and understanding.

And just because we know and understand something in our heads doesn't mean that we won't slip up when we're overwhelmed by emotion. I can't tell you how many times I have stood on a stage and said, "While it's hard to look at the areas in our lives where we feel shame, it's often much more painful to acknowledge that we've all used shame and caused others significant pain." Yet it took experiences like the one with Pamela, and my work with Diana, to fully understand how dangerous I can be when I'm backed into a corner.

Some of us, when backed into emotional corners, put our hands over our faces and slide down the wall onto the floor. We just want to hide. Some of us try to people-please our way out of that corner. Some of us come out swinging. What is important is to know who we are and how we tend to respond in these situations. As much as I despise that intense scene in *The Silence of the Lambs,* it opened my eyes to the fact that sometimes I'm the belittled Agent Starling, and sometimes, as much as I hate to admit it, I'm the one serving up people with "fava beans and a nice Chianti."

I'm slowly learning how to straddle the tension that comes with understanding that I am tough and tender, brave and afraid, strong and struggling—all of these things, all of the time. I'm working on letting go of having to be one or the other and embracing the wholeness of wholeheartedness.

The roles in my life—partner, mother, teacher, researcher, leader, entrepreneur—all require me to bring my whole self to the table. *We can't be "all in" if only parts of us show up. If we're not living, loving, parenting, or leading with our whole, integrated hearts, we're doing it halfheartedly.*

In the new, wholehearted story that I'm writing about my life, I'm acknowledging that my ten-year-old self—the four-square champion who also won the slingshot contest on our street—has saved my butt at least as many times as my well-mannered social scientist self. I can't rise strong unless I bring all of my wayward girls and fallen women back into the fold. I need them, and they need me.

On the complexity of our many diverse and sometimes contradictory parts, Walt Whitman wrote, "I am large . . . I contain multitudes." On the importance of understanding ourselves, Carl Jung wrote, "Your vision will become clear only when you can look into your own heart. Who looks outside, dreams; who looks inside, awakes." On the importance of understanding your past, loving yourself, and owning your shit so you can move forward in life, my dad wisely says, "You got to dance with them that brung you."

There is
NO GREATER THREAT
TO THE CRITICS AND CYNICS AND
FEARMONGERS
than those of us
who are WILLING TO FALL
BECAUSE WE HAVE LEARNED HOW TO
RISE.

Eleven

THE REVOLUTION

There is no greater threat to the critics and cynics
 and fearmongers
Than those of us who are willing to fall
Because we have learned how to rise.

don't use the term *revolution* lightly. I've learned a lot about
the difference between incremental, evolutionary change
and thundering, revolutionary upheaval from community
and organization leaders who often differentiate between
these two types of change. What's become clear to me in the
research captured in this book is that the rising strong process
can lead to deep, tumultuous, groundbreaking, no-turning-
back transformation. The process may be a series of incremental changes, but when the process becomes a practice—a way
of engaging with the world—there's no doubt that it ignites
revolutionary change. It changes us and it changes the people
around us.

In *The Gifts,* I describe this transformation as a whole-hearted revolution:

A small, quiet, grassroots movement that starts with each of us saying, "My story matters because I matter." A movement where we can take to the streets with our messy, imperfect, wild, stretch-marked, wonderful, heartbreaking, grace-filled, and joyful lives. A movement fueled by the freedom that comes when we stop pretending that everything is okay when it isn't. A call that rises up from our bellies when we find the courage to celebrate those intensely joyful moments even though we've convinced ourselves that savoring happiness is inviting disaster.

I look back now at how I once addressed the power and intention of the term *revolution* and I still feel completely committed to this idea. Even in 2010, I wrote in *The Gifts*:

Revolution might sound a little dramatic, but in this world, choosing authenticity and worthiness is an absolute act of resistance. Choosing to live and love with our whole hearts is an act of defiance. You're going to confuse, piss off, and terrify lots of people—including yourself. One minute you'll pray that the transformation stops, and the next minute you'll pray that it never ends. You'll also wonder how you can feel so brave and so afraid at the same time. At least that's how I feel most of the time . . . brave, afraid, and very, very alive.

Rising strong is the final piece of this transformation.

LET THE REVOLUTION BEGIN:
WHEN PROCESS BECOMES PRACTICE

All revolutions start with a new vision of what's possible. Our vision is that we can rise from our experiences of hurt and struggle in a way that allows us to live more wholehearted lives. However, transforming the way we live, love, parent, and work requires us to act on our vision: The rising strong *process* is nowhere near as powerful as the rising strong *practice*. The revolution starts when we own and embody what lives at the heart of rising strong—the story rumble—in our everyday lives.

When emotion washes over us and the first thing we think is, *Why am I so pissed? What's going on with me?* or *My gut says something's up and I need to get out my journal and figure this out,* that's when the uprising has officially started. In the introduction we talked about integration being the soul of rising strong. The ultimate act of integration is when the rising strong process becomes a daily practice—a way of thinking about our emotions and our stories. Rather than running from our SFDs, we dig into them knowing they can unlock the fears and doubts that get in the way of our wholeheartedness. We know that rumbling is going to be tough, but we head straight into it because we know running is harder. We wade into the brackish delta with open hearts and minds because we've come to learn that the wisdom in the stories of our falls makes us braver.

Let's take a look at what the revolution—moving from process to practice—can do for our organizations, families, and communities.

THE STORY RUMBLE AT WORK

In the last six chapters, we've explored what it looks like when we as individuals use the rising strong process. But what happens when an organization or a group within an organization experiences a conflict or a failure or a fall? Imagine the possibilities if organizations—corporations, small businesses, schools, places of worship, creative agencies, law firms—made the rising strong process part of their culture by training individuals and teams on the process and creating story rumble teams. Story rumble teams would be trained to use the rising strong process to facilitate large and small group discussions around pressing issues. We've found that these questions are helpful in an organizational setting:

1. How do we engage in this process with an open heart and an open mind?

2. What emotions are people experiencing?

3. How do we listen with empathy?

4. What do we need to get curious about?

5. What are the stories that people are making up?

6. What do our SFDs tell us about our relationships? About our communication? About leadership? About the culture? About what's working and what's not working?

7. Where do we need to rumble? What lines of inquiry do we need to open to better understand what's really happening and to reality-check our conspiracies and confabulations?

8. What's the delta between those first SFDs and the new information we're gathering in the rumble?

9. What are the key learnings?

10. How do we act on the key learnings?

11. How do we integrate these key learnings into the culture and leverage them as we work on new strategies?

At The Daring Way—the company I lead—the story rumble is central to the culture. These are the guiding principles for our organization, summarized in what we call the 5 Rs.

THE 5 Rs: THIS IS HOW WE WORK

- **Respect** for self, for others, for story, for the process
- **Rumble** on ideas, on strategies, on decisions, on creativity, on falls, on conflicts, on misunderstandings, on disappointments, on hurt feelings, on failures
- **Rally** together to own our decisions, own our successes, own our falls, own and integrate our key learnings into our culture and strategies, and practice gratitude
- **Recover** with family, friends, rest, and play
- **Reach out** to each other and the community with empathy, compassion and love

Our willingness and ability to rumble during big conflicts, like a missed project deadline or a financial loss, have kept us at The Daring Way from cratering during crisis moments that are extremely scary for all new and growing businesses—those moments that cause you to question if the endeavor is even worth it. But just as important, our rumbling skills have allowed us to keep our focus and "stay clear" with one another. Here's a great example of a rumble at The Daring Way that happened during the course of writing this book, and how we used the rising strong process to get through it.

We were two hours into a three-hour leadership team meeting when it became clear to me that we were not going to make it through our agenda. I took a quick inventory of the remaining items and asked the team if we could move one discussion from the middle of the agenda to the end. There were a few nods and some rustling of papers, and then we moved on. Not one minute after we started tackling the next issue on the agenda, one of my team members spoke up. "I need to circle back on something." Immediately every one of us sat straight up in our chairs, put our pens down, and gave him our full attention. *Circle back* is a serious term in our culture.

For us, *circle back* means "I moved forward too quickly and I'd like to revisit that conversation," or "I'd like to talk more about what happened," or "I need to make amends for something I did or said or for not showing up."

He drew a deep breath and said, "I know we're running out of time, but when you asked if we could move this item to the end of the agenda, I made up the story that we're moving it because it's no longer a priority for us. That really concerns me, because I'm spending 70 percent of my time on that project, and if it's no longer important, I need to know."

For me, there is no greater gift than working with people who are brave enough and trust the team enough to rumble like this. His SFD was on the table. There were no hidden resentments or fears. He wouldn't go back to his office and change his focus without checking in with the team. He just laid it out there. It was bold and professional.

I said, "Thank you for rumbling. I moved it because it's an issue that we can't afford to rush through. I'd rather meet again tomorrow than give it short shrift today."

He responded, "Thank you. That makes sense."

But it doesn't end there. What's the delta? What's the key learning? The key learning is that next time I will say, "The discussion about the global events needs an hour of our full attention. Let's move it to the bottom and schedule a time this week to devote a meeting to it." Respecting the passion and commitment of people means respecting their items on the agenda.

The conspiracies and confabulations that we tend to make up in the face of limited data can tear away at the heart of organizations. Allowing fifty employees to come up with fifty different stories about a leader's cryptic email is a tremendous waste of energy, time, and talent. Instead, we should put in place a system where people can go to their managers and say, "We need a rumble on that email about the new evaluation system." Curiosity, clean communication, circling back, and rumbling become part of the culture. Just like people, when organizations own their stories and take responsibility for their actions, they get to write the new endings. When they deny their stories, people on the outside, like the media, take over the story's authorship to write new narratives that could come to define the organization.

THE STORY RUMBLE AT HOME

As you can probably imagine after reading this book, Steve and I rumble all the time. At least once a week, one of us will need to say, "The story I'm making up is . . ." It's not hyperbole to state that it has revolutionized the way we deal with our conflicts. Even with as much as I understand about the power of emotion and as many years as we've been together, I'm still surprised by how many of our arguments are intensified by the fabrications we tell ourselves. What starts as a small disagreement about an unimportant issue becomes a fight over wrongly assigned intentions and hurt feelings.

The story rumble also permeates our family culture. We're doing our best to model and teach our children the rising strong process and help them integrate it as a practice in their lives. All children wrestle with belonging and wanting to be a part of something, so many of their SFDs are about these struggles. (For our kids, SFD stands for *stormy first drafts,* which also allows us to work a weather metaphor.)

When our kids feel lonely or scared, or when they convince themselves that they're "the only ones" who aren't out having a blast with a huge group of friends, or who can't watch a certain movie or go to a concert, or who don't have the latest technology, we try to get curious about the stories they're making up. We strongly encourage journaling and even drawing.

Practicing the story rumble during these times not only teaches them the process, but also almost always leads to an experience of connection between us. It's far more effective than relying on, "I don't care if everyone in the world is allowed to go to this music festival—you're not. Would you jump off a bridge if everyone else was doing it?" Or, worst of all in terms of undermining the respect our children have for us, "Because I said so."

When we ask our kids about their conspiracies and confabulations, it opens a discussion that otherwise we might not have. For example, Ellen might say, "I'm making up that I study hard and help around the house and try to be a responsible person, but you still don't trust me enough to let me go to this festival, and I'll probably never get to go." Her SFD gives us the opportunity to empathize and tell her how much we trust and appreciate her, and to explain that we're not making our decision based on her behavior, but on how the people around her will most likely be behaving. No matter how trustworthy our children are, when drugs, alcohol, and crowds are in play, it's easy to get in over your head and find yourself in unnecessarily dangerous situations.

It also gives us a chance to tell Ellen how much we love live music and that we're so happy that she does, too, and to assure her that there will be time in the near future when we will feel that it is appropriate for her to attend a music festival. It's been important in helping Ellen understand that we believe children need a place or time to grow into, to show them that they have new experiences and privileges and opportunities to look forward to. We get to tell her how proud we are that she's earned the fullest privileges that we believe are appropriate for someone her age.

Don't think for one minute that this changes her level of disappointment—it doesn't, and that's not our goal. It does, however, ensure that even if she disagrees with our decision and is angry with us (which is totally healthy and okay), she's not marinating in feelings of not being trusted or respected enough.

With social media, it's easy for children (and adults) to look at all the perfectly edited pictures on Facebook and Twitter and make up stories about how glorious everyone else's life is and how much our mundane existence sucks. Sometimes we've asked Ellen, "What are you making up about these pictures?"

And we might hear, "Every single person I know is out having a blast tonight while I'm home drowning in chemistry home-work." More often than not, by the time we're done with our rumble, we've learned that her closest friends are also at home studying, and even though she had invitations to go out, she chose to stay at home because she really wants to do well on her exam. That's a big difference.

Even with our ten-year-old, Charlie, the stormy first draft works great. He'll tell us that he's having a rotten time in school because he's the only one who doesn't understand what's happening with fractions. This is when we acknowl-edge his emotions and start the reckoning with empathy. Then we move to curiosity by asking questions. Sometimes I'll check in with the teacher, who 90 percent of the time says, "This is a tough unit. He's frustrated, but he's exactly where he's supposed to be. This is new for everyone." With this infor-mation in hand, we can begin a productive rumble and help him find the delta between the story he made up about his level of ability and the normal frustrations of learning new material.

There's another important parenting takeaway from this research. As we've discovered, we're wired for story and in the absence of data we will rely on confabulations and conspira-cies. When our children sense something is wrong—maybe a sick grandparent or a financial worry—or when they *know* something is wrong—an argument or a work crisis—they quickly jump to filling in the missing pieces of the story. And because our well-being is directly tied to their sense of safety, fear sets in and often dictates the story. It's important that we give them as much information as is appropriate for their developmental and emotional capacity, and that we provide a safe place for them to ask questions. Emotions are contagious and when we're stressed or anxious or afraid our children can be quickly engulfed in the same emotions. More information means less fear-based story-making.

THE STORY RUMBLE IN OUR COMMUNITIES

Many of the most difficult conversations I've had took place in classrooms at the University of Houston Graduate College of Social Work (GCSW) and centered on race, gender, class, and sexual identity/orientation. UH is one of the most diverse research universities in the United States, and I've taught courses on everything from research practice, women's issues, and empowerment to global justice and my own research findings. Over the past ten years, my classes have been approximately 25 percent African American, 25 percent Caucasian or Anglo, 25 percent Latino or Latina, 15 percent Asian American, and 10 percent Middle Eastern. Approximately 20 percent of my students have been lesbian, gay, bisexual, transgender, or questioning, and I have had American Sign Language interpreters in many of my courses. This is the miracle that is UH, the GCSW, and Houston. We are a microcosm of the world.

So much of who I am and what I believe in was forged in my bones by what I have experienced in the classroom. And although classrooms are a specific kind of community, the conversations we have mirror the exact conflicts that can unravel all communities—differences, fears, competing priorities, and conflicts of perspectives. It doesn't matter if your community is a parent-teacher organization or a Boy Scout troop or a neighborhood coalition, using our ability to navigate uncomfortable conversations, own our emotions, and rumble with our stories is how we build connection.

In our classroom community, we didn't call our difficult and almost always tearful conversations about issues of racism and homophobia and classism story rumbles, but I see now that that's exactly what they were. What makes a college of social work a unique laboratory for rumbling is the expectation that we must have uncomfortable conversations if we're going to work to empower people and change systems. Just a couple of years ago, we were processing a creative arts project on shame and an African American woman and a white woman got into a passionate discussion about the "angry black woman" stereotype. We talked about the pain, rage, and trauma that happen to us when labels are used to explain away our feelings and our complexity.

Last year, an Asian American student asked the class members to be honest about their first thought when a person cut them off on the freeway in Houston. A black student said, "Asian. No question." A young Latina said, "It's an old person." A white student who was shocked by the exchange replied, "I thought all of you would stick up for each other." The willingness of everyone in the classroom to reckon with these biases—some of which had been unconscious until this exercise—and to get curious about where they came from led us to transformative rumbles as a community.

Another example of the power of owning our stories occurred during a class discussion about privilege. I asked students to write down their first short response to the idea of privilege—a fast story that we could rumble on. One of the white women in the class wrote, "You don't know me. I came from nothing. I worked for everything I have. I didn't come from privilege—I'm just like you. Stop feeling sorry for yourself." This led to a painful discussion about the true nature of unearned privilege and how it has nothing to do with working hard. It's about being afforded special, almost invisible privileges because of our group membership.

After reading a powerful article on privilege by Peggy McIntosh, the class began to bring to the surface what privilege meant to them. A Latino man talked about the pain of having his daughter come home from kindergarten and tell him that they only had crayons with skin colors for white kids, so her self-portrait wasn't very good—it didn't look like her. A white student responded with her summary of race privilege: "I'm white and everything is made for me." A black female student said, "I'm straight. I can hold hands with my boyfriend without fearing violence." Another student said, "I'm a Christian. I can wear my cross necklace to school and no one calls me a terrorist." A white man said, "Unlike my wife, I'm not afraid to run in the morning when it's still dark, before it gets hot."

After listening to everyone rumble with both their pain and their privilege, the white woman who wrote the "you don't know me" note said, "I get it, but I can't spend my life focusing on the negative things—especially what the black and Hispanic students are talking about. It's too hard. Too painful." And before anyone could say a word, she had covered her face with her hands and started to cry. In an instant, we were all in that marshy, dark delta with her. She wiped her face

and said, "Oh my God. I get it: I can choose to be bothered
when it suits me. I don't have to live this every day."

I chose to use my social work classroom as a living example
of a community story rumble because there is so much pain
and trauma surrounding these same issues in our country and
across the globe. Racism, sexism, homophobia, classism—
they're all real and pervasive. And, if you think about it, the
stereotypes that fuel fear and discrimination are often no more
than shitty first drafts—stories we make up based on our own
lack of knowledge and experience, or stories handed down to
us by people who also had very little exposure or understanding. Unraveling stereotypes requires the reckoning and the
rumble—we have to acknowledge that emotion is at play, get
curious, and rumble.

What kind of revolution will change this reality? A revolution fueled by thousands of conversations like the ones my
amazing, brave students have every semester. Each of the stories we tell and hear is like a small flicker of light—when we
have enough of them, we will set the world on fire. But I don't
think we can do it without story. It doesn't matter what community is in question or what the conflict appears to be on the
surface, resolution and change will require people to own,
share, and rumble with stories.

Every part of the rising strong practice points to these questions: *Can we lean in to the vulnerability of emotion and stand in our
truth? Are we willing to lean in to the initial discomfort of curiosity and
creativity so we can be braver with our lives? Do we have the courage to
rumble with our story?* Imagine if people gathered to talk about the
real issues that fuel disconnection and asked the eleven rising
strong questions. What if we were willing to acknowledge our

own hurt and pain, and in doing so made sure not to diminish the hurt and pain of others? We could rise strong together.

MANIFESTO OF THE BRAVE AND BROKENHEARTED

There is no greater threat to the critics and cynics
    and fearmongers
Than those of us who are willing to fall
Because we have learned how to rise

With skinned knees and bruised hearts;
We choose owning our stories of struggle,
Over hiding, over hustling, over pretending.

When we deny our stories, they define us.
When we run from struggle, we are never free.
So we turn toward truth and look it in the eye.

We will not be characters in our stories.
Not villains, not victims, not even heroes.

We are the authors of our lives.
We write our own daring endings.

We craft love from heartbreak,
Compassion from shame,
Grace from disappointment,
Courage from failure.

Showing up is our power.
Story is our way home.
Truth is our song.
We are the brave and brokenhearted.
We are rising strong.

NOTES ON TRAUMA AND COMPLICATED GRIEF

TRAUMA

Having worked with vets, first responders, and survivors of tragedies ranging from 9/11 to genocide, I believe the body and brain store complex trauma in a way that often requires more than the tools we explore in this book—it requires help and support from professionals trained in trauma work. I do believe the process that emerged from this research can be extremely helpful in conjunction with trauma treatment. Reaching out for help is an act of courage.

COMPLICATED GRIEF

Falling often leads to some form of grieving, even if it's simply grieving the loss of an expectation or experience. This was a strong pattern in the data, and I've recognized it in my own life. But complicated grief is something more and, like trauma, requires professional support and help. The Center for Complicated Grief at the Columbia University School of Social Work is an invaluable resource for people struggling in this area. Here's how they define and explain complicated grief:

> Complicated grief is an intense and long-lasting form of grief that takes over a person's life. It is natural to experience acute grief after someone close dies, but complicated grief is different. Complicated grief is a form of grief that takes hold of a person's mind and won't let go. People with complicated grief often say that they feel "stuck."

For most people, grief never completely goes away but recedes into the background. Over time, healing diminishes the pain of a loss. Thoughts and memories of loved ones are deeply interwoven in people's minds, defining their history and coloring their view of the world. Missing deceased loved ones may be an ongoing part of the lives of bereaved people, but it does not interrupt life unless a person is suffering from complicated grief. For people with complicated grief, grief dominates their lives rather than receding.

The term "complicated" refers to factors that interfere with the natural healing process. These factors might be related to characteristics of the bereaved person, to the nature of the relationship with the deceased person, the circumstances of the death, or to things that occurred after the death.

Again, the rising strong process can be helpful if you're experiencing complicated grief, but it won't be enough. There are times we need help, and asking for it is pure courage.

FINDING A CERTIFIED DARING WAY HELPING PROFESSIONAL

The Daring Way™ is a highly experiential methodology based on the research of Dr. Brené Brown. The method was designed for work with individuals, couples, families, work teams, and organizational leaders. It can be facilitated in clinical, educational, and professional settings.

During the process, facilitators explore topics such as vulnerability, courage, shame, and worthiness. Participants are invited to examine the thoughts, emotions, and behaviors that are holding them back, and identify new choices and practices that will move them toward more authentic and wholehearted living. The primary focus is on developing shame resilience skills and developing daily practices that transform the way we live, love, parent, and lead.

These professionals do not work for The Daring Way— they are independent practitioners or members of larger organizations who are often trained in multiple models of work, including Brené's work.

To find a Certified Daring Way Facilitator, visit thedaringway.com.

THE GIFTS OF IMPERFECTION— SUMMARY OF KEY LEARNINGS

TEN GUIDEPOSTS FOR WHOLEHEARTED LIVING

1. Cultivating authenticity: letting go of what people think

2. Cultivating self-compassion: letting go of perfectionism

3. Cultivating a resilient spirit: letting go of numbing and powerlessness

4. Cultivating gratitude and joy: letting go of scarcity and fear of the dark

5. Cultivating intuition and trusting faith: letting go of the need for certainty

6. Cultivating creativity: letting go of comparison

7. Cultivating play and rest: letting go of exhaustion as a status symbol and productivity as self-worth

8. Cultivating calm and stillness: letting go of anxiety as a lifestyle

9. Cultivating meaningful work: letting go of self-doubt and "supposed to"

10. Cultivating laughter, song, and dance: letting go of being cool and "always in control"

A THEORY ON WHOLEHEARTED LIVING

1. Love and belonging are irreducible needs of all men, women, and children. We're hardwired for connection—it's what gives purpose and meaning to our lives. The absence of love, belonging, and connection always leads to suffering.

2. If you roughly divide the men and women I've interviewed into two groups—those who feel a deep sense of love and belonging, and those who struggle for it—there's only one variable that separates the groups: Those who feel lovable, who love, and who experience belonging simply believe they are *worthy* of love and belonging. They don't have better or easier lives, they don't have fewer struggles with addiction or depression, and they haven't survived fewer traumas or bankruptcies or divorces, but in the midst of all of these struggles, they have developed practices that enable them to hold on to the belief that they are worthy of love, belonging, and joy.

3. A strong belief in our worthiness doesn't just happen—it's cultivated when we understand the guideposts as choices and daily practices.

4. The main concern of wholehearted men and women is living a life defined by courage, engagement, and a clear sense of purpose.

5. The wholehearted identify vulnerability as the catalyst for courage, engagement, and a clear sense of purpose. In fact, the willingness to be vulnerable emerged as the single clearest value shared by all of the women and men whom I would describe as wholehearted. They attribute everything—from their professional success to their marriages to their proudest parenting moments—to their ability to be vulnerable.

DARING GREATLY—
SUMMARY OF KEY LEARNINGS

SCARCITY: LOOKING INSIDE
OUR CULTURE OF "NEVER ENOUGH"

Key Learning: We're living in a culture of scarcity, a culture of "never enough."

The opposite of "never enough" isn't abundance or "more than you could ever imagine." The opposite of scarcity is enough, or what I call *wholeheartedness*. There are ten guideposts to wholeheartedness, but at its core are vulnerability and worthiness: facing uncertainty, exposure, and emotional risk, and knowing that you are enough.

After doing this work for the past twelve years and watching scarcity ride roughshod over our families, organizations, and communities, I'd say the one thing we all have in common is that we're sick of feeling afraid. We want to dare greatly. We're tired of the national conversation centering on "What should we fear?" and "Who should we blame?" We all want to be brave.

DEBUNKING THE VULNERABILITY MYTHS

Key Learning: I define vulnerability as exposure, uncertainty, and emotional risk.

Yes, feeling vulnerable is at the core of difficult emotions like fear, grief, and disappointment, but it's also the birthplace of love, belonging, joy, empathy, innovation, and creativity. When we shut ourselves off from vulnerability, we distance ourselves from the experiences that bring purpose and meaning to our lives.

Myth #1: Vulnerability is weakness.
Myth #2: "I don't do vulnerability."
Myth #3: We can go it alone.
Myth #4: Trust comes before vulnerability.

UNDERSTANDING AND COMBATING SHAME

Key Learning: Shame derives its power from being unspeakable. That's why it loves perfectionists—we're so easy to keep quiet. If we cultivate enough awareness about shame to name it and speak to it, we've basically cut it off at the knees. Just the way exposure to light was deadly for the Gremlins, language and story bring light to shame and destroy it.

THE ARMORY

Key Learning: As children we found ways to protect ourselves from vulnerability, from being hurt, diminished, and disappointed. We put on armor; we used our thoughts, emotions, and behaviors as weapons; and we learned how to make ourselves scarce, even to disappear. Now as adults we realize that to live with courage, purpose, and connection—to be the people we long to be—we must again be vulnerable. The courage to be vulnerable means taking off the armor we use to protect ourselves, putting down the weapons that we use to keep people at a distance, showing up, and letting ourselves be seen.

MIND THE GAP: CULTIVATING CHANGE AND CLOSING THE DISENGAGEMENT DIVIDE

Key Learning: To reignite creativity, innovation, and learning, we must rehumanize education and work; we need DISRUPTIVE ENGAGEMENT.

Rehumanizing work and education requires courageous leadership. Honest conversations about vulnerability and shame are disruptive. The reason that we're not having these conversations in our organizations is that they shine light in the dark corners. Once there is language, awareness, and understanding, turning back is almost impossible and carries with it severe consequences. We all want to dare greatly. If you give us a glimpse into that possibility, we'll hold on to it as our vision. It can't be taken away.

WHOLEHEARTED PARENTING: DARING TO BE THE ADULTS WE WANT OUR CHILDREN TO BE

Key Learning: Who we are and how we engage with the world are much stronger predictors of how our children will do than what we know about parenting. In terms of teaching our children to dare greatly in the "never enough" culture, the question isn't so much "Are you parenting the right way?" as it is "Are you the adult that you want your child to grow up to be?" Our stories of worthiness—of being enough—begin in our first families. The narrative certainly doesn't end there, but what we learn about ourselves and how we learn to engage with the world as children set a course that either will require us to spend a significant part of our lives fighting to reclaim our self-worth or will give us hope, courage, and resilience for our journey.

＋

from "Braving the Wilderness"

True belonging does not require us to change who we are.
It requires us to _be_ who we are.

A Grateful Heart

To my team of rebels and rumblers—Suzanne Barrall, Barrett Guillen, Sarah-Margaret Hamman, Charles Kiley, Murdoch Mackinnon, Amy O'Hara, and Ashley Brown Ruiz: You're the finest group of dreamers, doers, and shit-starters I've ever met. *Plane landed, Murdoch.*

To my agent, Jennifer Rudolph Walsh, and the entire team at William Morris Endeavor, especially Tracy Fisher, Katie Giarla, Maggie Shapiro, and Eric Zohn: Thank you for your vision, tenacity, and friendship.

To Polly Koch: I literally couldn't do it without you. Thank you for helping me find my voice and hold on to it.

To Julie Grau and Gina Centrello at Random House: I'm so grateful that you invited me into your home. I know how much you care about people and how committed you are to doing meaningful work. It's an honor.

To Jessica Sindler: This is our second book together and I still feel like the luckiest writer in the world to get to work with you. Thank you.

To the entire Random House team—Debbie Aroff, Maria

Braeckel, Kate Childs, Sanyu Dillon, Benjamin Dreyer, Karen Dziekonski, Nancy Elgin, Sarah Goldberg, Leigh Marchant, Sally Marvin, Greg Mollica, Nicole Morano, Loren Noveck, Tom Perry, Erika Seyfried, Laura Van Der Veer, Theresa Zoro: You never cease to amaze me. Thank you for your passion, commitment, and creativity.

So grateful for the creatives who share their talents and make the world a more beautiful and connected place: Thank you to the Pixar magic makers; Kathleen Shannon, Tara Street, Liz Johnson, and Kristin Tate of Braid Creative and Consulting; coding and web developer Brandi Bernoski; Kelli Newman of Newman & Newman; designer and typographer Simon Walker; and book cover genius Greg Mollica.

Gratitude to the gang at Speakers Office—Jenny Canzoneri, Holli Catchpole, Kristen Fine, Cassie Glasgow, Marsha Horshok, Michele Rubino, and Kim Stark: *Y'all are just the best. It's that simple.*

To the people who inspire me every day—Jo Adams, Miles Adcox, Lorna Barrall, Jimmy Bartz, Negash Berhanu, Shiferaw Berhanu, Wendy Burks, Susan Cain, Katherine Center, Marsha Christ, Alan Conover, Ronda Dearing, Andy Doyle, Jessie Earl, Laura Easton, Beverly and Chip Edens, Ali Edwards, Margarita Flores, Liz Gilbert, Cameron and Matt Hammon, Karen Holmes, Alex Juden, Kat Juden, Michelle Juden, Jenny Lawson, Harriet Lerner, Elizabeth Lesser, Susie Loredo, Laura Mayes, Glennon Doyle Melton, Patrick Miller, John Newton, Shauna Niequist, Murray Powell, Joe Reynolds, Rondal Richardson, Kelly Rae Roberts, Gretchen Rubin, Eleanor Galtney Sharpe, Diana Storms, Karen Walrond, Yolanda Williams, and Maile Wilson.

Huge thanks to my soulful friends at HARPO/OWN—Kyle Alesio, Dana Brooks, Jahayra Guzman, Mamie Healey, Chelsea Hettrick, Noel Kehoe, Corny Koehl, Erik Logan, Mashawn Nix, Lauren Palmer, Peggy Panosh, Liz Reddinger, Sheri Salata, Harriet Seitler, Jon Sinclair, Jill Van Lokeren, Sue Yank, and Oprah Winfrey.

To Team Red, White, and Blue—#EaglesRisingStrong.

To the Daring Way Senior Faculty—Ronda L. Dearing, John Dietrich, Terrie Emel, Dawn Hedgepeth, Virginia Rondero Hernandez, Sonia Levine, Susan Mann, Cynthia Mulder, Cheryl Scoglio, Doug Sorenson, Eric Williams, and Amanda Yoder: I'm so proud to be a member of this team. Your courage makes the world a more wholehearted place.

To the Daring Way Community: Thank you for showing up, being seen, and living brave!

To my parents—Deanne Rogers and David Robinson, Molly May and Chuck Brown, Jacobina and Bill Alley, Corky and Jack Crisci: Thank you for being so brave with your love.

To my sibs—Ashley and Amaya Ruiz; Barrett, Frankie, and Gabi Guillen; Jason and Layla Brown and Gisel Prado; and Jen, David, and Larkin Alley: love and thanks. It's a wonderful, wild adventure—glad y'all are riding shotgun.

To Steve, Ellen, and Charlie: You are the great loves of my life. Thank you.

Notes

A NOTE ON RESEARCH AND STORYTELLING
AS METHODOLOGY

page xii **An editorial . . . written by Ann Hartman:** Hartman, A. (1990). Many ways of knowing [editorial]. *Social Work, 35,* 1: 3–4.

page xiv **Quoting a lyric from a Rush song in *Daring Greatly*:** Brown, B. (2012). *Daring greatly: How the courage to be vulnerable transforms the way we live, love, parent, and lead.* New York: Gotham Books.

page xiv **"You can't always get what you want":** Jagger, M., and Richards, K. (1969). "You Can't Always Get What You Want," on *Let It Bleed,* Decca Records.

TRUTH AND DARE: AN INTRODUCTION

page xvii **The Gifts of Imperfection and *Daring Greatly*:** Brown, B. (2010). *The gifts of imperfection: Let go of who you think you're supposed to be and embrace who you are.* Center City, Minn.: Hazelden; Brown, B. (2012). *Daring greatly: How the courage to be vulnerable transforms the way we live, love, parent, and lead.* New York: Gotham Books.

page xx **Roosevelt's powerful quote from his 1910 "Man in the Arena" speech:** Roosevelt, T. (1910). "Citizenship in a Republic," speech at the Sorbonne, Paris, April 23, 1910. www.theodore-roosevelt.com/images/research/speeches/maninthearena.pdf.

page xxii **Masterpiece's *Sherlock*:** Moffat, S. (2014). "His Last Vow," *Sherlock,* season 3, episode 3, directed by N. Hurran, aired February 2. BBC Home Entertainment.

page xxv **"'Tis better to have loved and lost":** Tennyson, A. (2003). *In memoriam A. H. H.,* ed. Gray, E. I. Norton Critical Edition. New York: W. W. Norton. First published in 1850 by Moxon.

page xxv **Ashley Good . . . the founder and CEO of Fail Forward:** failforward.org/vision and failforward.org/the-team.

CHAPTER ONE: THE PHYSICS OF VULNERABILITY

page 3 **David Gray's song "My Oh My":** Gray, D., and McClune, C. (1998). "My Oh My," on *White Ladder,* Iht Records.

page 6 **Neuroeconomist Paul Zak . . . cortisol and oxytocin:** Zak, P. J. (2012). *The moral molecule: The source of love and prosperity.* New York: Dutton.

page 10 **"You know after any truly initiating experience":** Rohr, R. (2004). *Adam's return: The five promises of male initiation.* New York: Crossroad Publishing.

CHAPTER TWO: CIVILIZATION STOPS AT THE WATERLINE

page 17 **"Hallelujah":** Cohen, L. (1984). "Hallelujah," on *Various Positions,* Columbia Records.

page 23 **"In Spite of Ourselves":** Prine, J. (1999). "In Spite of Ourselves," with DeMent, I., on *In Spite of Ourselves,* Oh Boy Records.

page 25 **The cover of *Fast Company*:** See the following articles in *Fast Company,* 184, April 2014: Catmull the wise, 68–74; Catmull, E., and Tetzeli, R. At some point, all our movies suck, 64–66; Inside the Pixar braintrust, 67–74.

page 25 ***Creativity, Inc.*:** Catmull, E., and Wallace, A. (2014). *Creativity, Inc.: Overcoming the unseen forces that stand in the way of true inspiration.* New York: Random House.

page 25 ***The Alchemist*:** Coelho, P. (1998). *The alchemist.* San Francisco: HarperCollins.

page 27 **Julius Caesar's famous *"Iacta alea est"*:** Suetonius. (2000). *The lives of the Caesars,* trans. Edwards, C. Oxford World's Classics. New York: Oxford University Press.

page 27 **The "form-storm-norm-perform" cycle:** Tuckman, B. W. (1965). Developmental sequence in small groups. *Psychological Bulletin, 63,* 6: 384–399.

page 30 ***Joseph Campbell's hero's journey*:** Campbell, J. (2008). *The hero with a thousand faces,* 3rd ed. Novato, Calif.: New World Library.

page 32 **Carl Jung and Joseph Campbell wrote about water:** Campbell, J. (2008) *The hero with a thousand faces,* 3rd ed. Novato, Calif.: New World Library; Jung, C. G. (1980) *The archetypes and the collec-*

tive unconscious, trans. Hull, R. F. C. Collected works, 2nd ed., vol. 9, pt. 1. Princeton, N.J.: Princeton University Press. First published in 1959 by Princeton University Press.

page 32 **"Civilization ends at the waterline":** Thompson, H. S. (1988). *Generation of swine: Tales of shame and degradation in the '80s.* Gonzo papers, vol. 2. New York: Summit Books.

page 35 **"Release the kraken!":** Elliott, T., and Rossio, T. (2006). *Pirates of the Caribbean: Dead Man's Chest,* directed by Verbinski, G. Walt Disney Studios Home Entertainment.

CHAPTER THREE: OWNING OUR STORIES

page 39 **A map does not just chart:** Larsen, R. (2009). *The selected works of T. S. Spivet.* New York: Penguin Press.

page 42 **"Creativity is just connecting things":** Wolf, G. (1996). Steve Jobs: The next insanely great thing. *Wired,* 4.02, February 1996. Retrieved from archive.wired.com/wired/archive/4.02/jobs_pr.html.

page 42 **Shonda Rhimes:** Interview conducted by Brené Brown on July 18, 2014.

CHAPTER FOUR: THE RECKONING

page 45 **The big question:** Campbell, J., and Moyers, B. (1991). *The power of myth.* New York: Anchor Books.

page 51 *Healing Through the Dark Emotions:* Greenspan, M. (2003). *Healing through the dark emotions: The wisdom of grief, fear, and despair.* Boston: Shambhala Publications.

page 51 **Miriam Greenspan . . . interviewed by Jungian therapist Barbara Platek:** Platek, B. (2008). Through a glass darkly: Miriam Greenspan on moving from grief to gratitude. *The Sun,* 385, January 2008. Retrieved from thesunmagazine.org/issues/385/through_a_glass_darkly.

page 52 **"The important thing is not to stop questioning":** Death of a genius: His fourth dimension, time, overtakes Einstein. (1955) *Life* 38, 18: 61–64.

page 52 **Curiosity is correlated with creativity, intelligence:** Gruber, M. J., Gelman, B. D., and Ranganath, C. (2014). States of curiosity modulate hippocampus-dependent learning via the dopaminergic circuit. *Neuron, 84,* 2: 486–496; Kang, M. J., Hsu, M., Krajbich, I. M., Loewenstein, G., McClure, S. M., Wang, J. T., and Camerer, C. F. (2009). The wick in the candle of learning: Epistemic curiosity activates reward circuitry and enhances memory. *Psychological Science, 20,* 8: 963–973; Leonard, N. H., and Harvey, M. (2007). The trait of curiosity as a predictor of emotional intelligence. *Journal of Applied Social Psychology, 37,* 8: 1545–1561; Leslie, I. (2014). *Curious: The desire to know and why your future depends on it.* New York: Basic Books; Tough, P. (2012). *How children succeed: Grit, curiosity, and the hidden power of character.* Boston: Houghton Mifflin Harcourt.

page 53 **William Plomer wrote, "Creativity is the power to connect":** Plomer, W. (1978). *Electric delights.* London: Jonathan Cape.

page 54 **The brain's chemistry changes when we become curious:** Gruber, M. J., Gelman, B. D., and Ranganath, C. (2014). States of curiosity modulate hippocampus-dependent learning via the dopaminergic circuit. *Neuron, 84,* 2: 486–496.

page 54 *Curious: The Desire to Know and Why Your Future Depends on It:* Leslie, I. (2014). *Curious: The desire to know and why your future depends on it.* New York: Basic Books.

page 54 **Groundbreaking 1994 article "The Psychology of Curiosity":** Loewenstein, G. (1994). The psychology of curiosity: A review and reinterpretation. *Psychological Bulletin, 116,* 1: 75–98.

page 58 **"Barn's burnt down / now / I can see the moon":** Mizuta Masahide (1994). In *The little Zen companion,* comp. Schiller, D. New York: Workman Publishing.

page 65 *The Body Keeps the Score:* van der Kolk, B. A. (2014). *The body keeps the score: Brain, mind, and body in the healing of trauma.* New York: Viking.

page 66 **You may not control all the events:** Angelou, M. (2008). *Letter to my daughter.* New York: Random House.

page 67 **Empirical evidence that not owning and integrating our stories:** Bloniasz, E. R. (2011). Caring for the caretaker: A nursing process approach. *Creative Nursing, 17,* 1: 12–15; Gottschall, J. (2012). *The storytelling animal: How stories make us human.* New York: Houghton Mifflin Harcourt; Horowitz, S. (2008). Evidence-based health outcomes of expressive writing. *Alternative and Complementary Therapies, 14,* 4: 194–198; Park, C. L., and Blumberg, C. J. (2002). Disclosing trauma through writing: Testing the meaning-making hypothesis. *Cognitive Therapy and Research, 26,* 5: 597–616; Singer, J. A. (2004). Narrative identity and meaning making across the adult lifespan: An introduction. *Journal of Personality, 72,* 3: 437–460.

page 67 **J. K. Rowling's character Dolores Umbridge:** Dolores Jane Umbridge first appeared in the Harry Potter series as the Defense Against the Dark Arts professor in the fifth book, *Harry Potter and the Order of the Phoenix.* Rowling, J. K. (2003). *Harry Potter and the order of the phoenix.* New York: Arthur A. Levine Books.

page 68 **The cat from *The LEGO Movie:*** Lord, P., and Miller, C. (2014). *The LEGO Movie,* directed by Lord, P., and Miller, C. Warner Bros. Entertainment, Inc.

page 68 ***Super Soul Sunday:*** Winfrey, O. Oprah and Brené Brown: Daring greatly. *Super Soul Sunday* (2013), season 5, episode 7, aired March 17. Harpo Productions.

page 70 **Mark Miller:** sofrep.com/author/mark-miller.

page 71 **Greater Good Science Center:** greatergood.berkeley.edu.

page 72 **Flow . . . Mihaly Csikszentmihalyi:** Csikszentmihalyi, M. (1990). *Flow: The psychology of optimal experience.* New York: Harper and Row.

page 73 **Newton's third law of motion:** Newton, I. (1999). *The Principia: Mathematical principles of natural philosophy,* trans. Cohen, I. B., and Whitman, A. Berkeley: University of California Press. First published in 1687.

page 74 ***The Empire Strikes Back:*** Lucas, G., Brackett, L., and Kasdan, L. (1980). *Star Wars Episode V—The Empire Strikes Back,* directed by Irvin Kershner. Lucasfilm, Ltd./20th Century Fox Home Entertainment.

CHAPTER FIVE: THE RUMBLE

page 77 **When you are in the middle of a story:** Atwood, M. (1996). *Alias grace.* London: Bloomsbury.

page 78 **"Civilization ends at the waterline":** Thompson, H. S. (1988). *Generation of swine: Tales of shame and degradation in the '80s.* Gonzo papers, vol. 2. New York: Summit Books.

page 79 **Our brains reward us with dopamine:** Burton, R. A. (2008). *On being certain: Believing you are right even when you're not.* New York: St. Martin's Press.

page 80 ***The Storytelling Animal:*** Gottschall, J. (2012). *The storytelling animal: How stories make us human.* New York: Houghton Mifflin Harcourt.

page 84 ***Bird by Bird:*** Lamott, A. (1995). *Bird by bird: Some instructions on writing and life.* New York: Anchor Books.

page 86 ***Writing to Heal:*** Pennebaker, J. W. (2004). *Writing to heal: A guided journal for recovering from trauma and emotional upheaval.* Oakland, Calif.: New Harbinger Publications.

page 86 **In an interview posted on the University of Texas's website, Pennebaker explains:** www.utexas.edu/features/2005/writing.

page 94 **"Delta":** Crosby, D. (1982). "Delta," on *Daylight Again,* Atlantic Records.

CHAPTER SIX: SEWER RATS AND SCOFFLAWS

page 105 *Flushed Away:* Clement, D., La Frenais, I., Lloyd, C., Keenan, J., and Davies, W. (2006). *Flushed Away,* directed by Bowers, D., and Fell, S. DreamWorks Animation and Aardman Animations.

page 119 *Daring Greatly:* Brown, B. (2012). *Daring greatly: How the courage to be vulnerable transforms the way we live, love, parent, and lead.* New York: Gotham Books.

page 119 "Hallelujah": Cohen, L. (1984). "Hallelujah," on *Various Positions,* Columbia Records.

page 124 Kelly Rae Roberts: kellyraeroberts.com.

page 129 Character—the willingness to accept responsibility: Didion, J. (2008). *Slouching towards Bethlehem: Essays.* New York: Farrar, Straus and Giroux. First published in 1968 by Farrar, Straus and Giroux.

page 129 Maria Popova . . . BrainPickings.org: www.brainpickings .org/about. Popova reprints the Didion essay "On Self-Respect," included in the volume cited above. Popova, M. (2012). Joan Didion on self-respect. Retrieved from www.brainpickings.org/2012/05/21/joan-didion-on-self-respect.

CHAPTER SEVEN: THE BRAVE AND BROKENHEARTED

page 139 "No one ever told me that grief": Lewis, C. S. [Clerk, N. W., pseud.]. (1989). *A grief observed.* New York: HarperCollins. First published in 1961 by Faber.

page 140 "Expectations are resentments": Lamott, A. (1998). *Crooked little heart.* New York: Anchor Books.

page 142 *Spirited Away:* Miyazaki, H. (2001). *Spirited Away,* directed by Miyazaki, H. Walt Disney Home Entertainment and Studio Ghibli.

page 142 "Resentment is like drinking poison": www.forbes.com/sites/mfonobongnsehe/2013/12/06/20-inspirational-quotes-from-nelson-mandela/.

page 146 *The Fault in Our Stars:* Green, J. (2012). *The fault in our stars.* New York: Dutton.

page 150 Forgiveness positively correlates with emotional, mental, and physical well-being: Bono, G., McCullough, M. E., and Root, L. M. (2008). Forgiveness, feeling connected to others, and well-being: Two longitudinal studies. *Personality and Social Psychology Bulletin, 34,* 2): 182–195; Larsen, B. A., Darby, R. S., Harris, C. R., Nelkin, D. K., Milam, P.-E., and Christenfeld, N. J. S. (2012). The immediate and delayed cardiovascular benefits of forgiving. *Psychosomatic Medicine, 74,* 7: 745–750; Worthington, E. L., Jr. (2006). *Forgiveness and reconciliation: Theory and application.* New York: Routledge; Worthington, E. L., Jr., Witvliet, C. V. O., Pietrini, P., and Miller, A. J. (2007). Forgiveness, health, and well-being: A review of evidence for emotional versus decisional forgiveness, dispositional forgivingness, and reduced unforgiveness. *Journal of Behavioral Medicine, 30,* 4: 291–302.

page 151 ***The Book of Forgiving: The Fourfold Path for Healing Ourselves and Our World:*** Tutu, D. M., and Tutu, M. A. (2014). *The book of forgiving: The fourfold path for healing ourselves and our world.* New York: HarperCollins.

page 154 ***The Places That Scare You:*** Chödrön, P. (2001). *The places that scare you: A guide to fearlessness in difficult times.* Boston: Shambhala Publications.

page 156 **"To love at all":** Lewis, C. S. (1991). *The four loves.* San Diego: Harcourt Books. First published in 1960 by Harcourt, Brace.

CHAPTER EIGHT: EASY MARK

page 160 **"The opposite of faith is not doubt":** twitter.com/annela mott/status/529295149554487298.

page 169 ***The Dance of Connection:*** Lerner, H. (2001). *The dance of connection: How to talk to someone when you're mad, hurt, scared, frustrated, insulted, betrayed, or desperate.* New York: HarperCollins.

page 181 **"May you always do for others":** Dylan, B. (1974). "Forever Young," on *Planet Waves,* Asylum Records.

page 182 ***The Gifts of Imperfection:*** Brown, B. (2010). *The gifts of imperfection: Let go of who you think you're supposed to be and embrace who you are.* Center City, Minn.: Hazelden.

CHAPTER NINE: COMPOSTING FAILURE

page 198 ***The Thin Book of Trust:*** Feltman, C. (2008). *The thin book of trust: An essential primer for building trust at work.* Bend, Ore.: Thin Book Publishing.

page 201 **Martin Luther King, Jr.'s definition of it:** "the ability to achieve our purpose and to effect change" paraphrases the following quote: "Power is the ability to achieve purpose, power is the ability to effect change, and we need power," in King M. L., Jr. (2011). All labor has dignity. *All labor has dignity,* ed. Honey, M. K. New York: Beacon Press, 167–179.

page 202 **Despair is a spiritual condition:** Bell, R. (2014). Speech at Oprah Winfrey's Life You Want Weekend Tour, various U.S. cities.

page 202 **Trilogy of "goals, pathways, and agency":** Snyder, C. R., ed.

(2001). *Handbook of hope: Theory, measures, and applications.* San Diego: Academic Press.

page 203 **I wrote my first book in 2002:** It was never published under its original title, *Hairy Toes and Sexy Rice: Women, Shame, and the Media,* but became *Women and Shame.*

page 205 **Women and Shame:** Brown, B. (2004). *Women and shame: Reaching out, speaking truths and building connection.* Austin, Tex.: 3C Press.

page 206 **I Thought It Was Just Me:** Brown, B. (2007). *I thought it was just me: Women reclaiming power and courage in a culture of shame.* New York: Gotham Books.

page 211 **We're the Millers:** Fisher, B., Faber, S., Anders, S., and Morris, J. (2013). *We're the Millers,* directed by Thurber, R. M. New Line Cinema.

page 211 **George Saunders's 2013 commencement address at Syracuse University:** Enslin, R. "George Saunders G'88 Delivers 2013 Convocation Address." *Syracuse University College of Arts and Sciences News,* May 20, 2013. asnews.syr.edu/newsevents_2013/releases/ george_saunders_convocation.html.

page 213 **The Rise:** Lewis, S. (2014). *The rise: Creativity, the gift of failure, and the search for mastery.* New York: Simon and Schuster.

CHAPTER TEN: YOU GOT TO DANCE WITH THEM THAT BRUNG YOU

page 226 **"The Devil Went Down to Georgia":** Daniels, C., Crain, J. T., Jr., DiGregorio, W. J., Edwards, F. L., Hayward, C. F., and Marshall, J. W. (1979) "The Devil Went Down to Georgia," on *Million Mile Reflections,* Epic Records.

page 231 **That dreadful scene in *The Silence of the Lambs*:** Harris, T., and Tally, T. (1991). *The Silence of the Lambs,* directed by Demme, J. Orion Home Video.

page 234 **Four elements of shame resilience:** Brown, B. (2007). *I thought it was just me: Women reclaiming power and courage in a culture of shame* New York, NY: Gotham Books; Brown, B. (2010). *The gifts of imperfection: Let go of who you think you're supposed to be and embrace who you are.* Center City, Minn: Hazelden; Brown, B. (2012). *Daring greatly: How the courage to be vulnerable transforms the way we live, love, parent, and lead.* New York: Gotham Books.

page 234 **I dearly love the state of Texas:** Ivins, M. (1994). *Nothin' but good times ahead.* New York: Vintage.

page 235 **Finding Meaning in the Second Half of Life:** Hollis, J. (2005).

Finding meaning in the second half of life: How to finally, really grow up. New York: Gotham Books.

page 242 **The Way We Never Were:** Coontz, S. (1992). *The way we never were: American families and the nostalgia trap.* New York: Basic Books.

page 243 **The Great Beauty:** Sorrentino, P., and Contarello, U. (2013) *The Great Beauty,* directed by Sorrentino, P. Indigo Film.

page 247 **"Definitions belong to the definers":** Morrison, T. (1988). *Beloved.* New York: Penguin Books.

page 250 **"Fava beans and a nice Chianti":** Harris, T., and Tally, T. (1991). *The Silence of the Lambs,* directed by Demme, J. Orion Home Video.

page 251 **"I am large . . . I contain multitudes":** Whitman, W. (2007). Song of myself. *Leaves of grass: The original 1855 edition,* ed. Pine, J. T. Mineola, N.Y.: Dover Publications. First published in 1855 by the author.

page 251 **"Your vision will become clear":** Jung, C. G. (1973). *C. G. Jung Letters, Volume 1: 1906–1950,* eds. Adler, G., and Jaffe, A., trans. Hull, R. F. C. Princeton, N.J.: Princeton University Press.

CHAPTER ELEVEN: THE REVOLUTION

page 253 **The Gifts:** Brown, B. (2010). *The gifts of imperfection: Let go of who you think you're supposed to be and embrace who you are.* Center City, Minn: Hazelden.

Index

About the Type

This book was set in Stone, a typeface created in 1988 by the type and graphic designer Sumner Stone (b. 1945). This typeface was designed to satisfy the requirements of low-resolution laser printing. Its traditional design blends harmoniously with many typefaces, making it appropriate for a variety of applications.